Embedded Control Systems in C/C++

An Introduction for Software Developers Using MATLAB

Jim Ledin

CMPBooks

San Francisco, CA • New York, NY • Lawrence, KS

Published byCMP Books
an imprint of CMP Media LLC
Main office: 600 Harrison Street, San Francisco, CA 94107 USA
Tel: 415-947-6615; fax: 415-947-6015
Editorial office: 4601 West 6th Street, Suite B, Lawrence, KS 66049 USA
www.cmpbooks.com
email: books@cmp.com

Distributed in the U.S. by:
Publishers Group West
1700 Fourth Street
Berkeley, California 94710
1-800-788-3123
www.pgw.com

Distributed in Canada by:
Jaguar Book Group
100 Armstrong Avenue
Georgetown, Ontario M6K 3E7 Canada
905-877-4483

For individual orders and for information on special discounts for quantity orders, please contact:
CMP Books Distribution Center, 6600 Silacci Way, Gilroy, CA 95020
email: cmp@rushorder.com; Web: www.cmpbooks.com
ISBN: 1-57820-127-6

To my loving and supportive wife, Lynda

Table of Contents

Preface

Designing a control system is a hard thing to do. To do it the "right" way, you must understand the mathematics of dynamic systems and control system design algorithms, which requires a strong background in calculus. What if you don't have this background and you find yourself working on a project that requires a control system design?

I wrote this book to answer that question. Recent advances in control system design software packages have placed the mathematics needed for control system design inside easy-to-use tools that can be applied by software developers who are not control engineers.

Using the techniques described in this book, embedded systems developers can design control systems with excellent performance characteristics. Mathematical derivations are avoided, making the methods accessible to developers with no background in control system engineering. The design approaches covered range from iterative experimental tuning procedures to advanced optimal control algorithms.

Although some of the design methods are mathematically complex, applying them need not be that difficult. It is only necessary for the user to understand the inputs required by a particular method and to provide them in a suitable form. For cases in which a controller design fails to produce satisfactory results, suggestions are provided for ways to adjust the inputs to enable the method to succeed. To compensate for the lack of mathematical rigor in the procedures, thorough testing of the resulting control system design is strongly advocated.

For the more advanced algorithms, this book demonstrates how to apply the best available software tools for control system design: MATLAB® and its toolboxes. Toolboxes are add-ons to the basic MATLAB product that enhance its capabilities to perform specific tasks. The primary toolbox discussed here is the Control System Toolbox. Other add-ons to MATLAB also are covered, including the System Identification Toolbox, Simulink, and SimMechanics.

Acknowledgments

I thank Al Williams for his assistance and advice while I wrote this book. I also thank the staff at CMP Books for their support in the writing and publishing of this book.

CHAPTER 1

CONTROL SYSTEMS BASICS

1.1 Introduction

A control system (also called a controller) manages a larger system's operation so that the overall response approximates commanded behavior. A common example of a control system is the cruise control in an automobile: The cruise control manipulates the throttle setting so that the vehicle speed tracks the commanded speed set by the driver.

In years past, mechanical or electrical hardware components performed most control functions in technological systems. When hardware solutions were insufficient, continuous human participation in the control loop was necessary.

In modern system designs, embedded processors have taken over many control functions. A well-designed embedded controller can provide excellent system performance under widely varying operating conditions. To ensure a consistently high level of performance and robustness, an embedded control system must be carefully designed and thoroughly tested.

This book presents a number of control system design techniques in a step-by-step manner and identifies situations in which the application of each is appropriate. It also covers the process of implementing a control system design in C or C++ in a resource-limited embedded system. Some useful approaches for thoroughly testing control system designs are also described.

There is no assumption of prior experience with control system engineering. The use of mathematics will be minimized and explanations of mathematically complex issues will appear in Advanced Concept sections. Study of those sections is recommended but is not required for understanding the remainder of the book. The focus is on presenting control system design and testing procedures in a format that lets you put them to immediate use.

This chapter introduces the fundamental concepts of control systems engineering and describes the steps of designing and testing a controller. It introduces the terminology of control system design and shows how to interpret block diagram representations of systems.

Many of the techniques of control system engineering rely on mathematical manipulations of system models. The easiest way to apply these methods is to use a good control system design software package such as the MATLAB® Control System Toolbox. MATLAB and related products, such as Simulink® and the Control System Toolbox, are used in later chapters to develop system models and apply control system design techniques.

Throughout this book, words and phrases that appear in the Glossary are displayed in italics the first time they appear.

1.2 Chapter Objectives

After reading this chapter, you should be able to

- describe the basic principles of feedback control systems,
- recognize the significant characteristics of a *plant* (a system to be controlled) as they relate to control system design,
- describe the two basic steps in control system design: controller structure selection and parameter specification,
- develop control system performance specifications,
- understand the concept of system stability, and
- describe the principal steps involved in testing a control system design.

1.3 Feedback Control Systems

The goal of a controller is to move a system from its initial condition to a desired state and, once there, maintain the desired state. For the cruise control system mentioned earlier, the initial condition is the vehicle speed at the time the cruise control is engaged. The desired state is the speed setting supplied by the driver. The difference between the desired and actual state is called the error signal. It is also possible that the desired state will change over time. When this happens, the controller must adjust the state of the system to track changes in the desired state.

Note: A control system that attempts to keep the output signal at a constant level for long periods of time is called a *regulator.* In a regulator, the desired output value is called the set point. A control system that attempts to track an input signal that changes frequently (perhaps continuously) is called a *servomechanism.*

Some examples will help clarify the control system elements in familiar systems. Control systems typically have a sensor that measures the output signal to be controlled and an actuator that changes the system's state in a way that affects the output signal. As Table 1.1 shows, many control systems are implemented with simple sensing hardware that turns an actuator such as a valve or switch on and off.

Table 1.1 Common control systems.

System	Sensor	Actuator
Home heating system	Temperature sensor	Furnace on/off switch
Automotive engine temperature control	Thermostat	Thermostat
Toilet tank water level control	Float	Valve operated by float

The systems shown in Table 1.1 are some of the simplest applications of control systems. More advanced control system applications appear in the fields of automotive and aerospace engineering, chemical processing, and many other areas This book focuses on the design and implementation of control systems in complex applications.

1.3.1 Comparison of Open-Loop Control and Feedback Control

In many control system designs, it is possible to use either open-loop control or feedback control. Feedback control systems measure the system parameter being controlled and use that information to determine the control actuator signal. Open-loop systems do not use feedback. All the systems described in Table 1.1 use feedback control. Example 1.1 below demonstrates why feedback control is the nearly universal choice for control system applications.

Example 1.1 Home heating system.

Consider a home heating system consisting of a furnace and a controller that cycles the furnace off and on to maintain a desired room temperature. I'll look at how this type of controller could be implemented with open-loop control and feedback control.

Open-Loop Control For a given combination of outdoor temperature and desired indoor temperature, it is possible to experimentally determine the ratio of furnace on time to off time that maintains the desired indoor temperature. Suppose a repeated cycle of 5 minutes of furnace on and 10 minutes of furnace off produces the desired indoor temperature for a specific outdoor temperature. An open-loop controller implementing this algorithm will produce the desired results only so long as the system and environment remain unchanged. If the outdoor temperature changes or if the furnace airflow changes because the air filter is replaced, the desired indoor temperature will no longer be maintained. This is clearly an unsatisfactory design.

Feedback Control A feedback controller for this system measures the indoor temperature and turns the furnace on when the temperature drops below a turn-on threshold. The controller turns the furnace off when the temperature reaches a higher turn-off threshold. The threshold temperatures are set slightly above and below the desired temperature to keep the furnace from rapidly cycling on and off. This controller adapts automatically to outside temperature changes and to changes in system parameters such as airflow.

This book focuses on control systems that use feedback because feedback controllers, in general, provide superior system performance in comparison to open-loop controllers.

Although it is possible to develop very simple feedback control systems through trial and error, for more complex applications, the only feasible approach is the application of design methods that have been proven over time. This book covers a number of control system design methods and shows you how to employ them directly. The emphasis is on understanding the input and results of each technique, without requiring a deep understanding of the mathematical basis for the method.

As the applications of embedded computing expand, an increasing number of controller functions are moving to software implementations. To function as a feedback controller, an embedded processor uses one or more sensors to measure the system state and drives one or more actuators that change the system state. The sensor measurements are inputs to a control algorithm that computes the actuator commands. The control system design process encompasses the development of a control algorithm and its implementation in software along with related issues such as the selection of sensors, actuators, and the sampling rate.

The design techniques described in this book can be used to develop mechanical and electrical hardware controllers, as well as software controller implementations. This approach allows you to defer the decision of whether to implement a control algorithm in hardware or software until after its initial design has been completed.

1.4 Plant Characteristics

In the context of control systems, a plant is a system to be controlled. From the controller's point of view, the plant has one or more outputs and one or more inputs. Sensors measure the plant outputs and actuators drive the plant inputs. The behavior of the plant itself can range from trivially simple to extremely complex. At the beginning of a control system design project, it is helpful to identify a number of plant characteristics relevant to the design process.

1.4.1 Linear and Nonlinear Systems

Important Point

A linear plant model is required for some of the control system design techniques covered in the following chapters. In simple terms, a linear system produces an output that is proportional to its input. Small changes in the input signal result in small changes in the output. Large changes in the input cause large changes in the output. A truly linear system must respond proportionally to any input signal, no matter how large. Note that this proportionality could also be negative: A positive input might produce a proportional negative output.

1.4.2 Definition of a Linear System

Advanced Concept

Consider a plant with one input and one output. Suppose you run the system for a period of time while recording the input and output signals. Call the input signal $u_1(t)$ and the output signal $y_1(t)$. Perform this experiment again with a different input signal. Name the input and output signals from this run $u_2(t)$ and $y_2(t)$, respectively. Now perform a third run of the experiment with the input signal $u_3(t) = u_1(t) + u_2(t)$.

The plant is linear if the output signal $y_3(t)$ is equal to the sum $y_1(t) + y_2(t)$ for any arbitrarily selected input signals $u_1(t)$ and $u_2(t)$.

Real-world systems are never precisely linear. Various factors always exist that introduce nonlinearities into the response of a system. For example, some nonlinearities in the automotive cruise control discussed earlier are:

- The force of air drag on the vehicle is proportional to the square of its speed through the air.
- Friction (a nonlinear effect) exists within the drive train and between the tires and the road.
- The speed of the vehicle is limited to a range between minimum and maximum values.

However, the linear idealization is extremely useful as a tool for system analysis and control system design. Several of the design methods in the following chapters require a linear plant model. This immediately raises a question: If you do not have a linear model of your plant, how do you obtain one?

The approach usually taught in engineering courses is to develop a set of mathematical equations based on the laws of physics as they apply to the operation of the plant. These equations are often nonlinear, in which case it is necessary to perform additional steps to linearize them. This procedure requires intimate knowledge of plant behavior, as well as a strong mathematical background.

In this book, I don't assume this type of background. My focus is on simpler methods of acquiring a linear plant model. For instance, if you need a linear plant model but don't want to develop one, you can always let someone else do it for you. Linear plant models are sometimes available from system data sheets or by request from experts familiar with the mathematics of a particular type of plant. Another approach is to perform a literature search to locate linear models of plants similar to the one of interest.

System identification is an alternative if none of the above approaches are suitable. System identification is a technique for performing semiautomated linear plant model development. This approach uses recorded plant input signal $u(t)$ and output signal $y(t)$ data to develop a linear system model that best fits the input and output data. I discuss system identification further in Chapter 3.

Simulation is another technique for developing a linear plant model. You can develop a nonlinear simulation of your plant with a tool such as Simulink and derive a linear plant model on the basis of the simulation. I will apply this approach in some of the examples presented in later chapters.

Perhaps you just don't want to expend the effort required to develop a linear plant model. With no plant model, an iterative procedure must be used to determine a suitable controller structure and parameter values. In Chapter 2, I discuss procedures for applying and tuning PID controllers. PID controller tuning is carried out with the results of experiments performed on the system consisting of plant plus controller.

1.4.3 Time Delays

Sometimes a linear model accurately represents the behavior of a plant, but a time delay exists between an actuator input and the start of the plant response to the input. This does not refer to sluggishness in the plant's response. A time delay exists only when there is absolutely no response for some time interval following a change to the plant input.

For example, a time delay occurs when controlling the temperature of a shower. Changes in the hot or cold water valve positions do not have immediate results. There is a delay while water with the adjusted temperature flows up to the shower head and then down onto the person taking the shower. Only then does feedback exist to indicate whether further temperature adjustments are needed.

Many industrial processes exhibit time delays. Control system design methods that rely on linear plant models can't directly work with time delays, but it is possible to extend a linear plant model to simulate the effects of a time delay. The resulting model is also linear and captures the approximate effects of the time delay. Linear control system design methods are applicable to the extended plant model. I discuss time delays further in Chapter 3.

1.4.4 Continuous-Time and Discrete-Time Systems

A *continuous-time system* has outputs with values defined at all points in time. The outputs of a *discrete-time system* are only updated or used at discrete points in time. Real-world plants are usually best represented as continuous-time systems. In other words, these systems have measurable parameters such as speed, temperature, weight, etc. defined at all points in time.

The discrete-time systems of interest in this book are embedded processors and their associated input/output (I/O) devices. An embedded computing system measures its inputs and produces its outputs at discrete points in time. The embedded software typically runs at a fixed sampling rate, which results in input and output device updates at equally spaced points in time.

I/O Between Discrete-Time Systems and Continuous-Time Systems

A class of I/O devices interfaces discrete-time embedded controllers with continuous plants by performing direct conversions between analog voltages and the digital data values used in the processor. The analog-to-digital converter (ADC) performs input from an analog plant sensor to a discrete-time embedded computer. Upon receiving a conversion command, the ADC samples its analog input voltage and converts it to a quantized digital value. The behavior of the analog input signal between samples is unknown to the embedded processor.

The digital-to-analog converter (DAC) converts a quantized digital value to an analog voltage, which drives an analog plant actuator. The output of the DAC remains constant until it is updated at the next control algorithm iteration.

Two basic approaches are available for developing control algorithms that run as discrete-time systems. The first is to perform the design entirely in the discrete-time domain. For design methods that require a linear plant model, this method requires conversion of the continuous-time plant model to a discrete-time equivalent. One drawback of this approach is that it is necessary to specify the sampling rate of the discrete-time controller at the very beginning of the design process. If the sampling rate changes, all the steps in the control algorithm development process must be repeated to compensate for the change.

An alternative procedure is to perform the control system design in the continuous-time domain followed by a final step to convert the control algorithm to a discrete-time representation. With the use of this method, changes to the sampling rate only require repetition of the final step. Another benefit of this approach is that the continuous-time control algorithm can be implemented directly in analog hardware if that turns out to be the best solution for a particular design. A final benefit of this approach is that the methods of control system design tend to be more intuitive in the continuous-time domain than in the discrete-time domain.

For these reasons, the design techniques covered in this book will be based in the continuous-time domain. In Chapter 8, I discuss the conversion of a continuous-time control algorithm to an implementation in a discrete-time embedded processor with the C/C++ programming languages.

1.4.5 Number of Inputs and Outputs

The simplest feedback control system, a single-input–single-output (*SISO*) system, has one input and one output. In a SISO system, a sensor measures one signal and the controller produces one signal to drive an actuator. All of the design procedures in this book are applicable to SISO systems.

Control systems with more than one input or output are called multiple-input–multiple-output (*MIMO*) systems. Because of the added complexity, fewer MIMO system design procedures are available. Only the pole placement and optimal control design techniques (covered in Chapters 5 and 6) are directly suitable for MIMO systems. In Chapter 7, I cover issues specific to MIMO control system design.

In many cases, MIMO systems can be decomposed into a number of approximately equivalent SISO systems. For example, flying an aircraft requires simultaneous operation of several independent control surfaces, including the rudder, ailerons, and elevator. This is clearly a MIMO system, but focusing on a particular aspect of behavior can result in a SISO system for control system design purposes. For instance, assume the aircraft is flying straight and level and must maintain a desired altitude. A SISO system for altitude control uses the measured altitude as its input and the commanded elevator position as its output. In this situation, the sensed parameter and the controlled parameter are directly related and have little or no interaction with other aspects of system control.

The critical factor that determines whether a MIMO system is suitable for decomposition into a number of SISO systems is the degree of coupling between inputs and outputs. If changes to a particular plant input result in significant changes to only one of its outputs, it is probably reasonable to represent the behavior of that I/O signal pair as a SISO system. When the application of this technique is appropriate, all of the SISO control system design approaches become available for use with the system.

However, when too much coupling exists from a plant input to multiple outputs, there is no alternative but to perform a control system design with the use of a MIMO method. Even in systems with weak cross-coupling, the use of a MIMO design procedure will generally produce a superior design compared to the multiple SISO designs developed assuming no cross-coupling between I/O signal pairs.

1.5 Controller Structure and Design Parameters

Important Point

The two fundamental steps in designing a controller are to

- specify the controller structure and
- determine the value of the design parameters within that structure.

The controller structure identifies the inputs, outputs, and mathematical form of the control algorithm. Each controller structure contains one or more adjustable design parameters. Given a controller structure, the control system designer must select a value for each parameter so that the overall system (consisting of the plant and the controller) satisfies performance requirements.

For example, in the root locus method described in Chapter 4, the controller structure might produce an actuator signal computed as a constant (called the gain) times the error signal. The adjustable parameter in this case is the value of the gain.

Like engineering design in other domains, control system design tends to be an iterative process. During the initial controller design iteration, it is best to begin with the simplest controller structure that could possibly provide adequate performance. Then, with the use of one or more of the design methods in the following chapters, the designer attempts to identify values for the controller parameters that result in acceptable system performance.

It might turn out that no combination of parameter values for a given controller structure results in satisfactory performance. When this happens, the controller structure must be altered in some way so that performance goals will be met. The designer then determines values for the adjustable parameters of the new structure. The cycle of controller structure modification and design parameter selection repeats until a final design with acceptable system performance has been achieved.

The following chapters contain several examples demonstrating the application of this two-step procedure by different control system design techniques. The examples come from engineering domains where control systems are regularly applied. Studying the steps in each example will help you develop an understanding of how to select an appropriate controller structure. For some of the design techniques, the determination of design parameter values is an automated process performed by control system design software. For the other design methods, you must follow the appropriate steps to select values for the design parameters.

Following each iteration of the two-step design procedure, you must evaluate the resulting controller to see whether it meets performance requirements. In Chapter 9, I cover techniques for testing control system designs, including simulation testing and tests of the controller operating in conjunction with the actual plant.

1.6 Block Diagrams

A *block diagram* of a plant and controller is a graphical means of representing the structure of a controller design and its interaction with the plant. Figure 1.1 is a block diagram of an elementary feedback control system. Each block in the figure represents a system component. The solid lines with arrows indicate the flow of signals between the components.

In block diagrams of SISO systems, a solid line represents a single scalar signal. In MIMO systems, a single line can represent multiple signals. The circle in the figure represents a summing junction, which combines its inputs by addition or subtraction depending on the + or – sign next to each input.

The contents of the dashed box in Figure 1.1 are the control system components. The controller inputs are the reference input (or set point) and the plant output signal (measured by the sensor), which is used as feedback. The controller output is the actuator signal that drives the plant.

Figure 1.1 Block diagram of a feedback control system.

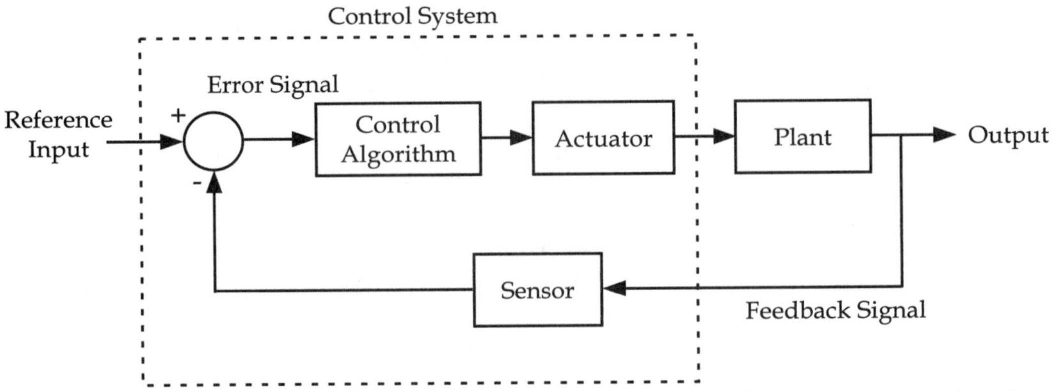

A block in a diagram can represent something as simple as a constant value that multiplies the block input or as complex as a nonlinear system with no known mathematical representation. The design techniques in Chapter 2 do not require a model of the Plant block of Figure 1.1, but methods in subsequent chapters will require a linear model of the plant.

Advanced Concept

1.6.1 Linear System Block Diagram Algebra

It is possible to manipulate block diagrams containing only linear components to achieve compact mathematical expressions representing system behavior. The goal of this manipulation is to determine the system output as a function of its input. The expression resulting from this exercise is useful in various control system analysis and design procedures.

Each block in the diagram must represent a linear system expressed in the form of a transfer function. I introduce transfer functions in Chapter 3. Detailed knowledge of transfer functions is not required to perform block diagram algebra.

Figure 1.2 is a block diagram of a simple linear feedback control system. Lowercase characters identify the signals in this system.

- r is the reference input.
- e is the error signal, computed by subtracting the sensor measurement from the reference input.
- y is the system output, which is measured and used as the feedback signal.

The blocks in the diagram represent linear system components. Each block can represent dynamic behavior with any degree of complexity as long as the requirement of linearity is satisfied.

- G_c is the linear controller algorithm.
- G_p is the linear plant model (including actuator dynamics).
- H is a linear model of the sensor, which can be modeled as a constant (1, for example) if the sensor dynamics are negligible.

Figure 1.2 Linear feedback control system.

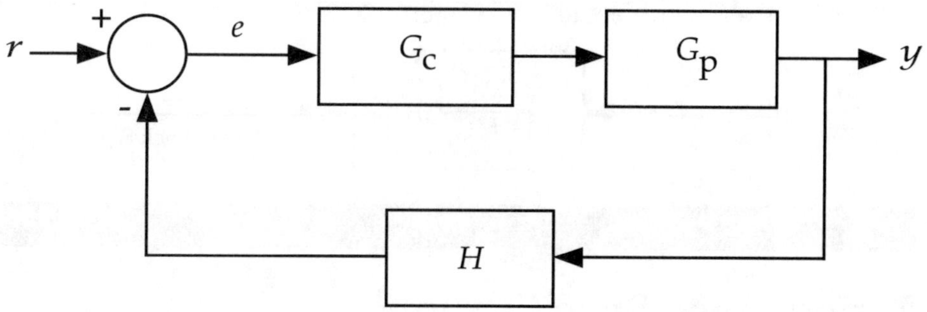

The fundamental rule of block diagram algebra states that the output of a block equals the block input multiplied by the block transfer function. Applying this rule twice results in Eq. 1.1. In words, Eq. 1.1 says the system output y is the error signal e multiplied by the controller transfer function G_c, and then multiplied again by the plant transfer function G_p.

$$y = (eG_c)G_p \qquad \text{Eq. 1.1}$$

Block diagram algebra obeys the usual rules of algebra. Multiplication and addition are commutative, so the parentheses in Eq. 1.1 are unnecessary. This also means that the positions of the G_c and G_p blocks in Figure 1.2 can be swapped without altering the external behavior of the system.

The error signal e is the output of a summing junction subtracting the sensor measurement from the reference input r. The sensor measurement is the system output y multiplied by the sensor transfer function H. This relationship appears in Eq. 1.2.

$$e = r - yH \qquad \text{Eq. 1.2}$$

Substituting Eq. 1.2 into Eq. 1.1 and rearranging algebraically results in Eq. 1.3.

$$\frac{y}{r} = \frac{G_c G_p}{1 + HG_c G_p} \qquad \text{Eq. 1.3}$$

Equation 1.3 is a transfer function giving the ratio of the system output to its reference input. This form of system model is suitable for use in numerous control system analysis and design tasks.

By employing the relation of Eq. 1.3, the entire system in Figure 1.2 can be replaced with the equivalent system shown in Figure 1.3. Remember, these manipulations are only valid when the components of the block diagram are all linear.

Figure 1.3 System equivalent to that in Figure 1.2.

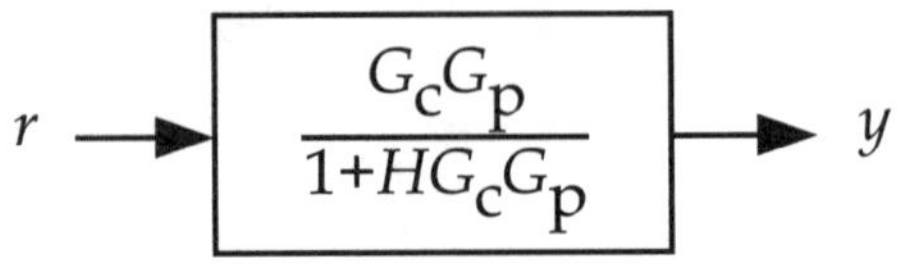

1.7 Performance Specifications

One of the first steps in the control system development process is the definition of a suitable set of system performance specifications. Performance specifications guide the design process and provide the means for determining when a controller design is satisfactory. Controller performance specifications can be stated in both the time domain and in the frequency domain.

Time domain specifications usually relate to performance in response to a step change in the reference input. An example of such a step input is instantaneously changing the reference input from 0 to 1. Time domain specifications include, but are not limited to, the following parameters [1].

- t_r is the rise time from 10 to 90 percent of the commanded value.
- t_p is the time to peak magnitude.
- M_p is peak magnitude. This is often expressed as the peak percentage by which the output signal overshoots the step input command.
- t_s is the settling time to within some fraction (such as 1 percent) of the step input command value.

Examples of these parameters appear in Figure 1.4, which shows the response of a hypothetical plant plus controller to a step input command with an amplitude of 1. The time axis zero location is the instant of application of the step input.

The step response in Figure 1.4 represents a system with a fair amount of overshoot (in terms of M_p) and oscillation before converging to the reference input. Sometimes the step response has no overshoot at all. When no overshoot occurs, the t_p parameter becomes meaningless and M_p is zero.

Figure 1.4 Time domain control system performance parameters.

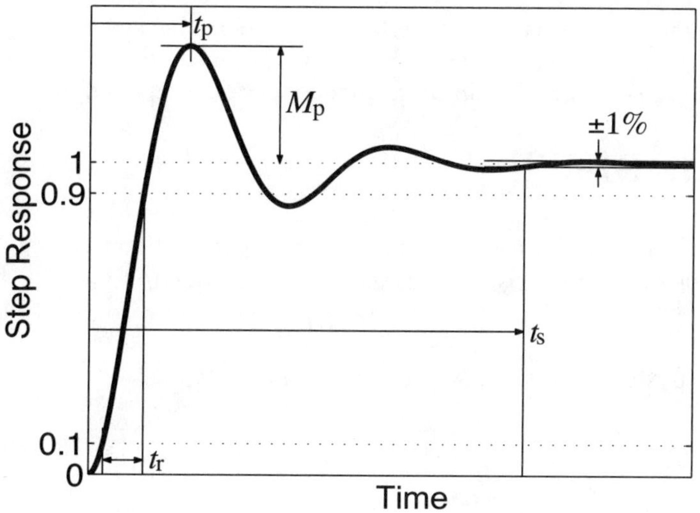

Tracking error is the error in the output that remains after the input function has been applied for a long time and all transients have died out. It is common to specify the steady-state controller tracking error characteristics in response to different commanded input functions such as steps, ramps, and parabolas.

The following are some example specifications of tracking error in response to different input functions.

- Zero tracking error in response to a step input.
- Less than X tracking error magnitude in response to a ramp input, where X is a nonzero value.

In addition to the time domain specifications discussed above, performance specifications can be stated in the frequency domain. The controller reference input is usually a low-frequency signal, while noise in the sensor measurement used by the controller often contains high-frequency components. It is normally desirable for the control system to suppress the high-frequency components related to sensor noise while responding to changes in the reference input. Performance specifications capturing these low and high frequency requirements would appear as follows.

- For sinusoidal reference input signals with frequencies below a cutoff point, the amplitude of the closed-loop (plant plus controller) response must be within X percent of the commanded amplitude.
- For sinusoidal reference input signals with frequencies above a higher cutoff point, the amplitude of the closed-loop response must be reduced by at least Y percent.

In other words, the frequency domain performance requirements given above say that the system response to expected changes in the reference input must be acceptable and simultaneously attenuate the effects of noise in the sensor measurement. Viewed in this way, the closed-loop system exhibits the characteristics of a lowpass filter.

I discuss frequency domain performance specifications in more detail in Chapter 4.

1.8 System Stability

Stability is a critical issue throughout the control system design process. A stable controller produces appropriate responses to changes in the reference input. If the system stops responding properly to changes in the reference input and does something else instead, it has become unstable.

Figure 1.5 System with an unstable oscillatory response.

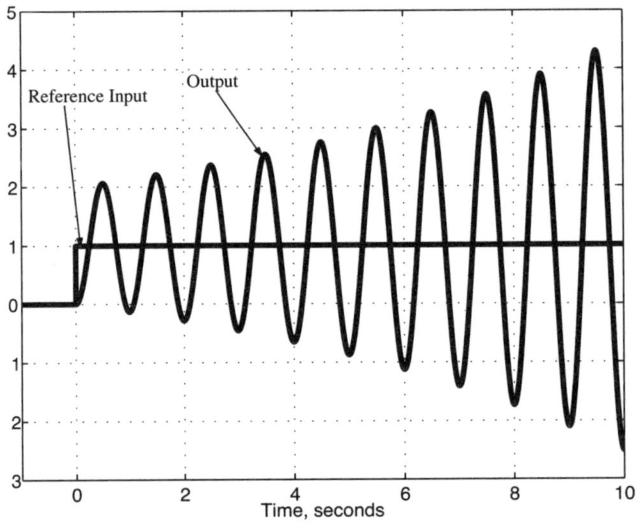

Figure 1.5 shows an example of unstable system behavior. The initial response to the step input overshoots the commanded value by a large amount. The response to that overshoot is an even larger overshoot in the other direction. This pattern continues, with increasing output amplitude over time. In a real system, an unstable oscillation like this grows in amplitude until some nonlinearity such as actuator saturation (or a system breakdown!) limits the response.

Important Point System instability is a risk when using feedback control. Avoiding instability is an important part of the control system design process.

In addition to achieving stability under nominal operating conditions, a control system must possess a degree of robustness. A robust controller can tolerate limited changes to the parameters of the plant and its operating environment while continuing to provide satisfactory, stable performance. For example, an automotive cruise control must maintain the desired vehicle speed by adjusting the throttle position in response to changes in road grade (a change in the external environment). The cruise control must also perform properly even if the vehicle is pulling a trailer (a change in system parameters).

Determining the allowable ranges of system and environmental parameter changes is part of the controller specification and design process. To demonstrate robustness, the designer must evaluate controller stability under worst-case combinations of expected plant and environment parameter variations. For each combination of parameter values, a robust controller must satisfy all of its performance requirements.

When working with linear models of plants and controllers, it is possible to precisely determine whether a particular plant and controller form a stable system. In Chapter 3, I describe how to determine linear system stability.

If no mathematical model for the plant exists, stability can only be evaluated by testing the plant and controller under a variety of operating conditions. In Chapter 2, I cover techniques for developing stable control systems without the use of a plant model. In Chapter 9, I describe methods for performing thorough control system testing.

1.9 Control System Testing

Testing is an integral part of the control system design process. Many of the design methods in this book rely on the use of a linear plant model. Creating a linear model always involves approximation and simplification of the true plant behavior. The implementation of a controller with the use of an embedded processor introduces nonlinear effects such as quantization. As a result, both the plant and the controller contain nonlinear effects that are not accounted for in a linear control system design.

The ideal way to demonstrate correct operation of the nonlinear plant and controller over the full range of system behavior is by performing thorough testing with an actual plant. This type of system-level testing normally occurs late in the product development process when prototype hardware becomes available. Problems found at this stage of the development cycle tend to be very expensive to fix.

Because of this, it is highly desirable to perform thorough testing at a much earlier stage of the development cycle. Early testing enables the discovery and repair of problems when they are relatively easy and inexpensive to fix. However, testing the controller early in the product development process might not be easy if a prototype plant does not exist on which to perform tests.

System simulation provides a solution to this problem [2]. A simulation containing detailed models of the plant and controller is extremely valuable for performing early-stage control system testing. This simulation should include all relevant nonlinear effects present in the actual plant and controller implementations. Although the simulation model of the plant must necessarily be a simplified approximation of the actual system, it should be a much more authentic representation than the linear plant model used in the controller design.

When you use simulation in the product development process, it is imperative to perform thorough simulation verification and validation.

- Verification demonstrates that the simulation has been implemented correctly according to its design specifications.
- Validation demonstrates that the simulation accurately represents the behavior of the simulated system and its environment for the intended purposes of the simulation.

The verification step is relevant for any software development process and simply shows that the software performs as its designers intended. In simulation work, verification can occur in the early stages of a product development project. It is possible (and common) to perform verification for a simulation of a system that does not yet exist. This consists of making sure that the models used in the simulation are correctly implemented and produce the expected results. Verification allows the construction and application of a simulation in the earliest phases of a product development project.

Validation is a demonstration that the simulation models the embedded system and the real-world operational environment with acceptable accuracy. A standard approach for validation is to use the results of system operational tests for comparison against simulation results. This involves running the simulation in a scenario that is identical to a test that was performed by the actual system in a real-world environment. The results of the two tests are compared, and the differences are analyzed to determine whether they represent significant deviations between the simulation and the actual system.

A drawback of this approach to validation is that it cannot happen until a complete system prototype is available. However, even when a prototype does not exist, it might be possible to perform validation at an earlier project phase at the component and subsystem level. You can perform tests on those system elements in a laboratory environment and duplicate the tests with the simulation. Comparing the results of the two tests provides confidence in the validity of the component or subsystem model.

The use of system simulation is common in the control engineering world. If you are unfamiliar with the tools and techniques of simulation, see Ledin (2001) [2] for an introduction to this topic.

1.10 Computer-Aided Control System Design

The classical control system analysis and design methods I discuss in Chapter 4 were originally developed and have been taught for years as techniques that rely on hand-drawn sketches. Although this approach leads to a level of design intuition in the student, it takes significant time and practice to develop the necessary skills.

Because I intend to enable the reader to rapidly apply a variety of control system design techniques, automated approaches will be emphasized in this book. Several commercially available software packages perform control system analysis and design functions and nonlinear system simulation as well. Some examples are listed below.

- *VisSim/Analyze™*. This product performs linearization of nonlinear plant models and supports compensator design and testing. This is an add-on to the VisSim product, which is a tool for performing modeling and simulation of complex dynamic systems. For more information, see `http://www.vissim.com/products/addons/analyze.html`.

- *Mathematica® Control System Professional*. This tool handles linear SISO and MIMO system analysis and design in the time and frequency domains. This is an add-on to the Mathematica product. Mathematica provides an environment for performing symbolic and numerical mathematical computations and programming. For more information, see `http://www.wolfram.com/products/applications/control/`.

- *MATLAB Control System Toolbox*. This is a collection of algorithms that implement common control system analysis, design, and modeling techniques. It covers classical design techniques as well as modern state-space methods. This is an add-on to the MATLAB product, which integrates mathematical computing, visualization, and a programming language to enable the development and application of sophisticated algorithms to large sets of data. For more information, see `http://www.mathworks.com/products/control/`.

Important Point

In this book, I use MATLAB, the Control System Toolbox, and other MATLAB add-on products to demonstrate a variety of control system modeling, design, and simulation techniques. These tools provide efficient, numerically robust algorithms to solve a variety of control system engineering problems. The MATLAB environment also provides powerful graphics capabilities for displaying the results of control system analysis and simulation procedures.

The MATLAB software is not cheap, but powerful tools like this seldom are. Pricing information is available online at `http://www.mathworks.com/store/index.html`. MATLAB products are available for a free 30-day trial period. If you are a student using the software in conjunction with a course at a degree-granting institution, you are entitled to purchase the MATLAB Student Version and Control System Toolbox at greatly reduced prices. For more information, see `http://www.mathworks.com/products/education/student_version/sc/index.shtml`.

1.11 Summary

Feedback control systems measure attributes of the system being controlled and use that information to determine the control actuator signal. Feedback control provides superior performance compared to open-loop control when environmental or system parameters change.

The system to be controlled is called a plant. Some characteristics of the plant as they relate to the control system design process follow.

- **Linearity.** A linear plant representation is required for some of the design methods presented in following chapters. All real-world systems are nonlinear, but it is often possible to develop a suitable linear approximation of a plant.

- **Continuous time or discrete time.** A continuous-time system is usually the best way to represent a plant. Embedded computing systems function in a discrete-time manner. Input/output devices such as DACs and ADCs are the interfaces between a continuous-time plant and a discrete-time controller.

- **Number of input and output signals.** A plant that has a single input and a single output is a SISO system. If it has more than one input or output, it is a MIMO system. MIMO systems can often be approximated as a set of SISO systems for design purposes.

- **Time delays.** Time delays in a plant add some difficulty to the problem of designing a controller.

The two fundamental steps in control system design are to

- specify the controller structure and
- determine the value of the design parameters within that structure.

The control system design process usually involves the iterative application of these two steps. In the first step, a candidate controller structure is selected. In the second step, a design method is used to determine suitable parameter values for that structure. If the resulting system performance is inadequate, the cycle is repeated with a new, usually more complex, controller structure.

A block diagram of a plant and controller graphically represents the structure of a controller design and its interaction with the plant. It is possible to perform algebraic operations on the linear components of a block diagram to reduce the diagram to a simpler form.

Performance specifications guide the design process and provide the means for determining when controller performance is satisfactory. Controller performance specifications can be stated in both the time domain and the frequency domain.

Stability is a critical issue throughout the control system design process. A stable controller produces appropriate system responses to changes in the reference input. Stability evaluation must be performed as part of the analysis of a controller design.

Testing is an integral part of the control system design process. It is highly desirable to perform thorough control system testing at an early stage of the development cycle, but prototype system hardware might be unavailable at that time. As an alternative, a simulation containing detailed models of the plant and controller is useful for performing early-stage control system testing. When prototype hardware is available, thorough testing of the control system across the intended range of operating conditions is imperative.

Several software packages are commercially available that perform control system analysis and design functions, as well as complete nonlinear system simulation. These tools can significantly speed the steps of the control system design and analysis processes. This book will emphasize the application of the MATLAB Control System Toolbox and other MATLAB-related products to control system design, analysis, and system simulation tasks.

1.12 Self-Test

1. A driver (the controller) operating an automobile (the plant) manipulates the steering wheel, accelerator, and brake pedal while processing information that is received visually. Is this an open-loop control system or a closed-loop control system? What are the actuators?
2. A home heating system turns a furnace on and off in response to variations in room temperature. The on/off switching can be assumed to take place instantaneously when the sensed temperature crosses a threshold. Is this a continuous-time system or a discrete-time system?
3. A robotic angular positioning system measures the angle of a shaft. The controller estimates the shaft angular velocity with the use of multiple position measurements over time. From the position measurements and velocity estimates, the controller computes a voltage that drives a direct current motor that moves the shaft. Is this a SISO system or a MIMO system?
4. True or false: It is generally best to begin the control system design process with a rich, complex controller structure and attempt to find optimum parameter values within that structure.
5. For a control system to most closely track changes in the input signal, should each of the following specifications be maximized or minimized: rise time, t_r; time to peak magnitude, t_p; settling time, t_s?
6. Given a plant that is inherently unstable, is it possible to develop a controller that results in a stable system consisting of plant plus controller?
7. Is there any reasonable way to test a controller other than operating it in conjunction with a real plant?

Advanced Concepts

8. You perform two tests on a system by presenting different input signals $u_1(t)$ and $u_2(t)$. The two output signals from those tests are $y_1(t)$ and $y_2(t)$. You then perform a third test with the input signal $u_3(t) = u_1(t) + u_2(t)$. The output signal is $y_3(t) = y_1(t) + y_2(t)$. Does this prove that the system under test is a linear system?
9. Simplify the block diagram in Figure 1.6 to a single block with input r and output y. Use the intermediate variables r' and e' to assist in the solution.

Figure 1.6 System block diagram.

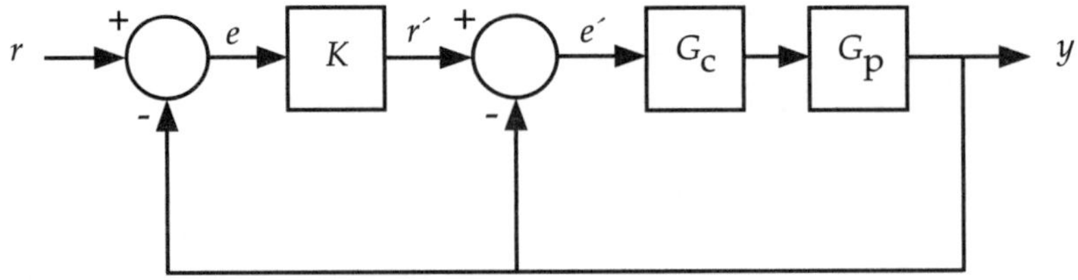

1.13 Answers to Self-Test

1. This is a closed-loop system. The feedback results from the driver's observation of the instruments and the external environment. The primary actuator inputs to the plant are the steering wheel, accelerator, and brake pedal positions.
2. This is a continuous-time system. All system parameters are defined at all points in time. The actuator signal to the furnace can occur at any point in time.
3. This is a SISO system. The controller has one input (shaft position) and one output (motor drive voltage). The controller internally estimates the velocity of the shaft, but that estimate is neither an input nor an output.
4. False. It is usually better to start with the simplest controller structure that could possibly meet performance requirements and only increase the controller complexity if the simplest structure fails to meet the requirements.
5. All of these parameters must be minimized to track the input signal most closely.
6. Yes. Automobile steering is one example: Releasing the steering wheel will eventually run the car off the road. Later chapters will present examples of controllers that stabilize unstable plants.
7. Yes. It is possible to perform thorough testing of a controller design by operating it in a simulation environment in conjunction with a mathematical model of the plant.

Advanced Concepts

8. No. The linearity test must be satisfied for all possible $u_1(t)$ and $u_2(t)$. Passing the test with only one pair of $u_1(t)$ and $u_2(t)$ does not prove linearity.
9. The solution is shown in Figures 1.7 and 1.8. As a first step in the solution, reduce the transfer function from r' to y to the expression

$$\frac{y}{r'} = \frac{G_c G_p}{1 + G_c G_p}$$

by the approach shown in the example in Section 1.6 with $H = 1$. Substitute that expression into the diagram. The result of this step appears in Figure 1.7.

Figure 1.7 Partially simplified system block diagram.

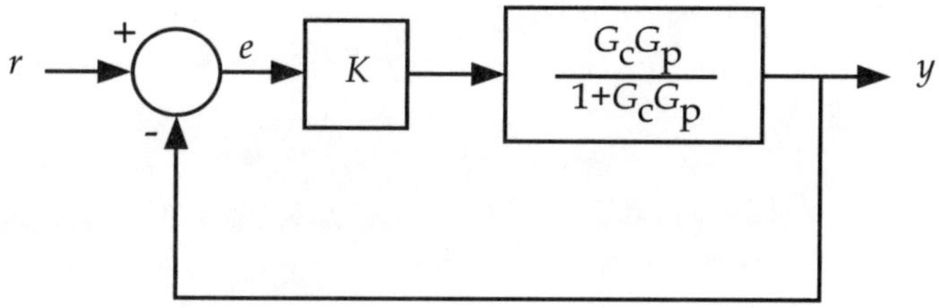

Repeat the diagram reduction procedure and simplify the resulting expression to arrive at the result of Figure 1.8.

Figure 1.8 Simplified system block diagram.

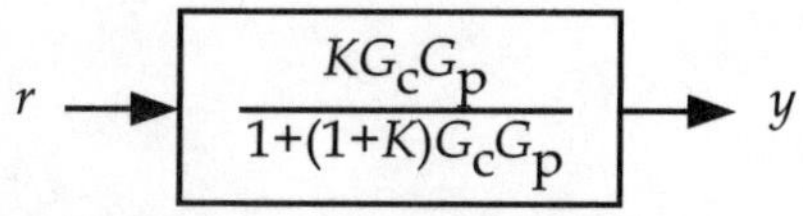

1.14 References

1. Gene F. Franklin, J. David Powell, and Abbas Emami-Naeini, *Feedback Control of Dynamic Systems* (Reading, MA: Addison Wesley, 1986).
2. Jim Ledin, *Simulation Engineering* (Lawrence, KS: CMP Books, 2001).

CHAPTER 2

PID CONTROL

2.1 Introduction

In this chapter, I introduce a method for implementing a control system when a plant model does not exist or is too complex to be useful for design purposes. This technique is suitable for use with plants that are approximately linear, although it can also provide satisfactory results with nonlinear plants.

The structure considered here is called the *PID controller.* The PID controller's output signal consists of a sum of terms proportional to the error signal, as well as to the integral and derivative of the error signal—hence, the name "PID." This is the most commonly used controller structure. By some estimates [1], 90 to 95 percent of all control problems are solved with PID control.

The input to a PID controller is the error signal created by subtracting the plant output from the reference input. The output of the PID controller is a weighted sum of the error signal and its integral and derivative. The designer determines a suitable weighting multiplier for each of the three terms by performing an iterative tuning procedure.

In this chapter, I describe iterative PID controller design techniques and show how they can be applied in practical situations.

2.2 Chapter Objectives

After reading this chapter, you should be able to

- describe when it is appropriate to apply PID controller design procedures;
- describe the structure and design parameters of a PID controller;

- describe when to use proportional-only, proportional plus derivative (PD), proportional plus integral (PI), and full PID controller structures;
- perform a tuning procedure on a PID controller operating in conjunction with a plant; and
- adapt a PID controller to perform well with a plant in which actuator saturation occurs in response to large reference input changes.

2.3 PID Control

The actuator command developed by a PID controller is a weighted sum of the error signal and its integral and derivative. PID stands for the Proportional, Integral, and Derivative terms that sum to create the controller output signal. Figure 2.1 shows a PID controller (represented by the G_c block) in a control loop. The G_p block represents the plant to be controlled.

Figure 2.1 Block diagram of a system with a PID controller.

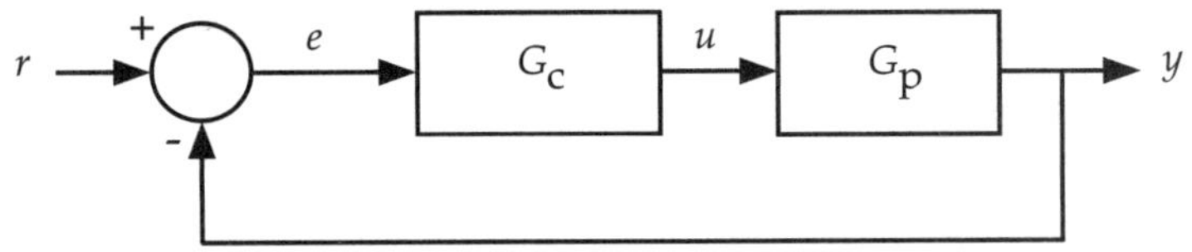

In Figure 2.1, the controller input is the error e. The output of the controller is the actuator command u. This diagram assumes the dynamics of the sensor to be negligible.

Integral and Derivative

The PID controller requires the integral and derivative of the error signal. These terms might be unfamiliar to readers who do not have a background in calculus.

In terms of a discrete-time controller, the integral of the error signal *e* can be approximated as the running sum of the *e* samples, each multiplied by the controller sampling interval *h*. In other words, the integral begins with an initial value (often 0), and at each controller update, the current *e* sample, multiplied by *h*, is added to the running sum. If *e* is greater than zero for a period of time, its integral will grow in value during that time.

The integral of *e* from time zero to the current time *t* is represented mathematically by the notation

$$\int_0^t e\, d\tau .$$

The derivative represents the rate of change, or slope, of *e*. In a discrete-time system, the derivative can be approximated by subtracting the value of *e* at the previous time step from the current *e* and dividing the result by *h*. When *e* increases in value from one sample to the next, the derivative is positive.

The derivative of *e* is represented mathematically by the notation $\frac{de}{dt}$.

The PID controller is suitable for use in SISO systems. As described in Chapter 1, it often is possible to approximate a MIMO system as a set of SISO systems for design purposes. When this approximation is reasonable, the design techniques described in this chapter can be applied to each SISO component of the larger MIMO system.

Equation 2.1 gives the mathematical formula for the continuous-time PID control algorithm.

$$u = K_p\left(e + K_i \int_0^t e \, d\tau + K_d \frac{de}{dt}\right) \qquad \text{Eq. 2.1}$$

The design parameters of the PID controller are the three constants K_p, K_i, and K_d, which are called the proportional, integral, and derivative gains, respectively. One or two of the gains can be set to zero, which simplifies the implementation of the algorithm. If K_i is zero, the result is a PD controller with no integral term. A PI controller contains proportional and integral terms, but no derivative term. The simplest mode of control consists of a proportional term only, with no derivative or integral terms.

PID Controller Parameters

The various branches of control system engineering do not use identical names for the PID controller parameters appearing in Eq. 2.1.

In the process control industries, the K_i constant is replaced with a constant defined as $1/T_I$, where T_I is defined as the integral time (also called reset time) and $1/T_I$ is called the reset rate. Also in process control, the K_d constant is renamed T_D, the derivative time.

Figure 2.2 shows a unit step response for an example plant with a full PID controller. A unit step is an instantaneous change in the reference input from 0 to 1. The four graphs show the system output y, the error signal e, the error derivative de/dt, and the error integral

$$\int_0^t e \, d\tau.$$

Observe how the response y in the top graph of Figure 2.2 overshoots the commanded value and slowly approaches it from above. This is caused by the integral term. As the bottom graph shows, the integral builds up to a value of approximately 1 at about $t = 2$ seconds and slowly decays toward 0. This behavior is an inherent attribute of integral control in response to large errors, such as those caused by step inputs. I address the issue of controller overshoot due to the integration of a large error signal later in this chapter.

As I suggested in Chapter 1, if you don't already know that a particular controller structure is required for a given application, you should begin with the simplest one you believe can work. This rule suggests that you should start PID controller design with just a proportional gain term and add derivative and integral terms only if testing proves them to be necessary.

Figure 2.2 Step response of a system with a PID controller.

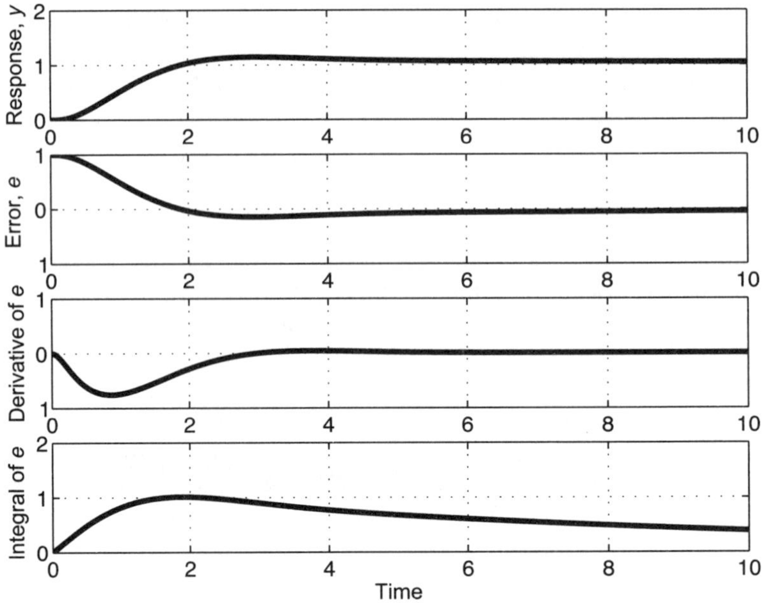

Advanced Concept

The plant used in the examples in this chapter is modeled as

$$G_p = \frac{1}{s^2(0.1s + 1)}.$$

I introduce the s notation employed here in Chapter 3. This model represents a rotating mass (with no friction) described by $1/s^2$. The actuator is modeled as a motor that rotates the mass and has the transfer function $1/(0.1s + 1)$. The expression for G_p combines the dynamics of the mass and the motor. The plant input is the voltage applied to the motor and the output is the angular position of the rotating mass. The controller goal is to rotate the mass to a commanded angular position by driving it with the motor.

2.3.1 Proportional Control

Setting both the K_i and K_d parameters to 0 in the PID control algorithm of Eq. 2.1 gives the proportional control algorithm shown in Eq. 2.2.

$$u = K_p e \qquad \text{Eq. 2.2}$$

Proportional control develops an actuator signal by multiplying the error in the system response by the constant K_p. If K_p is chosen with the correct sign, proportional control will always attempt to drive the error e to zero.

The design procedure for a proportional controller consists of selecting an appropriate value for K_p. In Chapter 4, I cover some methods for performing this selection when a plant model is available. In this chapter, no plant model is assumed, so a trial-and-error approach is necessary.

Important Point

The test setup for controller tuning should be carefully selected for safety reasons. It is entirely possible that system oscillation and instability will occur during the tuning procedure. The plant should have sufficient safeguards in its operation such that there is no risk of damage or injury as a result of the controller tuning process.

Tuning a Proportional Controller

1. Start by implementing a controller with the algorithm of Eq. 2.2 and choose a small value for K_p. A small value will minimize the possibility of excessive overshoot and oscillation.
2. Select an appropriate input signal such as a step input. Perform a test run by driving the controller and plant with that input signal. The result should be a sluggish response that slowly drives the error in the output toward zero.
3. Increase the value of K_p by a small amount and repeat the test. The speed of the response should increase. If K_p becomes too large, overshoot and oscillation could occur.
4. Continue increasing the value of K_p and repeating the test. If satisfactory system performance is achieved, you are done. If excessive overshoot and oscillation occur before acceptable response time is achieved, you will need to add a derivative term. If the steady-state error (the error that persists after the transient response has died out) fails to converge to a sufficiently small value, you will need to add an integral term.

Proportional-only controllers often suffer from two modes in which they fail to meet design specifications.

1. Because it is usually desirable to make the system respond as fast as possible, the K_p gain must be of large magnitude. This can result in overshoot and oscillation in the system response.
2. In many cases, the steady-state system response does not converge to zero error. The steady-state error could have an unacceptably large magnitude. An example of this would be a cruise control that allows the vehicle speed to drop to a significantly reduced value while traveling up a constant slope.

The first of these problems can be addressed by the addition of a derivative term to the controller. The effect of the derivative term is to anticipate overshoot and reduce the controller output during periods of rapid actuator change. An increase in the magnitude of the derivative gain K_d increases the damping of the system response. This controller structure is the topic of the next section.

The second problem, nonzero steady-state error, can be solved by adding an integral term to the controller. I cover this approach later in the chapter.

2.3.2 Proportional Plus Derivative (PD) Control

Setting $K_i = 0$ in the PID control algorithm of Eq. 2.1 produces the PD control algorithm shown in Eq. 2.3. With the correct choice of signs for K_p and K_d, a PD controller will generate an actuator command that attempts to drive both the error and the rate of change of the error to zero.

$$u = K_p\left(e + K_d \frac{de}{dt}\right) \quad \text{Eq. 2.3}$$

The top graph in Figure 2.3 shows the unit step response of the example plant with a proportional controller and $K_p = 1$. This controller produces an unstable (growing amplitude) oscillation and is clearly unacceptable.

The bottom graph in Figure 2.3 shows the response after adding a derivative term (with $K_d = 1.6$) to the controller. The same proportional gain is used in both controllers. Note how the overshoot and oscillation essentially have been eliminated. In addition, the system has become stable.

The time to peak response (t_p) for the PD controller in Figure 2.3 is 5.1 seconds. This is significantly longer than the time to the first peak for the (unstable) proportional controller, which was 3.2 seconds. This is because adding a derivative term has the effect of reducing the speed of the response. However, the damping provided by the derivative term allows the proportional gain K_p to be increased, resulting in a faster response. Increases in K_p typically require adjustments to K_d to maintain appropriate damping.

Figure 2.4 shows the response of the plant after adjusting the gains to $K_p = 10$ and $K_d = 0.5$. As a result of the higher proportional gain, t_p has been reduced to 1.2 seconds. These gain values were selected with the use of the PD controller tuning procedure described below.

Figure 2.3 Comparison of proportional and PD controller responses.

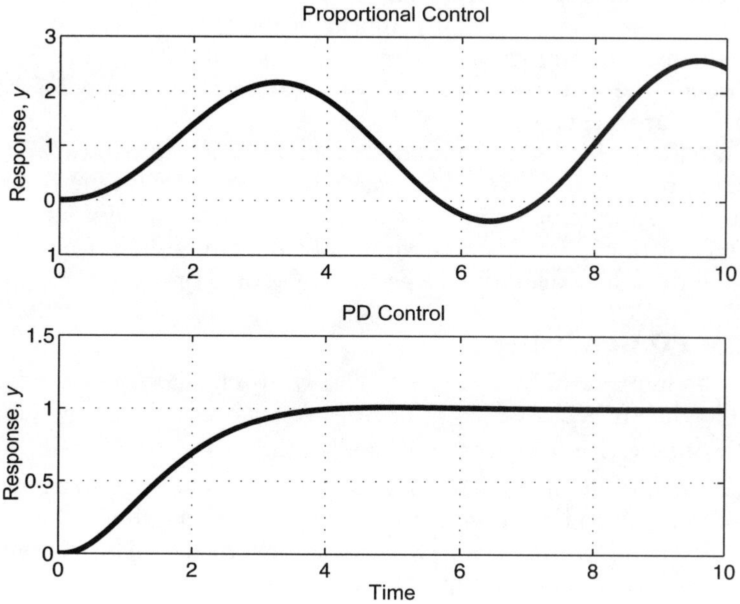

Figure 2.4 PD controller with $K_p = 10$ and $K_d = 0.5$.

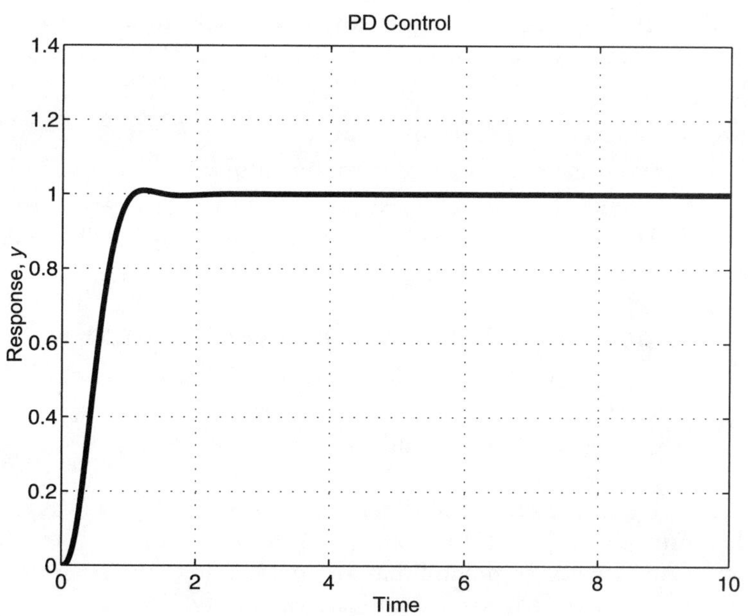

It is possible to increase the K_p gain further to get an even faster response, but that requires additional actuator effort. At some point, a real actuator will reach its limits of performance. These limits typically appear in the form of actuator position or rate-of-change bounds. This limiting behavior is called *actuator saturation*. When actuator saturation occurs, the system's response to increasing controller gains becomes nonlinear and could be unacceptable.

It is usually preferable to avoid actuator saturation in control systems. An example where actuator saturation would be unacceptable is in an automotive cruise control system. Saturating the actuator in this case would involve opening the throttle valve to its maximum position. Most drivers would not be happy with a cruise control that performed full-throttle acceleration as part of its normal operation.

Tuning a PD Controller

1. Start by implementing a PD controller with the algorithm of Eq. 2.3 and choose a small value for K_p. Set $K_d = 0$ for now. A small value of K_p will minimize the possibility of excessive overshoot and oscillation.
2. Select an appropriate input signal such as a step input. Perform a test run by driving the controller and plant with that input. The result should be a sluggish response that slowly drives the error in the output toward zero. The response might be unstable, as shown in the top graph of Figure 2.3. If it is unstable or highly oscillatory, go to step 4.
3. Increase the value of K_p and repeat the test. The speed of the response should increase. If K_p becomes too large, overshoot and oscillation can occur.
4. Increase the value of K_d to reduce any overshoot and oscillation to an acceptable level. If the speed of the response becomes unacceptably slow, try reducing the value of K_d.
5. Continue increasing the value of K_p and adjusting K_d as needed while repeating the test. Watch for the appearance of actuator saturation and reduce K_p if unacceptable saturation occurs. If satisfactory system performance is achieved, you are done. If the steady-state error fails to converge to a sufficiently small value, you will need to add an integral term.

2.3.3 Proportional Plus Integral (PI) Control

The addition of an integral term to a proportional controller results in a PI controller. An integral term eliminates steady-state errors in the plant response. The K_i gain of the integral term is usually set to a small value so that the steady-state error is gradually reduced.

Setting $K_d = 0$ in the PID control algorithm of Eq. 2.1 produces the PI control algorithm shown in Eq. 2.4. With the correct choice of signs for K_p and K_i, a PI controller will generate an actuator command that attempts to drive the error to 0 with the proportional gain and removes any steady-state error with the integral gain.

$$u = K_p\left(e + K_i\int_0^t e\,d\tau\right) \qquad \text{Eq. 2.4}$$

Use a PI controller in situations in which a proportional controller achieves acceptable performance, except that the steady-state error in the response is unacceptably large.

Tuning a PI Controller

1. Start by implementing a controller with the algorithm of Eq. 2.4 and choose a small value of K_p. Set $K_i = 0$ for now. A small value of K_p will minimize the possibility of excessive overshoot and oscillation.
2. Select an appropriate input signal such as a step input. Perform a test run by driving the controller and plant with that input signal. The result should be a sluggish response that slowly drives the error in the output toward zero.
3. Increase the value of K_p by a small amount and repeat the test. The speed of the response should increase. If K_p becomes too large, overshoot and oscillation can occur.
4. Continue increasing the value of K_p and repeating the test. If satisfactory system performance (other than steady-state error) is achieved, go to step 5. If excessive overshoot and oscillation occur before acceptable response time is achieved, you will need to add a derivative term as described in Section 2.3.4.
5. Set K_i to a small value and repeat the test. Observe the time it takes to reduce the steady-state error to an acceptably small level.
6. Continue increasing K_i and repeating the test. If K_i becomes too large, the overshoot in the response will become excessive. Select a value of K_i that gives acceptable overshoot while reducing the steady-state error at a sufficient rate. Watch for actuator saturation, which will increase the overshoot in the response. If actuator saturation is a problem, see Section 2.3.5.

2.3.4 Proportional Plus Integral Plus Derivative (PID) Control

Combining derivative and integral terms with a proportional controller produces a PID controller. The derivative term adds damping to the system response and the integral term eliminates steady-state errors in the response.

The full PID controller algorithm is shown again in Eq. 2.5. With the correct choice of signs for K_p, K_i, and K_d, a PID controller will generate an actuator command that attempts to drive the error to zero with the proportional gain, remove the steady-state error with the integral gain, and dampen the response with the derivative gain.

$$u = K_p\left(e + K_i\int_0^t e\,d\tau + K_d\frac{de}{dt}\right) \qquad \text{Eq. 2.5}$$

Use a PID controller in situations where a proportional-only controller exhibits excessive overshoot and oscillation and the steady-state error in the response is unacceptably large.

Tuning a PID Controller

1. Start by implementing a controller with the algorithm of Eq. 2.5 and choose a small value of K_p. Set $K_i = K_d = 0$ for now. A small value of K_p will minimize the possibility of excessive overshoot and oscillation.
2. Select an appropriate input signal such as a step input. Perform a test run by driving the controller and plant with that input. The result should be a sluggish response that slowly drives the error in the output toward zero. The response can be unstable, as shown in the top graph of Figure 2.3. If it is unstable or highly oscillatory, go to step 4.
3. Increase the value of K_p and repeat the test. The speed of the response should increase. If K_p becomes too large, overshoot and oscillation can occur.
4. Increase the value of K_d to reduce any overshoot and oscillation to an acceptable level. If the speed of the response becomes unacceptably slow, try reducing the value of K_d.
5. Continue increasing the value of K_p and adjusting K_d as needed while repeating the test. Watch for the appearance of actuator saturation and reduce K_p if unacceptable saturation occurs.
6. Set K_i to a small value and repeat the test. Observe the time it takes to reduce the steady-state error to an acceptable level.
7. Continue increasing K_i and repeating the test. If K_i becomes too large, the overshoot in response to a step input will become excessive. Select a value of K_i that gives acceptable overshoot while reducing the steady-state error at a sufficient rate. Watch for actuator saturation to occur, which will increase the overshoot in the response. If actuator saturation is a problem, continue with Section 2.3.5.

2.3.5 PID Control and Actuator Saturation

When actuator saturation occurs, a PI or PID controller experiences a phenomenon known as *integrator windup*, also called reset windup in process control applications. Integrator windup is the result of integrating a large error signal during periods when the actuator is unable to respond fully to its commanded behavior. The problem is that the integrated error term can reach a very large value during these periods, which results in significant overshoot in the system response. Oscillation is also a possibility, with the actuator banging from one end of its range of motion to the other. Clearly, integrator windup should be reduced to an acceptable level in a good controller design.

One way to reduce the effect of integrator windup is to turn the integration off when the amplitude (absolute value) of the error signal is above a cutoff level. This result can be achieved by setting the integrator input to zero during periods of large error.

In addition to improving controller response in the presence of actuator saturation, this technique can also reduce the overshoot in situations where the system response is linear. Earlier in this chapter, Figure 2.2 showed an example PID controller response for a linear plant that had significant overshoot because of the integral term. The overshoot in that example would be reduced substantially by the addition of integrator windup reduction to the controller.

Equation 2.6 shows the PID controller algorithm with integrator windup reduction included. The function q has the value 1 when the absolute value of the error is less than the threshold E and 0 otherwise. This freezes the value of the integrated error during periods of large error.

$$u = K_p\left(e + K_i \int_0^t qe\, d\tau + K_d \frac{de}{dt}\right) \qquad \begin{matrix} \text{where } q = 1 \text{ if } |e| < E, \\ \text{else } q = 0 \end{matrix} \qquad \text{Eq. 2.6}$$

This approach adds a parameter to the controller design process: The designer must determine the cutoff level E, where the error amplitude becomes “large.” This level must be high enough that normal steady-state errors are eliminated. It must also be small enough that the effects of integrator windup are reduced to an acceptable level. Selecting the cutoff level might require some iterative testing similar to the tuning that was done to select the controller gains.

The integrator error cutoff level should be selected after completing the PI or PID tuning procedure described above. If actuator saturation occurred during the initial controller tuning procedure, it might be necessary to retune the controller after the error cutoff level has been set.

Figure 2.5 shows an example of this technique. The plant and actuator in this figure are the same as those used in the previous examples of this chapter, except the actuator now saturates at ±0.5. With no integrator windup reduction, the response (the solid line in Figure 2.5) has 23 percent overshoot and converges slowly to the commanded value. With windup compensation enabled and the error cutoff level E set to 0.1, the response (the dashed line) has only 6 percent overshoot and quicker convergence to the commanded value. The same controller gains are used in both cases: $K_p = 10$, $K_i = 0.1$, and $K_d = 0.8$.

2.4 PID Controller Implementation in C/C++

Listing 2.1 is an implementation of the full PID controller algorithm (including windup reduction) in the C programming language. Note that this code only permits a single instance of a PID controller in a program. The extension of the code to support multiple controllers is left as an exercise for the reader.

Figure 2.5 PID controller with and without integrator windup reduction.

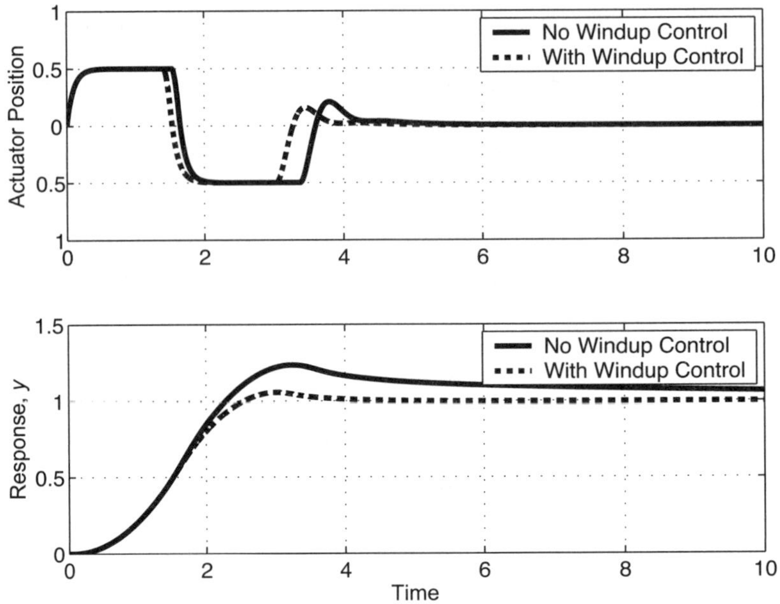

Simpler forms of the PID structure, including PD, PI, and proportional-only control, can be realized by setting one or both of the `ki` and `kd` parameters (the integral and derivative gains) in the `PID_Initialize()` function call to zero. To disable windup reduction, set the `error_thresh` input to a very large value.

The `step_time` input is the time interval (usually in seconds) between controller updates. In general, the smaller the value of `step_time`, the more closely the embedded controller performance will agree with the performance of the ideal PID controller described by Eq. 2.6. If `step_time` is set to a value that is too large, the system could exhibit oscillation or instability.

If the controller input signal is very noisy or has a large quantization step size, the simple derivative estimation technique used in this code might not produce meaningful results for PD and PID controllers. In this situation, lowpass filtering should be used to smooth the input signal used in the derivative calculation. Alternatively, you might want to employ a more advanced control system design technique from Chapters 4, 5, or 6 instead of PID control.

To use this code in a real-time application, call `PID_Initialize()` to set up the controller parameters, then call `PID_Update()` at time intervals equal to `step_time`. The error input to `PID_Update()` is the e signal in Figure 2.1. The output from `PID_Update()` is the u signal in Figure 2.1.

Listing 2.1 PID controller in C.

```
#include <math.h>

/* Select 'double' or 'float' here: */
typedef double real;

void PID_Initialize(real kp, real ki, real kd,
    real error_thresh, real step_time);
real PID_Update(real error);

static int m_started;
static real m_kp, m_ki, m_kd, m_h, m_inv_h, m_prev_error,
        m_error_thresh, m_integral;

void PID_Initialize(real kp, real ki,
    real kd, real error_thresh, real step_time)
{
    /* Initialize controller parameters */
    m_kp = kp;
    m_ki = ki;
    m_kd = kd;
    m_error_thresh = error_thresh;

    /* Controller step time and its inverse */
    m_h = step_time;
    m_inv_h = 1 / step_time;

    /* Initialize integral and derivative calculations */
    m_integral = 0;
    m_started = 0;
}

real PID_Update(real error)
{
    real q, deriv;

    /* Set q to 1 if the error magnitude is below
```

```
        the threshold and 0 otherwise */
    if (fabs(error) < m_error_thresh)
        q = 1;
    else
        q = 0;

    /* Update the error integral */
    m_integral += m_h*q*error;

    /* Compute the error derivative */
    if (!m_started)
    {
        m_started = 1;
        deriv = 0;
    }
    else
        deriv = (error - m_prev_error) * m_inv_h;

    m_prev_error = error;

    /* Return the PID controller actuator command */
    return m_kp*(error + m_ki*m_integral + m_kd*deriv);
}
```

Listing 2.2 provides an implementation of the full PID controller algorithm including windup reduction in the C++ programming language. The C++ implementation permits an unlimited number of instances of PID controllers in a program. Each controller in the application requires the instantiation of one object of the `PID_Controller` class.

The parameters to the `PID_Controller::Initialize` and `PID_Controller::Update` methods are identical to the parameters of the `PID_Initialize()` and `PID_Update()` functions in Listing 2.1. The usage of the C++ methods is identical to the corresponding functions in Listing 2.1.

Listing 2.2 PID controller in C++.

```
#include <cmath>

// Select 'double' or 'float' here:
typedef double real;
```

```
class PID_Controller
{
public:
    void Initialize(real kp, real ki, real kd,
        real error_thresh, real step_time);
    real Update(real error);

private:
    bool m_started;
    real m_kp, m_ki, m_kd, m_h, m_inv_h, m_prev_error,
        m_error_thresh, m_integral;
};

void PID_Controller::Initialize(real kp, real ki,
    real kd, real error_thresh, real step_time)
{
    // Initialize controller parameters
    m_kp = kp;
    m_ki = ki;
    m_kd = kd;
    m_error_thresh = error_thresh;

    // Controller step time and its inverse
    m_h = step_time;
    m_inv_h = 1 / step_time;

    // Initialize integral and derivative calculations
    m_integral = 0;
    m_started = false;
}

real PID_Controller::Update(real error)
{
    // Set q to 1 if the error magnitude is below
    // the threshold and 0 otherwise
    real q;
```

```
    if (fabs(error) < m_error_thresh)
        q = 1;
    else
        q = 0;

    // Update the error integral
    m_integral += m_h*q*error;

    // Compute the error derivative
    real deriv;
    if (!m_started)
    {
        m_started = true;
        deriv = 0;
    }
    else
        deriv = (error - m_prev_error) * m_inv_h;

    m_prev_error = error;

    // Return the PID controller actuator command
    return m_kp*(error + m_ki*m_integral + m_kd*deriv);
}
```

2.5 Summary

In this chapter, I discussed the design of PID controllers when a plant model does not exist. Because no mathematical model is assumed to be available, the design method requires iterative tuning of controller parameters in response to test runs of the closed-loop system.

A PID controller computes an actuator command by computing a weighted sum of the error signal and its integral and derivative. The weights applied to each of these terms are called the proportional, integral, and derivative gains, respectively.

The full PID controller structure can be simplified in several ways. Setting one or two of the gains in the PID controller to zero results in the proportional-only, PD, and PI structures. In general, the simplest controller structure that provides acceptable performance should be selected.

Proportional-only control multiplies the error signal by the proportional gain to develop the actuator command. If the proportional gain is set to a large value to achieve fast system response, overshoot and oscillation can occur. Adding a derivative term (to create a PD controller) reduces the overshoot and oscillation while allowing larger values of proportional gain.

If the steady-state error in the step response does not converge to an acceptably small value, adding an integral term will remove the error. The integral gain is usually set to a small value to slowly eliminate steady-state error.

In controllers with an integral term (PI and PID structures), actuator saturation can cause integrator windup. The result of integrator windup is excessive overshoot and slow convergence of the response to the commanded value. The technique of freezing the value of the integrator during periods of large error significantly reduces the effect of integrator windup.

2.6 Self-Test

1. The two basic steps in controller design are controller structure selection and parameter specification. Describe how these steps relate to the controller design procedures covered in this chapter.
2. An automobile using a PI cruise control is traveling along a level road at a constant speed. The slope of the road increases as the car goes up a hill. How does the controller adjust to maintain the desired steady-state speed?
3. An alternative way of writing the formula for the PID controller algorithm of Eq. 2.1 is to remove the parentheses around the terms multiplied by K_p as shown here.

$$u = \overline{K}_p e + \overline{K}_i \int_0^t e \, d\tau + \overline{K}_d \frac{de}{dt}$$

   Determine the values of the gains $\overline{K}_p$, $\overline{K}_i$, and $\overline{K}_d$ as they relate to the K_p, K_i, and K_d gains in Eq. 2.1.
4. How does the integrator windup reduction method discussed in this chapter improve the performance of a PI controller with a linear plant?
5. A system contains a significant time delay between an actuator change and the start of the measured response to that change. How does the addition of a time delay affect the resulting PID controller design?

2.7 Answers to Self-Test

1. In the context of PID controller design, structure selection consists of the choice of a proportional-only, PD, PI, or PID controller. Iterative tuning procedures are carried out to determine the parameter values.
2. The integral term must adjust to increase the throttle setting to account for the change in the slope of the road.
3. $\overline{K}_p = K_p$, $\overline{K}_i = K_p K_i$, $\overline{K}_d = K_p K_d$.

4. The windup reduction stops the error integration when the error has large amplitude. Even with a linear plant, the response to a large step input results in a large error integral if windup reduction is not employed. Windup reduction limits the integrator operation to times when the system output is in the vicinity of the commanded value. This results in a smaller integral value in response to large errors; consequently, there is less overshoot in the system response.
5. The addition of a time delay makes the occurrence of oscillation more likely. The controller must use a lower proportional gain compared to an equivalent system without the time delay. The result will be slower system response to changes in the reference input.

2.8 References

1. Karl J. Åström and Tore Hägglund, "PID Control," in *The Control Handbook*, ed. William S. Levine (Boca Raton, FL: CRC Press, 1996).

CHAPTER 3

PLANT MODELS

3.1 Introduction

In this chapter, I introduce techniques for developing linear time-invariant plant models. This type of model provides a simplified representation of the dynamic behavior of a real-world system. The control system design methods covered in subsequent chapters require plant models of this type. Linear time-invariant models possess a number of desirable mathematical properties that the upcoming design methods will utilize.

The standard approach for developing linear time-invariant models taught in engineering courses is to apply the laws of physics to a given system and develop a set of differential equations describing its behavior. The resulting equations are often nonlinear, so an additional step must be performed to linearize them. *Linearization* is the development of a set of linear equations that approximate the nonlinear equations in the vicinity of an *equilibrium point*. An equilibrium point is an operating point where the system is in a steady state and all the derivatives in the equations are zero. In many systems of interest, the response of the plant to small perturbations about an equilibrium point is approximately linear.

An example of an equilibrium point is an automobile operating under cruise control that is traveling at a steady speed on a level road. Because the vehicle speed is constant, the acceleration (the derivative of the speed) is zero.

The physics-based approach works well when the designer possesses the mathematical and engineering background to perform the analysis and linearization procedures. However, it is often the case that insufficient information exists to develop an accurate model by the physics-based technique alone. In this situation, the only way to gather the required information is to perform experiments on the actual system or on a model of the system.

An example of this type of experiment is the testing of a subscale aircraft model in a wind tunnel. The plant model resulting from this approach is a hybrid of the physics-based and experimental techniques. In this example, a physics-based approach is used to develop the basic form of the plant model equations using Newton's law of motion. Experimental results fill in the values of parameters in the equations.

Another approach for developing plant models uses *system identification* techniques to develop a model on the basis of time histories of experimental plant input and response data. This approach has several advantages compared to the physics-based model development method described above:

- Specialized engineering knowledge of the system physics is not required.
- The system identification approach uses real test data, so the possibility of oversimplifying the model by making unjustified assumptions is reduced.
- It is possible to develop system identification models for systems in situations where insufficient information exists to develop a physics-based model.

Plant model development that uses system identification has some potential drawbacks as well:

- The designer must make some careful decisions about the basic model structure, such as the selection of model order.
- The data used for system identification must accurately represent approximately linear system operation over all significant modes of the system's behavior.

System identification is the primary plant model development method advocated in this book. If you have the knowledge and adequate data to develop physics-based models, the use of that approach should usually result in a superior model. On the other hand, if you want to develop a plant model quickly and have the ability to perform a few tests on the system while recording input and output data, system identification could be the quickest and simplest way to create a useful plant model.

System identification involves the application of sophisticated numerical methods to create accurate plant models on the basis of test data. In this book, I will not cover the algorithms used in system identification. Instead, the System Identification Toolbox for MATLAB, which implements a number of the best available identification algorithms, will be employed as a tool here.

In this chapter, I begin with an introduction to linear system models and the most common model representation formats: transfer function, state-space, and frequency domain. I describe how to combine a time delay with a linear model and how to evaluate model stability. I include descriptions of the basic model development techniques described above (physics-based modeling and system identification).

3.2 Chapter Objectives

After reading this chapter, you should be able to

- describe linear time-invariant plant models and their application to control system design;
- understand the transfer function, state-space, and frequency domain representations for linear time-invariant models;
- evaluate plant stability given a linear time-invariant model of the plant;
- understand the approach used in developing system models based on physical laws;
- describe how linear approximations can be developed for nonlinear plant models;
- describe the technique of system identification; and
- explain when it is appropriate to use physics-based modeling, experimental modeling, and system identification for creating plant models.

3.3 Linear Time-Invariant Plant Models

In the following chapters, I present a number of control system design approaches that require a linear time-invariant plant model. The design methods use some combination of manual and automated procedures in conjunction with the plant model to develop a controller that satisfies a set of performance specifications. In this chapter, I cover some commonly used approaches for developing a linear time-invariant plant model suitable for use with the design methods.

As I discussed in Chapter 1, a linear system produces an output that is proportional to its input. Small changes in the input signal result in small changes in the output. Large changes in the input cause large changes in the output. A time-invariant model does not change its properties over time.

Example 3.1 Time-varying versus time-invariant behavior.

An example of a system that exhibits time-varying behavior is an aircraft on a very long flight. The dynamic behavior of this system changes as fuel is burned off, and as a result, the aircraft mass properties change during the flight. However, the response time to control inputs of interest (such as making a turn or an altitude change) is typically very short compared to the rate at which the plant properties change. The assumption of time-invariance is reasonable for control system analysis and design purposes at a given point in the flight. However, the controller parameters might need to be adjusted as the plant properties change during the flight.

Linear time-invariant models are developed with the use of a number of different approaches and can be represented mathematically in various ways. In the next three sections, I describe the three most commonly used formats for representing linear time-invariant models in control system design: transfer function, frequency response, and state-space.

3.3.1 Transfer Function Representation

The transfer function representation is based on the Laplace transform [1] of a linear differential equation with constant coefficients. A differential equation contains a function and one or more of its derivatives. The form of a linear differential equation with constant coefficients is shown in Eq. 3.1. Here, the function to be determined is y, its first derivative is $\dot{y}$, and so on. The constant coefficients are the numerical values such as 1.8 and 100.

The Laplace technique is widely applied in classical control system analysis and design. Transfer functions are used to represent linear models of SISO components such as plants, actuators, and sensors.

A transfer function is a ratio of polynomials in the variable s that represents the ratio of a system's output to its input. Each transfer function corresponds directly to a linear differential equation.

Equation 3.1 is an example of a linear differential equation. The corresponding transfer function representation is shown in Eq. 3.2. The lowercase x and y in Eq. 3.1 indicate the component input and output signals in the time domain and the uppercase X and Y in Eq. 3.2 represent the signals in the s domain (transfer function domain).

$$\ddot{y} + 1.8\dot{y} + 100y = 100x \qquad \text{Eq. 3.1}$$

$$\frac{Y}{X} = \frac{100}{s^2 + 1.8s + 100} \qquad \text{Eq. 3.2}$$

In a transfer function, each power of the variable s represents a derivative. For example, the expression $Ys^2 = X$ is equivalent to the differential equation $\ddot{y} = x$. The transfer function representation assumes that the initial conditions of all states in the differential equation are zero.

Most control system design software is capable of accepting plant models in transfer function form. Many manufacturers of control system components, such as sensors and actuators, provide linear models of those components as transfer functions.

Some familiarity with the transfer function format will be necessary to effectively use the control system design approaches in the following chapters. The most important thing to remember about transfer functions is that they represent linear differential equations.

In the MATLAB Control System Toolbox, `tf()` creates transfer function models. The following MATLAB command shows how to create a linear time-invariant model (named `tfplant`) of the transfer function shown in Eq. 3.2.

```
>> tfplant = tf(100, [1 1.8 100])
```

Note: The characters >> represent the MATLAB command line prompt and should not be entered.

The two arguments to `tf()` are vectors containing the polynomial coefficients of the transfer function numerator and denominator. The square brackets create a vector from the enclosed values and are optional when an argument is a scalar.

The output of the above command is shown here.

```
Transfer function:
 100
-----------------
s^2 + 1.8 s + 100
```

After this command executes, the MATLAB workspace variable `tfplant` is available for use with other Control System Toolbox functions.

3.3.2 Frequency Response Format

The frequency response format describes a system's behavior in terms of its response to a sinusoidal input signal across a range of frequencies. This format assumes linearity of the system and is applicable to SISO systems. The frequency response format is used for control system design as well as in areas such as the design of electronic filters.

When a linear system receives an input signal that is a sinusoid at some frequency ω (omega), the steady-state output is a sinusoid at the same frequency, but possibly with different amplitude and phase. The frequency response format indicates the amplitude of the output sinusoid relative to the input sinusoid, as well as the phase shift of the output relative to the input. The amplitude and phase shift information is displayed for a range of frequencies.

The frequency response of a system can be determined analytically or experimentally. The experimental approach is useful for systems that are not understood well enough to model with the equations of physics.

Figure 3.1 shows the frequency response representation of the linear system described by the transfer function of Eq. 3.2. The magnitude and phase of the transfer function are displayed in the form of a *Bode plot.* A Bode plot shows the ratio of the magnitude of the output signal to the input in *decibels* and the phase of the output signal relative to the input in degrees. The horizontal axis in both plots is the frequency of the input signal in radians per second displayed on a logarithmic scale.

You can create a plot similar to Figure 3.1 with the `bode()` command in the Control System Toolbox. The input to `bode()` is a linear time-invariant model in transfer function, state-space, or frequency response format.

```
>> bode(tfplant)
```

The Bode design method discussed in Chapter 4 uses a plant model in the frequency response format.

Figure 3.1 Bode plots of the system of Eq. 3.2.

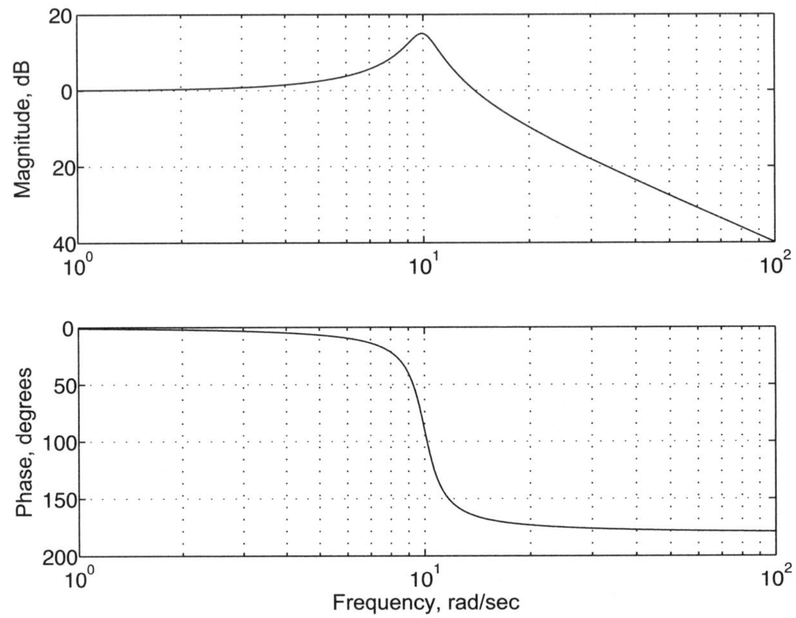

The Decibel

The decibel (dB) expresses the ratio of two quantities. The decibel is used rather than a simple ratio because it can describe very large and very small ratios with numbers of reasonable size. Another reason for using decibels is that two ratios can be multiplied or divided by adding or subtracting their values in decibels, thus simplifying calculations.

The mathematical definition of gain in decibels appears in Eq. 3.3, where z is the ratio of the amplitudes of the output sinusoid y and the input sinusoid x, expressed in decibels.

$$z = 20 \log_{10}\left|\frac{y}{x}\right| \text{ dB} \qquad \text{Eq. 3.3}$$

The vertical bars around the quantity y/x represent the absolute value of the ratio. The value of z will be negative if the magnitude of y is smaller than that of x. With this formula, if y is 1/1,000 of x, z will equal –60dB. Some other examples: If $z = -1$dB, the ratio y/x is 0.89. If $z = -6$dB, the ratio y/x is 0.50. Finally, if $z = +6$dB, the ratio y/x is 2.0.

The "bel" in decibel is named in honor of Alexander Graham Bell, inventor of the telephone.

In the MATLAB Control System Toolbox, it is possible to convert a transfer function model to a frequency response representation given a specified set of frequencies. The first step is to create a vector containing the desired frequencies. For example, `logspace()` can generate a vector of 50 logarithmically spaced frequencies from 10^0 to 10^2 with the following command.

```
>> freqs = logspace(0, 2);
```

Note: A semicolon at the end of a MATLAB command suppresses the display of output from that command. This is useful when executing commands that generate large amounts of output, such as the `logspace()` command shown here.

Convert the `tfplant` transfer function model (created in the previous section) to a frequency response representation with the following command.

```
>> frplant = frd(tfplant, freqs);
```

Alternatively, you can create a frequency domain model by providing a vector of frequencies and the measured response at each frequency to `frd()` as follows.

```
>> frplant = frd(response, freqs);
```

In the above command, the response vector contains complex numbers that represent the system response at each frequency. The magnitude and phase of each complex number represent the magnitude and phase of the output sinusoid relative to the input sinusoid at the corresponding frequency.

In the MATLAB Control System Toolbox, it is not possible to convert a linear model from the frequency domain format to transfer function or state-space representation.

3.3.3 State-Space Representation

The state-space representation models a system as a set of first-order linear differential equations with matrix methods, as shown in Example 3.2.

Example 3.2 Newton's Law

Newton's law for a mass M moving in one dimension x under the influence of a force F is shown in Eq. 3.4. A state-space representation of this second-order linear differential equation is shown in Eq. 3.5. In this representation, the variable x_1 is the position of the mass and x_2 is its velocity.

$$Mx'' = F \qquad \text{Eq. 3.4}$$

$$\begin{bmatrix} x_1' \\ x_2' \end{bmatrix} = \begin{bmatrix} 0 & 1 \\ 0 & 0 \end{bmatrix} \begin{bmatrix} x_1 \\ x_2 \end{bmatrix} + \begin{bmatrix} 0 \\ 1 \end{bmatrix} \frac{F}{M} \qquad \text{Eq. 3.5}$$

When working with linear time-invariant systems, it is possible to transform a state-space model to an equivalent transfer function and vice versa. It is also possible to convert a SISO state-space model containing N first-order differential equations into a single Nth-order differential equation.

The general form of a SISO continuous-time state-space model is shown in Eq. 3.6 .

$$\begin{aligned} \dot{\mathbf{x}} &= \mathbf{A}\mathbf{x} + \mathbf{B}u \\ y &= \mathbf{C}\mathbf{x} + du \end{aligned} \qquad \text{Eq. 3.6}$$

In Eq. 3.6, $\mathbf{x}$ is a column vector containing n elements. This is the state vector, which describes the state of the system and n is the order of the system. **A** is a matrix with n rows and n columns. Because this is a SISO system, u is the scalar system input and y is the scalar output. **B** is a vector with n rows and 1 column, and **C** is a vector with 1 row and n columns. d is a scalar value indicating the direct feedthrough of the system input to its output, if any. For a linear time-invariant system, the matrix **A**, the vectors **B** and **C**, and the scalar d are constants.

The dynamic behavior of a linear time-invariant SISO system is fully described by the contents of the matrix **A**, the vectors **B** and **C**, and the scalar d. In many models of real-world systems, the value of d is 0.

The state-space representation is very general and is directly applicable to MIMO as well as SISO systems. For MIMO applications, the vectors **B** and **C** and the scalar d all become matrices with appropriate numbers of rows and columns. I cover the use of state-space representation for MIMO systems in Chapter 7.

Important Point

When using control system design software (such as the Control System Toolbox) the preferred linear model representation is the state-space format. It exhibits superior numerical properties and provides more precise results compared with equivalent manipulations of transfer function models.

In the MATLAB Control System Toolbox, the `ss()` command creates a state-space model. The usual format for this command is as follows.

```
>> sys = ss(A, B, C, D)
```

Here, `A`, `B`, `C`, and `D` are scalars, vectors, or matrices with appropriate dimensions. It is also possible to convert a model from transfer function format to state-space format as shown here.

```
>> ssplant = ss(tfplant)
```

The output of this command (from the `tfplant` model created previously) displays the values of the resulting **A**, **B**, **C**, and **D** matrices.

```
a =
              x1       x2
   x1       -1.8   -3.125
   x2         32        0


b =
         u1
   x1     2
   x2     0


c =
            x1      x2
   y1        0   1.563


d =
         u1
   y1     0

Continuous-time model.
```

It is also possible to convert a model from state-space format to transfer function format as shown here.

```
>> tfplant2 = tf(ssplant)
```

3.4 Time Delays

In creating a linear plant model, a time delay can be considered an effect separate from the dynamic equations of its behavior. Looked at in this way, a plant model can be described by a transfer function or state-space model combined with a time delay. In MATLAB's representation of linear time-invariant models, a time delay can be added at the input or at the output of the model.

For example, the output is shown below for the command that adds a delay of 0.1 second at the input of the state-space model created in the previous section.

```
>> ssplant.inputdelay = 0.1
```

```
a =
                x1        x2
       x1     -1.8    -3.125
       x2       32         0


b =
           u1
       x1   2
       x2   0


c =
               x1      x2
       y1       0   1.563


d =
           u1
       y1   0

Input delays (listed by channel): 0.1

Continuous-time model.
```

Similarly, a delay could be placed at the plant output as shown here.

```
>> ssplant.outputdelay = 0.1
```

The external behavior of the plant will not differ if the location of a given delay is switched between the system input and its output. However, the internal behavior of the plant states will be affected if that switch is made. You should try to place the delay at the appropriate location (input or output) that best models the behavior of the actual system.

Time Invariance

The three system representation formats described above rely on the assumption that the system being modeled is linear and time invariant. These assumptions are only reasonable under specific conditions. For example, an aircraft can be represented as a linear time-invariant system when it is in a steady-state cruise condition, in which the velocity, altitude, and pitch orientation are approximately constant over a period of time that is long compared with the controller response time. Under these circumstances, it is reasonable (and accurate) for control system design purposes to assume that the response of the aircraft to the small actuator changes used to maintain altitude, heading, and airspeed is linear and time invariant.

It is not reasonable to expect a linear time-invariant model to be useful for modeling the flight of the aircraft from the start of its takeoff run until it reaches cruising altitude because the flight conditions change drastically in the transition from a low-speed, low-altitude takeoff environment to a high-speed, high-altitude cruise condition. Part of the craftsmanship of control system design is identifying conditions in which linear time-invariant models are applicable and using those models effectively in the design process.

3.5 Stability of Linear Models

Given a linear system model in the state-space format, you can determine its stability with the following two steps.

1. Determine the *eigenvalues* (poles) of the state-space model's **A** matrix.
2. Note whether any of the eigenvalues has a real part that is greater than or equal to zero. If any of the eigenvalue real parts are greater than zero, the system is unstable. If there is a pole at the origin of the complex plane, the system is unstable (this configuration is an integrator; a constant input results in an output that grows without bound). If the real parts of any complex eigenvalue pair are equal to zero, the system is *neutrally stable*. A system with neutral stability oscillates indefinitely in response to a change in input. If all the real parts are less than zero, the linear system is stable.

Any square matrix with n rows and n columns has n eigenvalues associated with it, some of which may be repeated. Linear algebra provides algorithms to compute the eigenvalues of a given matrix.

I will not delve into the algorithms used for this computation. Instead, I will note that the MATLAB Control System Toolbox contains the command `eig()`, which determines the eigenvalues of a transfer function or state-space model as follows:

```
>> eig(tfplant)
```

or

```
>> eig(ssplant)
```

The output of both of these commands is identical for the plant models created earlier, and is shown here.

```
ans =
  -0.9000 + 9.9594i
  -0.9000 - 9.9594i
```

This system has two eigenvalues, both of which have the real part –0.9. Because the real parts are all negative, the system is stable.

Complex Numbers and the Complex Plane

In this book, I frequently refer to complex numbers and the complex plane. A common application of these concepts is in solving for the zeros of polynomials. As an example, the formula $x^2 - 5x + 6 = 0$ has the solutions $x = 2$ and $x = 3$. However, the formula $x^2 - 4x + 5 = 0$ has no solutions consisting of real numbers.

Introducing the "imaginary" number $i = \sqrt{-1}$ allows the solution of this type of problem. The solutions of $x^2 - 4x + 5 = 0$ are $x = 2 + i$ and $x = 2 - i$. A pair of complex numbers such as this, where the only difference is the sign of the complex part, is called a complex conjugate pair. You work with complex numbers using the same techniques as in the algebra of real numbers. Whenever you come across a term of i^2, just replace it with –1.

I won't be performing math directly with complex numbers, although I will present plots that display such numbers on the complex plane. The complex plane is a two-dimensional plane with a complex number's real component measured along the horizontal axis and its imaginary component along the vertical axis. A complex number of the form $a + bi$ is graphed as a point on the complex plane with the horizontal coordinate equal to a and the vertical coordinate equal to b.

3.6 Model Development Methods

In the previous sections, I described three ways to represent linear models of dynamic systems. Now that you know how to represent a model in these formats, the next step is to create an accurate linear model of the plant portion of your control system. Two primary approaches are available for performing this task: physics-based modeling and empirical modeling.

3.6.1 Physics-Based Modeling

Figure 3.2 shows a pendulum suspended from a string of length l under the influence of gravitational acceleration g. The pendulum angular deflection with respect to the vertical is θ, in radians. The mass of the pendulum bob is defined to be m.

It is necessary to evaluate the relevant physical effects and determine which ones to include in a model of this system. Here are some effects to consider for this example.

- Gravity must be modeled because the pendulum would not move without it.
- The mass of the pendulum bob must be modeled for the same reason.
- If the size of the bob is small in comparison to the length of the string, the bob can be modeled as a point mass. This simplifies the model significantly.
- If the mass of the string is much less than that of the bob, the mass of the string can be ignored.
- Friction within the string is assumed to have a small effect and will be ignored.
- The pendulum is assumed to move slowly enough that air resistance is not a significant factor over a short time period.

Figure 3.2 Simple pendulum.

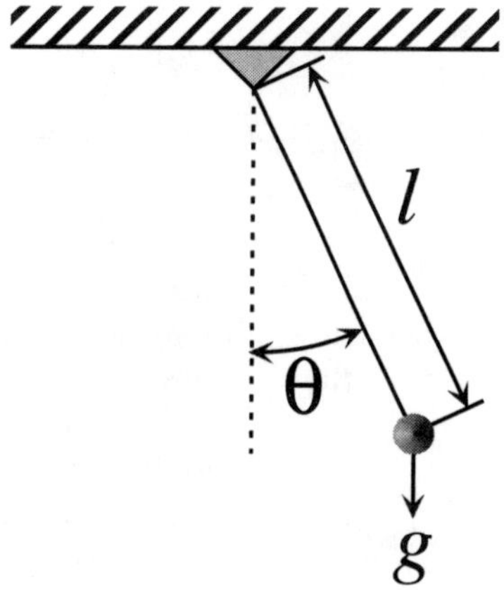

The simplifying assumptions given above will ease the model development task. In the next step, the laws of physics are applied to develop dynamic equations for this system.

The component of gravitational force affecting the motion of the pendulum bob is in the vertical plane perpendicular to the string. This force is defined in Eq. 3.7. The gravitational force component parallel to the string creates tension in the string but does not affect the motion of the bob, so it will be ignored.

$$F = -mg\sin\theta \qquad \text{Eq. 3.7}$$

Note that the force F will always be acting to move the bob back toward the center position. Applying Newton's law $F = ma$ to the problem leads to Eq. 3.8, in which a is the tangential acceleration of the bob.

$$a = -g\sin\theta \qquad \text{Eq. 3.8}$$

The acceleration a is related to the angle θ by the equation $a = l\ddot{\theta}$. This leads to the final dynamic equation of Eq. 3.9.

$$\ddot{\theta} = -\frac{g}{l}\sin\theta \qquad \text{Eq. 3.9}$$

Note that this equation does not depend on the mass of the bob m; however, it does depend on the assumptions listed above. It is also a nonlinear differential equation because it contains the term $\sin\theta$. To uniquely determine a solution for this equation, the initial conditions of the system must be specified as shown in Eq. 3.10. The parameter θ_0 in Eq. 3.10 is the angle from which the bob is released at time zero with an initial velocity of zero. For this system, the possible values for θ_0 are assumed to lie in the range $[-\pi/2, \pi/2]$.

$$\begin{aligned} \theta(0) &= \theta_0 \\ \dot{\theta}(0) &= 0 \end{aligned} \qquad \text{Eq. 3.10}$$

3.6.2 Linearization of Nonlinear Models

The technique of *linearization* is common in engineering, and it is worthwhile to examine some of the effects that can occur when it is used. The approach used in linearization is to identify a stable point or trajectory for a nonlinear system and model small variations about that point or trajectory with linear equations. As an example, I will linearize the pendulum model from the previous section about the stable point at which the pendulum hangs straight down with zero velocity.

The nonlinear term in the pendulum model is the $\sin\theta$ term. Assuming that the value of θ_0 is "small," Eq. 3.9 can be modified with the approximation $\sin\theta \approx \theta$ (in radians). The limit for this approximation depends on the tolerable amount of error in the solution. This approximation results in Eq. 3.11, which is now a linear differential equation that is solvable with standard calculus techniques. The solution to this equation incorporating the initial conditions of Eq. 3.10 is shown in Eq. 3.12.

$$\ddot{\theta} = -\frac{g}{l}\theta \qquad \text{Eq. 3.11}$$

$$\theta(t) = \theta_0 \cos\sqrt{\frac{g}{l}}t \qquad \text{Eq. 3.12}$$

Equation 3.12 has an oscillation period of $2\pi\sqrt{l/g}$ seconds. Note that this period is independent of θ_0.

Figure 3.3 shows the results of numerically solving the nonlinear model of Eq. 3.9 for values of θ_0 ranging from 0 to 90° and determining the oscillation period of each solution from the simulation output data. It also shows the oscillation period derived from the linear approximation to the solution, which is constant for all θ_0. It is clear that in the limit as θ_0 approaches 0, the linear approximation becomes a good match to the nonlinear model. It is also clear that using the linearized model will result in significant errors if θ_0 is large.

This example demonstrates the basic approach for developing a linearized physics-based mathematical model of a dynamic system. Similar model development techniques are useful in other disciplines such as electronics and chemistry. These techniques are applicable as long as the dynamic equations describing the system are well defined and the data values used in the equations are known with sufficient precision. In the pendulum example, the data values required were the gravitational acceleration g, the string length l, and the initial displacement θ_0. It is also necessary to examine additional data to verify that the assumptions used in the model development are reasonable, such as the assumption that the mass of the string is reasonably small relative to the mass of the bob.

Figure 3.3 Comparison of nonlinear and linear pendulum model oscillation periods.

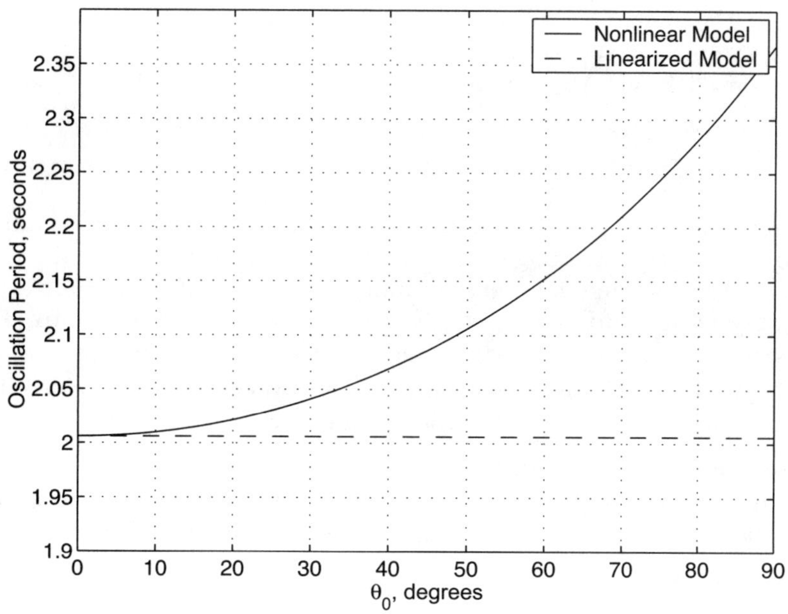

Linear approximations of dynamic systems are used frequently in control system engineering, but their limitations should be well understood. The assumptions used in linearization are only valid when the deviations from the stable point or trajectory are small.

In situations where the dynamic equations or data values for linear model development are not known to a sufficient degree of precision, it is necessary to use an experimental method for model development. In the next section, I discuss an approach for linear model development that avoids the need for a mathematical derivation of system equations.

3.7 System Identification Techniques

System identification [2] is the technique of developing models of dynamic systems from experimental input and output data. To perform system identification, one or more test input data sequences and the measured output data sequences are required for the system being modeled. Typically, tests of a real-world system are designed and executed to generate this data. By applying system identification algorithms, it is possible to derive an estimate of the system transfer function from input to output. The resulting model is linear and time-invariant, so the developer must verify that this is an adequate representation of the system.

I will not examine the mathematical details of the algorithms used in system identification. Instead, I will present an example that uses the MATLAB System Identification Toolbox. The System Identification Toolbox contains several different system identification algorithms and supporting routines. To duplicate the results shown in this section, you will need MATLAB, the Control System Toolbox, and the System Identification Toolbox.

3.7.1 Experiment Design

Assuming you have the software tools needed to perform system identification, the first step in this process is to design one or more experiments to capture the system's dynamic behavior. The collected data must contain histories of the system input and output signals sampled at uniform time intervals during the experiments. To provide the best results, the experiments must satisfy the following criteria.

- **All modes of system behavior must be represented.** The system identification process cannot model behavior if it is not contained in the measured data.

- **Transient and steady-state behavior must be represented.** The transient behavior provides information about the system's dynamic behavior, whereas the steady-state behavior enables determination of the steady-state gain from input to output.

- **The experiments must not damage the plant or drive it to nonlinearity.** System identification experiments, in many cases, can only be performed on a plant that is in operation. A controller might even be driving the plant (presumably a controller that is inadequate in some way). A system identification experiment for this type of system would involve adding perturbation signals at the plant input and measuring the plant's response to the controller's command plus the perturbation. The perturbations must not damage the plant hardware or drive it into nonlinear behavior.

It is important to remember that system identification experiments are used to develop *linear* plant models. The input signals for these experiments must be chosen so the plant behavior remains (at least approximately) linear. This usually means the amplitude of the input signal (and possibly its rate of change) must be limited to a range in which the plant response is approximately linear. However, the amplitude of the driving signal also must be large enough that corrupting effects such as noise and quantization in the measured output signal are minimized relative to the expected response.

A straightforward way to excite a system across a range of frequencies is to use a swept frequency sine wave as the input signal. Equation 3.13 shows the equations for generating a swept frequency sine wave over a period from $t = 0$ to $t = t_f$. These equations generate a signal that sweeps in frequency linearly from f_0 to f_f cycles per second (hertz) with a sine amplitude A.

$$\begin{aligned} \omega(t) &= 2\pi\left[f_0 + (f_f - f_0)\frac{t}{t_f}\right] \\ u(t) &= A\sin\left(\omega(t)\frac{t}{2}\right) \end{aligned} \qquad \text{Eq. 3.13}$$

The frequency range defined by f_0 to f_f and amplitude A must be selected to excite the frequency range of interest while maintaining approximately linear system behavior. The signal $u(t)$ drives the system at its input, and the plant response appears at its output. Both the input and output signal must be recorded during this test.

A swept frequency sine wave will do a good job of providing information about the dynamic behavior of a system for the system identification process, but the resulting model might not provide an accurate representation of the steady-state system response. To provide good steady-state accuracy in the system identification model, an additional test should be performed. A simple way to gather steady-state response data is to perform a step input test on the system.

In a step input test, the input $u(t) = 0$ (or perhaps some other value) prior to the time of the step (t_0) and instantaneously jumps by the step amplitude A at time t_0. The value of A must be chosen so that nonlinearities such as actuator saturation are avoided, or at least minimized. The input and output signals must be recorded from before the time of the step until the system has reached its steady-state response to the step and has remained there for some time.

The combination of a swept frequency sine wave test and a step response test should provide sufficient information to generate a linear plant model with system identification. You might want to perform each of the tests several times to ensure that system behavior is consistent from test to test and to provide data for validation of the linear model.

The tests described above might not be suitable for some types of systems. For example, a system with on/off control such as a simple electrical heating element could not use the swept sine wave as an input signal. For this type of system, an appropriate input signal would be a pseudorandom binary sequence. In this test, the input signal is switched on and off at pseudorandomly generated points in time. The test must last long enough that a good statistical distribution of time intervals between switches is produced. The pseudorandom binary sequence does a good job of exciting system behavior across a wide range of frequencies and should be used when appropriate.

3.7.2 Data Collection

The sampling rate for recording the input and output data during these tests must be high enough that all frequencies of interest are retained in the results. According to the Nyquist sampling theorem [3], the sampling rate (samples per second) must be at least twice the highest frequency of interest to enable reconstruction of the original signal. In practice, the sampling rate must be a bit higher than this limit to ensure the resulting data will be useful. For example, if the highest frequency of interest was 20 hertz (Hz), a sampling rate of 50Hz might be sufficient.

It is also important that corrupting effects such as noise and quantization are kept to a minimum relative to the measured signals. The amplitudes of test input signals must be large enough that the resulting outputs will be large relative to noise and quantization effects. This requirement must be balanced against the need to maintain the system in an approximately linear mode of operation, which typically requires that the input signal amplitudes be small.

3.7.3 Creating a System Identification Model

In this section, I use the MATLAB System Identification Toolbox to generate an example of a linear model of a system. An arbitrarily selected linear fourth-order system is created and experiments are performed on it to generate test results. This test data is then used by the System Identification Toolbox to generate a linear model, which will be compared to the original system.

The linear model used in this example is shown in Eq. 3.14.

$$\frac{-11s^3 + 54s^2 - 87s + 65}{s^4 + 12s^3 + 54s^2 + 108s + 65} \qquad \text{Eq. 3.14}$$

The first step in the system identification process is to perform a set of experiments on this system while recording input and output signals. In this example, a sampling rate of 100Hz is chosen for recording the data. This rate was selected with a knowledge of the dynamics of the system. If you aren't sure what sampling rate to use, it is better to select a rate that is too high than one that is too low.

Figure 3.4 shows the input and output data from a set of two experiments performed on the model. Each experiment runs for 20 seconds. The top graph shows the results from a swept frequency experiment, where the frequency linearly ramps from 0 to 2Hz over the test period. The bottom graph shows the system's response to a step input with amplitude 1. The sequence of MATLAB commands used to generate the input signals and produce the output signals for these tests is contained in the file `sys_id.m` in the `Examples\Ch03` directory of the companion CD-ROM.

The data collected during the above tests is contained in four MATLAB vectors: `u1` and `y1` are the input and output signals from the swept frequency experiment, and `u2` and `y2` are the input and output signals from the step response experiment. Each vector contains 2,001 data points.

The System Identification Toolbox can work with data from multiple experiments simultaneously. An object of the `iddata` type containing data from both experiments is created as follows with the `merge()` command.

```
>> dt = 0.01; % Time step between samples
>> data = merge(iddata(y1, u1, dt), iddata(y2, u2, dt));
```

The System Identification Toolbox contains several routines for performing the actual identification procedure. This example will use the `n4sid()` toolbox function, which creates a discrete-time state-space model. The user must specify the order of the model to create. You can either analyze the system to determine an appropriate order or simply guess several different values and try them out to see which one creates the best model. This example will use the correct system order, which is 4. You might want to repeat these steps with other orders such as 2 and 6 and examine the quality of the resulting model.

```
>>order = 4;
>>id_sys = n4sid(data, order, 'focus', 'simulation');
```

In this example, the focus of the system identification process is to produce a model that most effectively simulates the behavior seen in the data. Other choices for the focus, such as the best prediction of future behavior, are available. See the n4sid() command documentation for more information about identification focus.

The resulting model is converted from discrete time to continuous time and is displayed as a transfer function with the following commands.

```
>>id_sys = d2c(id_sys);
>>tf(id_sys)
```

The d2c() command name stands for "discrete to continuous." The tf() command displays the identified system in transfer function form, as shown here.

```
Transfer function from input "u1" to output "y1":
-10.71 s^3 + 55.03 s^2 - 86.49 s + 65.07
----------------------------------------
   s^4 + 12 s^3 + 54 s^2 + 108 s + 65
```

Figure 3.4 Input and output data from system identification experiments.

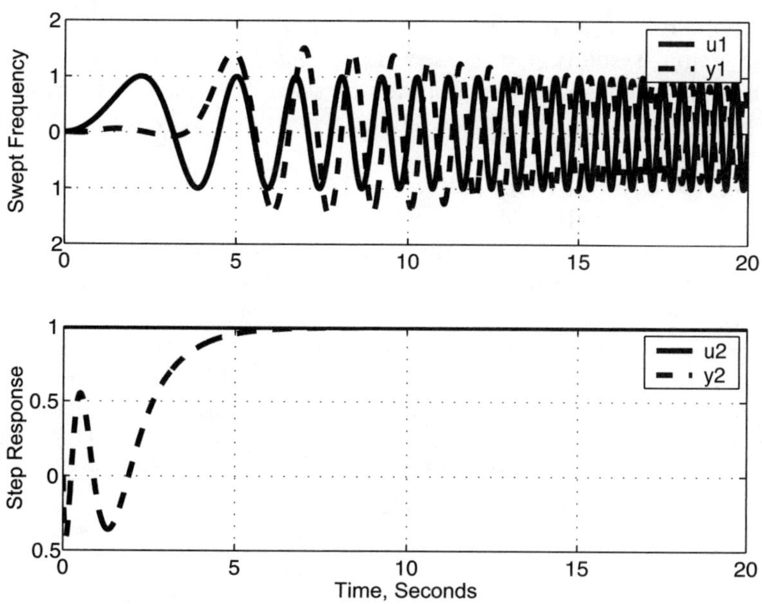

Comparing this result to Eq. 3.14, you see that the numerator is close to that of the original system, whereas the denominator is an exact match to the original. The zeros (the values of s where the numerator goes to 0) of the original system are at 2.8713 and $1.0189 \pm 1.0099i$. The zeros of the identified system are at 3.2118 and $0.9623 \pm 0.9823i$. These results show a very good, though not perfect, match between the original linear model and the model created through the system identification process.

Note, however, that this example used a somewhat artificial process for generating the data used in the system identification procedure.

- The original model was a purely linear system.
- No noise was introduced during the collection of test measurements.

In performing system identification of real-world systems, both of those factors will generally be violated to some degree. The closer you can get to satisfying the ideals of system linearity and noise-free measurements, the more likely the system identification process will produce an accurate, useful model.

System identification is a broad topic, with many techniques applicable to different problem areas. The System Identification Toolbox contains numerous algorithms and supporting functions for use in various modeling situations. In this section, I provided only a brief introduction to the toolbox and one of its algorithms (the `n4sid()` function). For additional information, see Ljung (1999) [2] and the documentation for the System Identification Toolbox.

3.8 Summary

In this chapter, I introduced the concepts involved in creating linear time-invariant models of dynamic systems. I discussed the transfer function, state-space, and frequency domain representations of linear time-invariant models. I also presented a number of ways to create and convert between these types of models in the MATLAB Control System Toolbox.

I presented a simple technique (with MATLAB, at least) to evaluate plant stability by examining the eigenvalues of the state-space model **A** matrix.

Physics-based and empirical approaches to model development were described. The use of a purely physics-based approach is rare. For real-world systems, a physics-based modeling approach relies on the use of at least some experimental data.

I described and demonstrated the technique of system identification for linear time-invariant model development with the use of the MATLAB System Identification Toolbox. System identification is particularly suitable in situations where insufficient physical knowledge of a plant exists to create a physics-based model. The system identification algorithms do their work with only the input and output data sequences collected during one or more tests performed on the plant.

3.9 Self-Test

1. Determine the eigenvalues of the matrix $\mathbf{A} = \begin{bmatrix} -1 & 1 \\ 1 & 0 \end{bmatrix}$.
2. Determine the eigenvalues of the following transfer function model. Is this system stable?

$$\frac{Y}{X} = \frac{1}{s^2 + s + 1}$$

3. Convert the following system to state-space form. Is the state-space representation of this system unique?

$$\frac{Y}{X} = \frac{10}{s^2 + 2.4s + 10}$$

4. Convert the state-space result from problem 3 back to transfer function form. Is the resulting transfer function identical to the transfer function of problem 3?
5. Repeat the system identification example of Section 3.7.3, but this time quantize the measured system outputs (`y1` and `y2`) to the ranges $\pm 2/2^{n-1}$, where n has the values 10, 12, 14, and 16. This simulates the quantization of an n-bit ADC with an input range of ±2. Comment on the results.
6. What steps could you take to improve the results of problem 5 if you could only use a 12-bit ADC?

3.10 Answers to Self-Test

1. The eigenvalues are $-\frac{1}{2} \pm \frac{\sqrt{3}}{2}i$.
2. The system is stable because the real parts of the eigenvalues, listed below, are negative.

$$-\frac{1}{2} \pm \frac{\sqrt{3}}{2}i$$

3. The `ss()` function produces the result shown in Eq. 3.15. The state-space representation is not unique. For instance, the `ssbal()` command (type `help ssbal` on the MATLAB command line for more information about this command) applied to this system produces the equivalent system shown in Eq. 3.16.

$$\dot{x} = \begin{bmatrix} -2.4 & -1.25 \\ 8 & 0 \end{bmatrix} x + \begin{bmatrix} 0.25 \\ 0 \end{bmatrix} u, \quad y = \begin{bmatrix} 0 & 0.5 \end{bmatrix} x \qquad \text{Eq. 3.15}$$

$$\dot{x} = \begin{bmatrix} -2.4 & -2.5 \\ 4 & 0 \end{bmatrix} x + \begin{bmatrix} 0.5 \\ 0 \end{bmatrix} u, \qquad y = \begin{bmatrix} 0 & 0.5 \end{bmatrix} x \qquad \text{Eq. 3.16}$$

4. When `tf()` is applied to either of the results in the answer for problem 3, it returns the original transfer function. The result of converting a model from transfer function form to state-space form and back is always the original transfer function (with the possible exception that the numerator and denominator might both be multiplied by the same constant.)
5. The use of a 16-bit ADC causes very little difference in the measured system. As the number of bits of ADC resolution decreases, the quality of the identified model degrades quickly.
6. Some tips for improving system identification performance are:

   - Design and execute additional types of experiments. Use the results of these experiments in the identification process.
   - Filter the measured data to reduce noise. Be careful not to alter the system's dynamic behavior of interest in the filtering process.
   - Try different system identification algorithms (the System Identification Toolbox contains several.)
   - Adjust the parameters used by the system identification algorithms, such as the model order.
   - Ensure that nonlinearities (such as actuator saturation) are not affecting the experimental results.

3.11 References

1. Churchill, Ruel V., *Operational Mathematics* (Boston, MA: McGraw-Hill, 1972).
2. Ljung, Lennart, *System Identification: Theory for the User*, 2nd ed. (Upper Saddle River, NJ: Prentice Hall PTR, 1999).
3. Oppenheim, Alan V., and Ronald W. Schafer, *Discrete-Time Signal Processing* (Englewood Cliffs, NJ: Prentice Hall, 1989), §3.2.

CHAPTER 4

CLASSICAL CONTROL SYSTEM DESIGN

4.1 Introduction

In this chapter, I introduce two classical control system design methods: root locus design and Bode diagram design. Bode diagram design is also known as the frequency response design method. Both methods require a linear time-invariant plant model. In Chapter 3, I described some approaches for developing plant models suitable for use with these design methods.

In the root locus method, the designer creates a graph showing all possible values (the "locus") of the closed-loop system transfer function poles as a design parameter varies over a specified range. The poles are the values of s for which the transfer function denominator is zero. Poles may be real numbers or may appear as complex conjugate pairs. The varying design parameter is typically the controller gain.

The root locus diagram displays a portion of the complex plane and plots the closed-loop poles as the gain parameter varies. By selecting a value for the gain that places the poles within a suitable region of the complex plane, it is possible to determine the dynamic behavior of the controlled system. If a gain change alone does not result in satisfactory performance, the compensator structure must be modified to improve the closed-loop pole locations.

The root locus method is a direct, graphical approach for controller design. The MATLAB Control System Toolbox provides tools for creating root locus plots, selecting gain values, and altering compensator structures in a quick, interactive manner. In this chapter, I introduce the use of MATLAB-based tools for root locus design.

In the Bode diagram design method, the designer works with plots displaying the open-loop system gain and phase responses. Adjustments to the controller structure and parameter values cause the Bode diagrams to change. The goal is to design a controller that meets stability margin specifications while providing sufficient system responsiveness.

The MATLAB Control System Toolbox supports Bode diagram design with immediate feedback indicating system performance and stability margins in response to design changes. In this chapter, I introduce the MATLAB Control System Toolbox tools for Bode diagram design.

Both the root locus and Bode diagram design methods are presented here as tools for SISO control system design. As discussed in Chapter 1, it is often possible to approximate a MIMO system as multiple SISO systems and use SISO design tools with those systems.

4.2 Chapter Objectives

After reading this chapter, you should be able to

- describe how to construct a root locus plot;
- given a set of system performance specifications, identify the portion of the complex plane that must contain the roots of the closed-loop transfer function to meet those specifications;
- use the MATLAB Control System Toolbox to perform root locus control system design;
- define the terms "gain margin" and "phase margin";
- identify system stability margins from Bode diagrams; and
- use the MATLAB Control System Toolbox to perform Bode diagram design.

4.3 Root Locus Design

Before beginning the root locus design process, you must have a linear time-invariant plant model in transfer function or state-space form. If you don't have such a model, I described some approaches in Chapter 3 for developing a plant model that is based on the laws of physics or the results of experiments performed on an actual plant. The model must accurately represent plant behavior in response to small-magnitude input signals, which implies that the plant itself must exhibit approximately linear behavior in response to small changes in its input.

Once you have a plant model, you can describe it in MATLAB and use the Control System Toolbox to perform root locus design. For the first example, I will use the second-order plant shown earlier in Eq. 3.2. Create a transfer function model of this system in MATLAB with the following command.

```
>> tfplant = tf(100, [1 1.8 100])
```

Next, open the Control System Toolbox SISO Design Tool Root Locus Editor and load the plant model with this command.

```
>> sisotool('rlocus', tfplant)
```

This opens a window (Figure 4.1) showing a root locus plot of the plant model with a proportional feedback controller that has its gain set to 1. In Figure 4.1, the plot aspect ratio has been set to Equal in the dialog reached by right-clicking on the Root Locus Editor window and selecting the Properties... item.

Figure 4.1 SISO Design Tool displaying a plant and proportional controller.

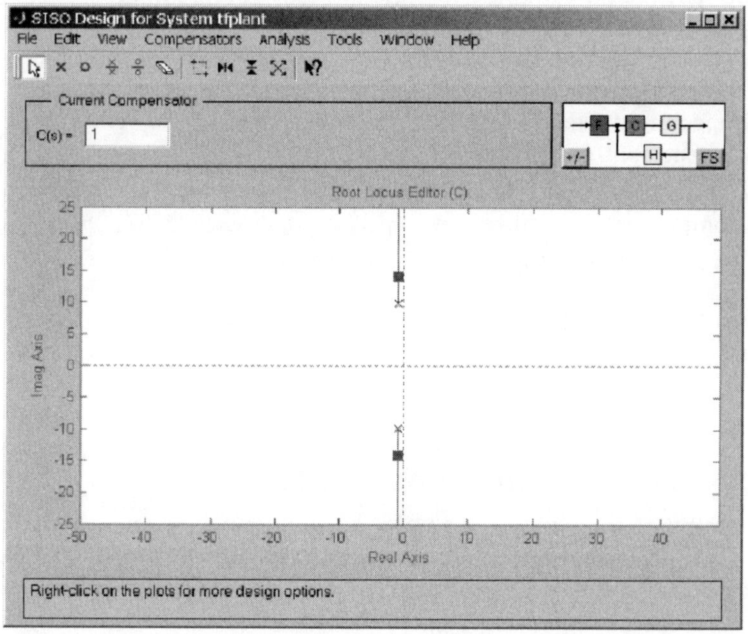

The SISO Design Tool displays a plot with blue x symbols as the plant pole locations and magenta squares as the closed-loop pole locations. The root locus appears as blue lines showing possible pole locations that can be selected by changing the gain parameter in the Current Compensator box.

To examine the numerical values of plant and closed-loop system pole locations, select the System Data item on the View menu to display the plant poles. Select the Closed-Loop Poles item on the View menu to display the closed-loop pole locations. In this example, the plant poles are located at $-0.9 \pm 9.96i$, and the closed-loop poles (with the compensator gain equal to 1) are at $-0.9 \pm 14.1i$.

The small diagram in the top right section of Figure 4.1 displays the controller structure. The blocks in this diagram represent the following components.

- *G* is the plant model given as an argument to the `sisotool()` command. In this example,

$$G = \frac{100}{s^2 + 1.8s + 100}.$$

- C is the control compensator, which by default is a proportional gain with the value 1.
- H is the sensor model and defaults to a gain of 1.
- F is a prefilter, which also is a default gain of 1.

In addition to this default controller structure, several other structures are available. I will consider only the default structure and will use the prefilter F as an adjustable gain. The sensor model H will be left unchanged. With these simplifications, the remaining steps in the root locus design process are as follows.

- Attempt to find a gain value that places the closed-loop system poles in suitable locations in the complex plane.
- If no gain value results in satisfactory pole locations, change the structure of the control compensator C and repeat step 1.
- Adjust the prefilter gain F to eliminate any steady-state error.

To satisfy system performance specifications, constraints must be defined for the acceptable closed-loop pole locations in the complex plane. The next section describes how to convert design specifications into pole location constraints with the SISO Design Tool.

4.3.1 Pole Location Constraints

The locations of the closed-loop poles in the complex plane are directly related to the stability and performance of the combined plant and controller. The poles are the values of s for which the closed-loop transfer function denominator is zero.

Important Point If any closed-loop pole has a positive real part, the system is unstable.

The first pole location constraint to consider is related to stability. On the root locus diagram, an unstable closed-loop pole (displayed as a magenta box) appears to the right of the vertical (imaginary) axis. A neutrally stable pole lies on the imaginary axis and has a real part of 0. For reasonable system performance, closed-loop poles must generally have negative real parts. In other words, the closed-loop poles must appear in the complex plane to the left of the vertical axis.

The next constraint relates to the damping ratio of complex conjugate pole pairs. A damping ratio of 1 results in critical damping, in which overshoot in the system response is eliminated. Smaller damping ratios lead to increased overshoot and faster rise time. Selecting an appropriate damping ratio involves a trade-off between speed of response and the acceptable amount of overshoot and oscillation.

Table 4.1 shows the relationship between damping ratio and percent overshoot in the system response for a second-order transfer function containing no zeros. For more complex systems, although the relationship is not exactly represented, this table is still a useful starting point for relating performance specifications to pole locations in the *s*-plane.

Table 4.1 Relation between damping ratio and percent overshoot.

Damping Ratio	Step Response (% Overshoot)
1.0	0.0
0.9	0.2
0.8	1.5
0.7	4.6
0.6	9.5

As Table 4.1 shows, choosing a smaller damping ratio increases the amount of overshoot. For many control system designs, a damping ratio of about 0.7 is the smallest that is acceptable.

A minimum damping ratio constraint can be directly represented as a region of the complex plane. Continuing the previous example, you can draw a 0.7 damping ratio constraint in the Root Locus Editor window of Figure 4.1 as follows.

- Right-click on the Root Locus Editor window and select Design Constraints from the menu, then select New... from the submenu.
- In the dialog box that appears, select Damping Ratio as the Constraint Type, then set the Damping Ratio > field value to 0.7. Click OK.

Two diagonal lines will be drawn from the origin into the left half of the complex plane as shown in Figure 4.2. The pole locations that satisfy the damping ratio constraint of 0.7 are located in the region to the left of these two lines.

The remaining constraint I will consider is the response settling time. Pole locations that result in a settling time less than a specified value appear to the left of a vertical line in the complex plane. The SISO Design Tool's default tolerance for determining the settling time is when the response converges to within 2 percent of the steady-state response. For this example, I will use a settling time specification of 1 second.

Draw a 1-second settling time constraint in the Root Locus Editor as follows.

- Right-click on the Root Locus Editor window and select Design Constraints from the menu, then select New... from the submenu.
- In the dialog box that appears, select Settling Time as the Constraint Type then set the Settling Time < field value to 1 second. Click OK.

Figure 4.2 Root Locus Editor showing damping ratio constraint.

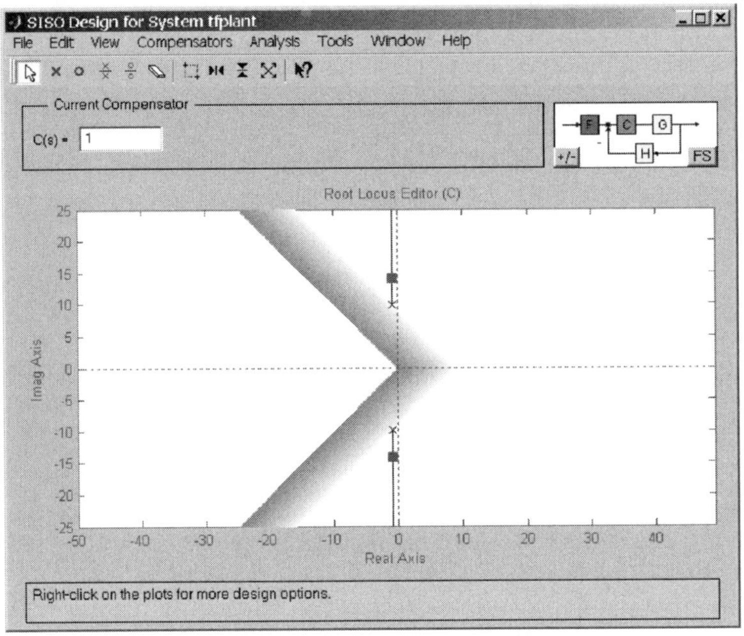

A straight vertical line will be drawn in the left half of the complex plane as shown in Figure 4.3. The pole locations that satisfy the settling time constraint of 1 second are located to the left of this line.

The existing compensator structure is clearly inadequate for this plant. The blue lines of the root locus never enter the region of the complex plane where the damping ratio and settling time specifications are met. Because this controller structure is unacceptable, the next step is to modify the structure in a way that results in acceptable performance.

4.3.2 Pole Cancellation

In this situation, which occurs frequently in control system design, pole cancellation provides a useful method for satisfying performance specifications. *Pole cancellation* involves the placement of compensator zeros at the locations of the undesired plant poles, thus canceling out the dynamic behavior resulting from those poles.

As previously stated, the plant poles are located at $-0.9 \pm 9.96i$. To cancel these poles, it is necessary to modify the compensator C to place zeros at these locations:

- Left-click on the box labeled C in the system diagram in the top right part of the SISO Design Tool. A dialog will appear with the title Edit Compensator C.
- In the Zeros section of the Edit Compensator C dialog, click Add Complex Zero.
- Enter –0.9 as the real part and 9.96 as the imaginary part and click Apply.

Figure 4.3 Root Locus Editor showing damping ratio and settling time constraints.

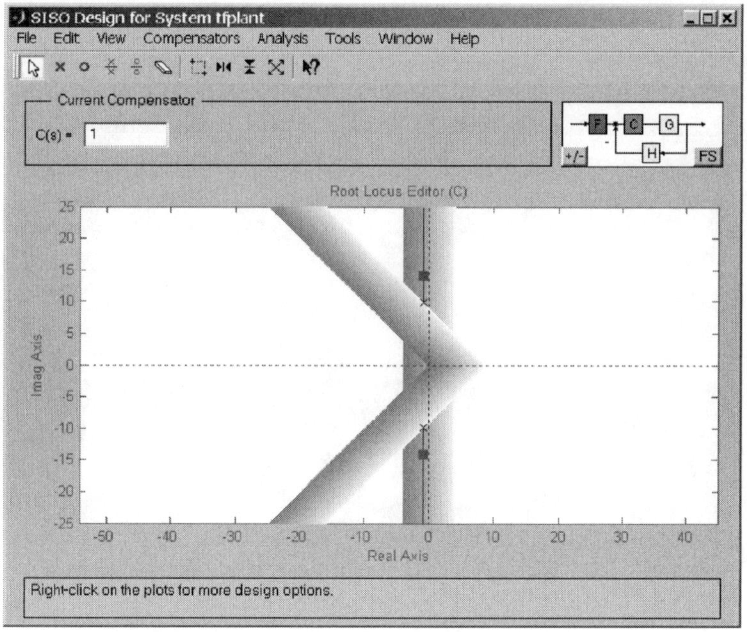

The poles have been canceled, but now it is necessary to add poles that meet the design specifications.

Important Point When designing a compensator, it is necessary for the transfer function to have a denominator order at least as large as the numerator order.

This compensator currently has numerator order 2 and denominator order 0. You need to add two poles. Placing two compensator poles at –5 on the real axis will satisfy the damping ratio and settling time constraints.

- In the Poles section of the Edit Compensator C dialog, click the Add Real Pole button two times.
- Enter –5 as the real part for both poles. Click Apply.

The Root Locus Editor window will now appear as in Figure 4.4.

The canceled poles still appear as isolated magenta boxes, but the zeros placed at the same locations effectively eliminate their influence on the dynamic behavior. The remaining two poles are slightly outside the boundaries defined by the performance specifications. Note that the vertical root locus line now passes through the region of the complex plane satisfying the performance specifications. It is possible to position the closed-loop poles within the acceptable region by adjusting the gain value.

Figure 4.4 Root Locus Editor showing compensator after editing.

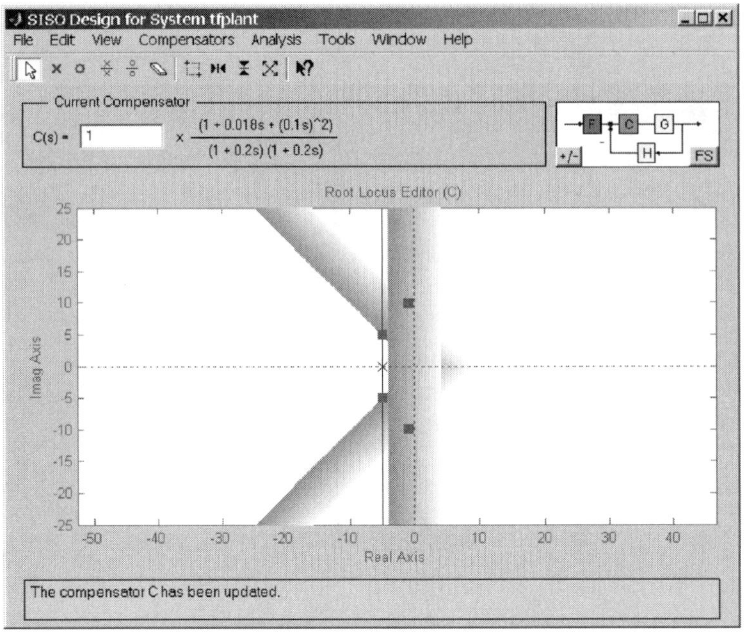

Grab the upper pole on the root locus curve by left-clicking on it. Drag it downward to position it just inside the region of acceptable performance and release the mouse button. The gain shown in the Current Compensator area should change to a value between 0.5 and 0.8. You can also type a gain value directly into the edit box inside the Current Compensator area. Change the compensator gain to 0.5 by typing this value into the edit box, then press Enter.

The damping ratio and settling time specifications are now satisfied by the closed-loop pole locations on the root locus plot. Next, take a look at the closed-loop response to a step input. On the Analysis menu, select Other Loop Responses... and click OK in the dialog box that appears. An LTI (linear time-invariant system) Viewer window will appear (see Figure 4.5) displaying the step response from input to system output.

Note: In Figure 4.5, the Input to Compensator Output display was turned off by right-clicking the Step Response plot area, selecting the Systems item, then clicking to remove the check mark from the item Closed Loop: r to u.

Although Figure 4.5 shows that the damping and settling time are satisfactory, the steady-state error in the step response is quite large. In response to a commanded step of 1, the response settles at a value of 0.333, a 67 percent error. To see the numerical steady-state value, right-click on the plot and select Characteristics → Steady-state from the context menu. A blue circle will appear at the rightmost point of the step response trace. Left-click on that circle to display the steady-state value.

Figure 4.5 Step response of pole-canceling compensator.

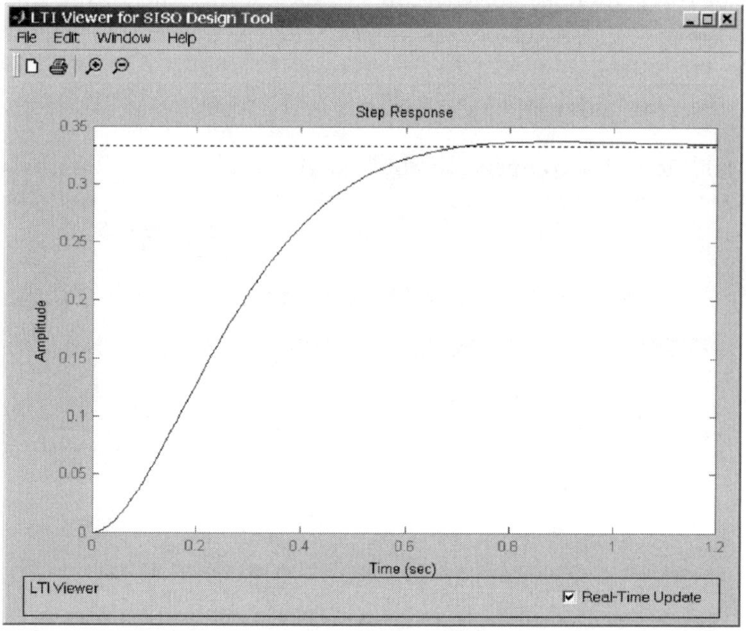

Setting the prefilter gain term *F* to the inverse of the steady-state step response eliminates any steady-state error. In this example, *F* should be set to 3. To make this change, left-click on the box labeled *F* in the system diagram in the top-right part of the SISO Design Tool. This brings up the Edit Compensator F dialog. Change the gain to 3 and click OK. The Step Response diagram will update and display the new steady-state response of 1.

Although adjusting the *F* gain term as described above eliminates steady-state error for the given plant model, modeling inaccuracies can result in a nonzero steady-state error in the final implementation. As I discussed in Chapter 3, all plant models are approximations containing some degree of error. To ensure that the steady-state error remains zero in the presence of plant modeling errors, it is necessary to add an integrator to the compensator.

4.3.3 Adding an Integrator

As discussed in Chapter 2, the way to eliminate steady-state error in PID controller design is to add an integrator term. You can do this in the Root Locus Editor by adding a compensator pole at the origin as follows.

- Remove the prefilter gain because the integrator will now perform its function: Left-click on the box labeled *F* in the system diagram in the top right part of the SISO Design Tool. A dialog will appear with the title Edit Compensator F. Set the gain back to 1 then click OK.
- Left-click on the box labeled C in the system diagram in the top right part of the SISO Design Tool. A dialog will appear with the title Edit Compensator C.
- In the Poles section of the Edit Compensator C dialog, click Add Real Pole.
- Enter 0 as the real part. Click Apply.

The addition of a compensator pole at the origin eliminates any steady-state error, but it also causes the two rightmost closed-loop poles to move to the right of the settling time specification limit. The result of this appears in Figure 4.6.

Figure 4.6 **Root Locus Editor after adding an integrator (a pole at the origin).**

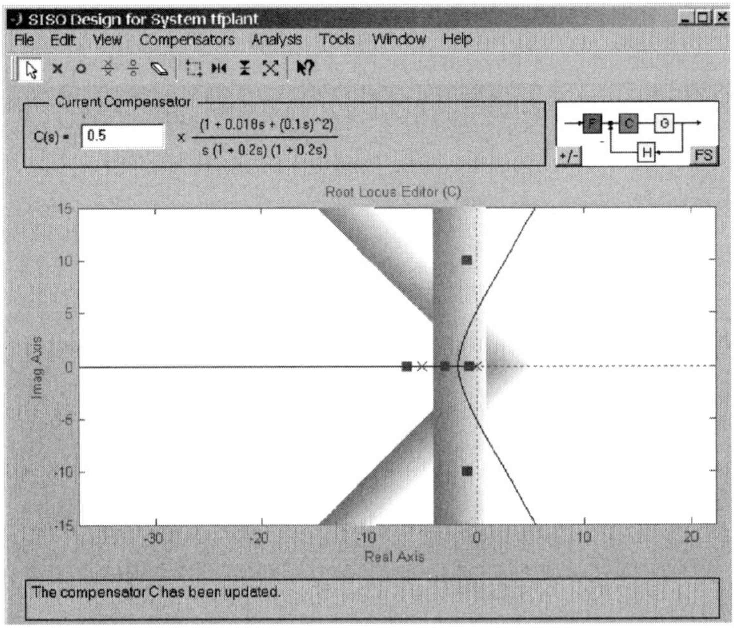

You need to "pull" the root locus to the left, back into the area of the complex plane that satisfies the performance specifications. The root locus tends to follow the average location of the poles, so by moving compensator poles to the left, this goal can be achieved. You can't move the pole at the origin because it would no longer perform the integration function that eliminates steady-state error. However, you can move the two compensator poles currently located at –5 on the real axis.

Grab the red X symbol at –5 and move it to the left to about –15. The other X remains at –5 when you do this. Move the other pole from –5 to –15 as well. Observe how the root locus curve moves as you move the poles. To precisely position the poles, open the Edit Compensator C dialog (left-click on the box labeled C in the system diagram in the top-right part of the SISO Design Tool) and set the locations of the first two poles to –15, then click Apply.

Figure 4.7 Root Locus Editor showing final compensator design.

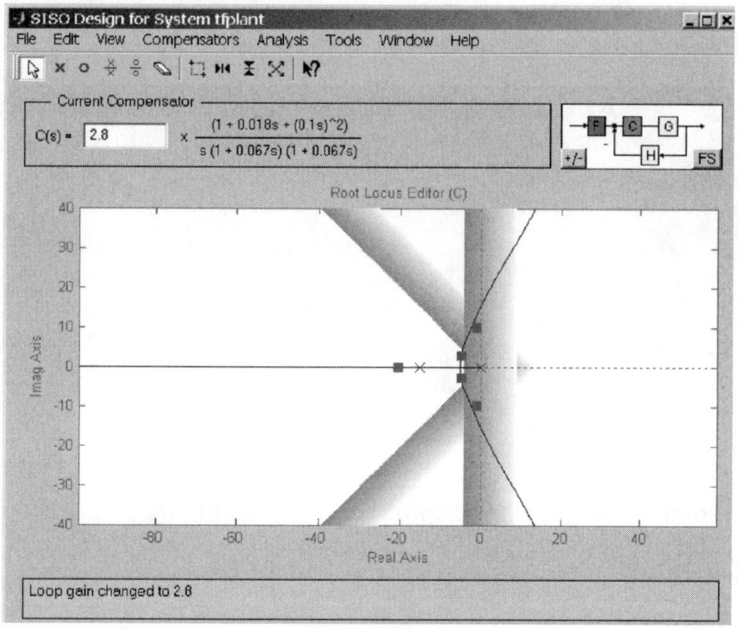

The only remaining design step is to adjust the gain to position the closed-loop poles within the area of the complex plane satisfying performance specifications. Try dragging the magenta boxes to locations within the region to the left of the performance boundaries. A gain of 2.8 provides satisfactory pole locations, as shown in Figure 4.7, and a step response with zero steady-state error, as shown in Figure 4.8.

The final compensator design provides zero steady error, a settling time less than 1 second, and very little overshoot. This compensator has the form shown in Eq. 4.1.

$$C(s) = 2.8\left[\frac{(0.1s)^2 + 0.018s + 1}{s(1 + 0.067s)^2}\right] \qquad \text{Eq. 4.1}$$

In Chapters 8 and 9, I discuss techniques for implementing compensator transfer functions such as this using C/C++ in an embedded processor.

Figure 4.8 Closed-loop step response.

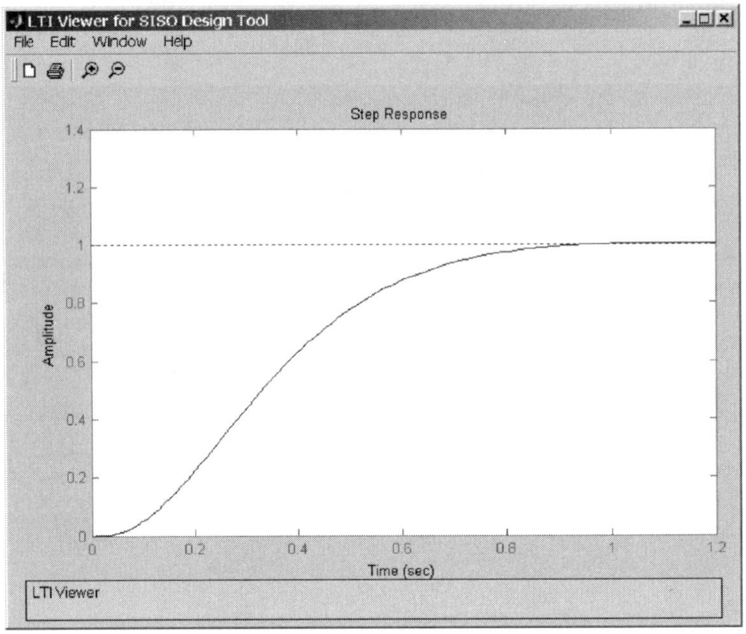

The compensator of Eq. 4.1 must be placed within the larger control system configuration. This arrangement is shown in Figure 4.9, in which the box labeled C represents the compensator.

Figure 4.9 System block diagram with a root locus–designed compensator.

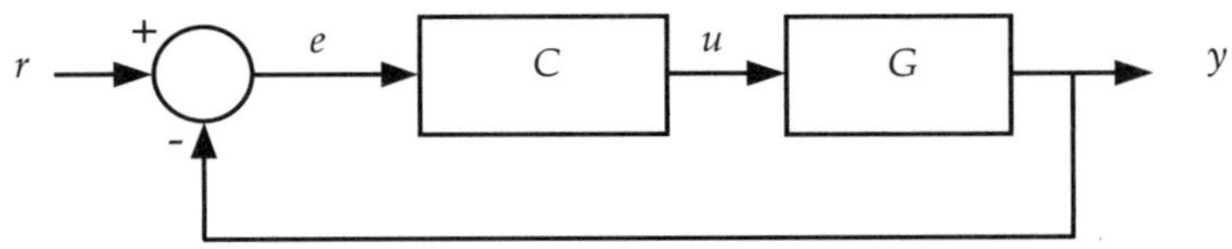

4.3.4 Lead and Lag Compensators

Although the pole cancellation technique is useful for many designs, in some situations, it is not appropriate. One example of such a situation is a plant that has one or more unstable poles. An attempt to cancel the unstable pole is inappropriate because any error in the cancellation results in an unstable closed-loop system. Because the model used in the root locus design process is always an approximation of the real-world system, pole cancellation generally fails to produce a stable design if any of the canceled poles are unstable.

Pole cancellation also might not be the best approach when the simplest controller that meets requirements is desired. The example in the previous section resulted in a third-order compensator design, which could involve more mathematical manipulation than an embedded processor has time to perform. Depending on system performance requirements, such as acceptable steady-state error and percent overshoot, it might be possible to develop a satisfactory first- or second-order compensator with the technique described next.

Instead of performing pole cancellation, an alternative approach is to add a real zero and a real pole to the compensator. If the added pole is to the right of the added zero in the complex plane, the result is called a lag compensator. If the zero is on the right, it is called a lead compensator.

Continuing with the previous example, begin by deleting any existing compensator poles and zeros and setting the compensator gain to 1. Add a real pole and a real zero to the compensator in the SISO Design Tool with the techniques described previously. Observe the effects on the shape and position of the root locus while moving the location of the pole and the zero to various positions.

Placing the pole at –40 and the zero at –1 and setting the compensator gain to 0.13 results in a system that meets the settling time requirement, although it suffers from 470 percent overshoot and –88 percent steady-state error. Although this is unlikely to be a satisfactory design, it suggests that some extra design effort could lead to a simpler compensator implementation.

Some basic rules for choosing lead or lag compensation and locating the compensator pole and zero are summarized here.

- A lead compensator approximates derivative control. Use lead compensation to increase the speed of the response. To achieve this effect, both the pole and the zero must be on the negative real axis, and the magnitude of the pole location should be 3 to 10 times the magnitude of the zero location.
- A lag compensator approximates integral control. Use lag compensation to improve low-frequency gain and steady-state accuracy. To achieve this effect, both the pole and the zero must be on the negative real axis, and the magnitude of the zero location should be 3 to 10 times the magnitude of the pole location.
- Moving the compensator pole to the left pulls the root locus to the left. This increases the speed of the response.
- Moving the compensator zero to the right also pulls the root locus to the left, which also increases the speed of the response.

4.3.5 Root Locus Summary

In the previous sections, I carried out a series of steps to design a controller for a specific plant. It is possible to generalize the design steps to a form that is applicable in a variety of situations.

1. Develop a linear model of the plant in MATLAB with the techniques discussed in Chapter 3.
2. Open the SISO Design Tool and load the plant model into it.

3. Create design constraints for closed-loop pole locations in terms of damping ratio and settling time.
4. Using the default controller structure (a proportional gain), attempt to select a gain value that places all of the closed-loop poles within the region of the complex plane where the specifications are met. If such a gain can be found, continue with step 7; otherwise, continue with step 5.
5. Cancel the rightmost plant pole (if it is on the real axis) or poles (if they are a conjugate pair) by adding zeros to the compensator. Add an equivalent number of poles to the compensator with locations on the real axis to the left of the settling time boundary in the complex plane. Experiment with the locations of the added poles to move the root locus into the acceptable region of the plane.
6. Try to find a gain value that places the closed-loop poles in the region of acceptable system performance. If no such gain can be found, return to step 5 and cancel one or two more of the plant poles with compensator zeros and add new compensator poles farther to the left.
7. Examine the steady-state step response. If it is not 1, set the compensator prefilter F to the inverse of the steady-state response. Verify that the step response now converges to 1.
8. If the elimination of steady-state error resulting from modeling errors is a requirement, add a compensator pole at the origin. Move the other compensator poles to the left as needed to pull the root locus to the left. Adjust the compensator gain to position the poles so performance specifications are met.

If the plant contains unstable poles, or if the above steps do not produce a satisfactory result, try adding lead or lag compensation. Adjust the newly added pole and zero locations and the compensator gain to achieve satisfactory pole locations and system response.

In following these steps, be careful to avoid placing compensator poles too far to the left in the complex plane. The locations should be just far enough to the left to satisfy the design constraints and no farther. Compensator poles that are too far to the left represent overdesign and can lead to the following problems.

- The actuator attempts to respond faster than needed to meet performance requirements, which might result in actuator saturation, excessive power use, and wear in the actuator system.
- As the compensator poles move to the left, the sampling rate of a digital controller that implements the compensator must increase.

After the controller design has been completed, you should perform robustness testing by altering the plant model to simulate realistic variations in the plant and observe how the closed-loop system copes with those changes. In Chapter 9, I suggest some approaches for thoroughly testing a controller design.

4.4 Bode Design

The Bode design method, also called the frequency response method, is probably the most common control system design approach (other than PID control) used in industry [8]. It is popular because this approach results in good controller designs even when there is significant uncertainty in the plant model.

Bode design is based on the use of open-loop frequency response plots of the plant plus controller. The open-loop system configuration from which this data is generated appears in Figure 4.10. The only difference between Figure 4.9 and Figure 4.10 is that the feedback path and the summing junction have been removed.

Figure 4.10 Open-loop system configuration used in Bode design.

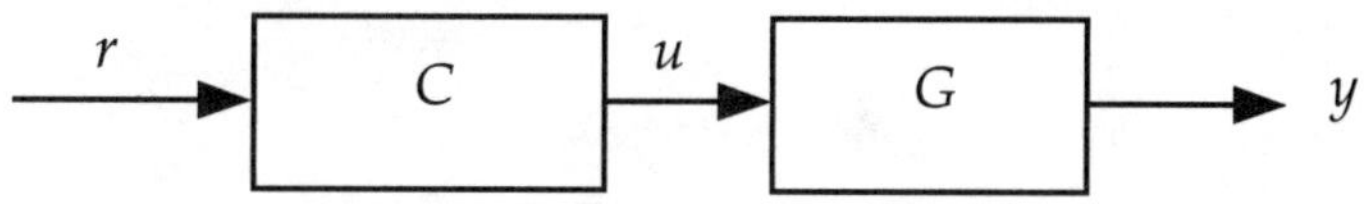

The MATLAB Control System Toolbox provides limited support for the Bode design approach. You can view Bode diagrams within the SISO Design Tool and use those diagrams in the design process. You can also view the gain margin and phase margin (defined in Section 4.4.1) of your design as you make changes. The Bode diagrams provide a useful alternate view of the system when working with a root locus design.

The default behavior of the SISO Design Tool is to display both a root locus plot and a set of Bode diagrams. Figure 4.11 shows the resulting dialog when the following commands are issued. Note that the only difference from the method previously used to start the SISO Design Tool is that the `rlocus` argument to the `sisotool()` command has been omitted.

```
>> tfplant = tf(100, [1 1.8 100])
>> sisotool(tfplant)
```

The Bode diagrams on the right side of the SISO Design Tool display the magnitude and phase of the open-loop frequency response on the upper and lower plots, respectively. The horizontal axis frequency range is automatically selected on the basis of the plant model characteristics. The magnitude plot is in units of decibels, and the phase plot is in degrees.

Together, the Bode diagrams indicate the steady-state amplitude and phase of an output sine wave relative to an input sine wave across the frequency range shown on the horizontal axis.

4.4.1 Phase Margin and Gain Margin

In a stable system, all closed-loop poles are in the left half of the complex plane. The point of neutral stability occurs when one or more of the poles are located directly on the imaginary axis. Instability results when any closed-loop pole moves into the right half of the plane.

Figure 4.11 SISO Design Tool displaying root locus and Bode views.

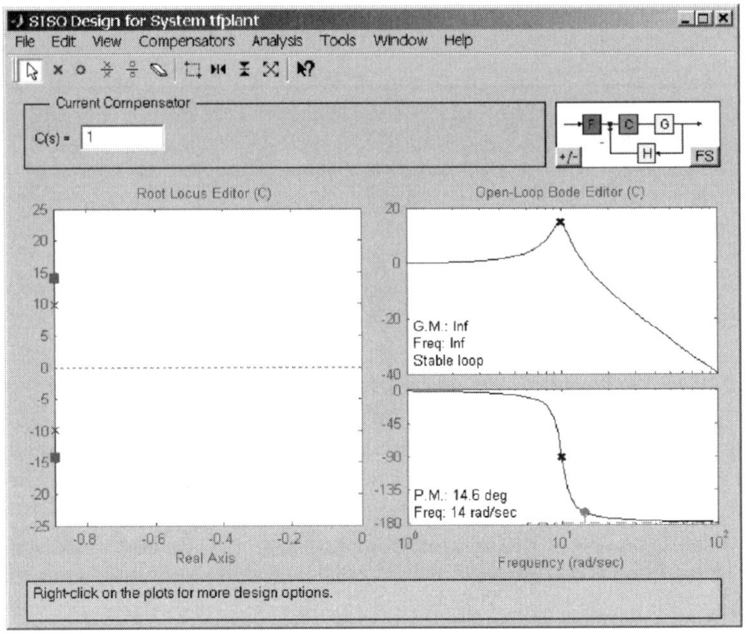

It is valuable to understand "how far" a design is from instability. This notion is captured in the concept of stability margin. Two measures of the stability margin are directly available from the open-loop Bode diagrams: *gain margin* and *phase margin*.

In a neutrally stable system, the open-loop gain is unity (0dB) at the frequency where the open-loop response is 180° out of phase from the input. If the gain at that frequency is less than 0dB, the system is stable. A gain greater than 0dB at that frequency produces an unstable system.

On the Bode diagrams, the frequency of interest for this test is where the phase plot has a value of –180°. For a stable system, the gain curve passes downward through 0dB at a frequency where the phase plot has a value greater than –180°. The phase margin is defined as the number of degrees the phase curve is above –180° at the frequency where the gain plot passes through 0dB.

The SISO Design Tool automatically determines the phase margin, displays it on the plot, and gives its value in degrees. In Figure 4.11, the phase margin is indicated by the text "P.M.: 14.6 deg." The phase margin is shown on the phase plot as a small circle with a line drawn downward to the –180° value to indicate its magnitude. The frequency indicated by "Freq: 14 rad/sec" below the phase margin is the frequency at which the gain plot passes through 0dB.

The gain margin is defined as the negative of the open-loop gain (in dB) at the frequency where the phase is –180°. A stable system has a gain less than 0dB at that frequency, so the negative of that value will result in a positive gain margin. The gain margin indicates the amount by which the compensator gain can be increased before the system becomes neutrally stable.

In Figure 4.11, the phase never reaches –180°, no matter how large the controller gain becomes, so the gain margin for this system is infinite. This is indicated by the text "G.M.: Inf." The frequency indicated below the gain margin is the frequency at which the phase is –180° if it exists or "Inf" if no such frequency exists. The line of text below that indicates whether the system is stable or unstable. If the gain margin is finite, it will be drawn on the Bode gain plot in a manner similar to that of the phase margin.

Phase margin is used more frequently than gain margin as a specification and performance metric for control system design. Gain margin is not easily translated into a meaningful measure of system performance. The following two rules guide the application of a phase margin to control system design.

- The damping ratio is approximately 0.01 multiplied by the phase margin in degrees.
- For good transient response characteristics, the phase margin should normally be at least 60°. A value of less than 45° will tend to produce unacceptable overshoot and oscillation in the response.

After repeating the steps of the example in Section 4.3 that place the pole location constraints in the Root Locus Editor, add poles and zeros to the compensator, and adjust the compensator gain, the resulting compensator design appears in Figure 4.12. The phase margin is 69.5° and the gain margin is 20.6dB.

4.5 Summary

In this chapter, I covered two classical control system design methods: root locus design and Bode diagram design. These methods both require a linear plant model.

The root locus method is based on a graph showing the possible locations of the closed-loop transfer function poles in the complex plane as a gain parameter varies over a specified range. By selecting a suitable value for the compensator gain, the closed-loop poles can be located as desired along the root locus curves.

System performance specifications, such as damping ratio and settling time constraints, translate directly into regions of acceptable pole location in the complex plane. By placing all the closed-loop poles within those regions, the specifications will be met. The root locus design process involves choosing an appropriate compensator structure and gain value to place the closed-loop poles in the acceptable region of the complex plane. A prefilter gain might also need to be adjusted to produce the correct steady-state response magnitude.

Figure 4.12 SISO Design Tool displaying root locus and Bode diagram views.

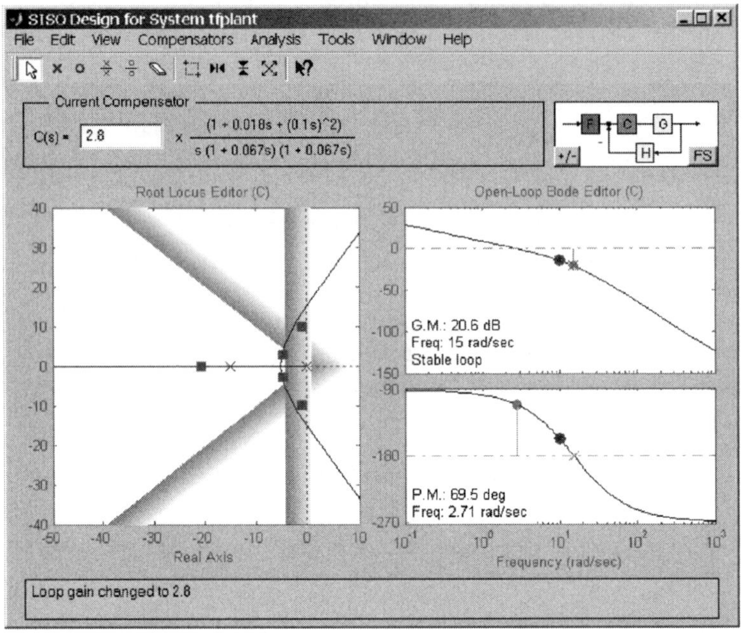

However, these steps can result in a controller with unacceptable steady-state error in the presence of modeling errors. The addition of an integrator to the compensator can eliminate any steady-state error but will likely require adjustment of the other compensator pole locations and gain in order to meet performance requirements.

In the Bode diagram design method, the designer works with Bode diagrams displaying the open-loop system response. Gain margin and phase margin are measures of stability that are easily determined from open-loop Bode diagrams. Phase margin is approximately proportional to the damping ratio of the closed-loop system.

The MATLAB Control System Toolbox provides tools for performing root locus and Bode diagram design with immediate feedback indicating system performance in response to design changes. In this chapter, I introduced the MATLAB-based tools available for root locus and Bode diagram design.

4.6 Self-Test

1. An electrohydraulic servomechanism has a control voltage as its input and hydraulic ram position as its output. The transfer function for this plant follows. Enter this transfer function into MATLAB and load it into the SISO Design Tool root locus editor.

$$G(s) = \frac{4 \times 10^7}{s(s+250)(s^2+40s+9\times 10^4)}$$

2. Apply the following design constraints: rise time < 0.05 seconds, damping ratio > 0.7.
3. Observe that two of the root locus curves do not pass through the acceptable region of the plane. Take the next step: Define a compensator with zeros that cancel the complex poles of the plant. Add any necessary compensator poles farther to the left on the real axis.
4. Attempt to change the compensator gain to place all the poles in the acceptable region of the complex plane. If this is not possible, move the compensator poles farther to the left and try again. Continue this iteration until satisfactory, but not over-designed, pole locations are found. View the step response of the closed-loop system and see whether it is acceptable.
5. Observe what happens when imperfect pole cancellation occurs. Increase the magnitude of the compensator zero real components by 10 percent and examine the step response. Increase the magnitude of the compensator zero imaginary components by 10 percent and examine the step response. Try some larger compensation error magnitudes and observe the effects.
6. A first-order unstable plant has the transfer function $G(s) = 1/(s - 1)$. The design specifications are a 1-second settling time and zero steady-state error. Design a compensator and examine the step response of the system.
7. A linear model of a DC electric motor has voltage as its input and motor rotation speed as its output. Consider the motor model that follows. Design a compensator that provides a 70° phase margin, a 0.5-second step time, and zero steady-state error in the presence of modeling errors.

$$G(s) = \frac{2}{s^2 + 16s + 50}$$

4.7 Answers

1. The plant transfer function can be rewritten as the product of three simpler transfer functions.

$$G(s) = \left(\frac{1}{s}\right)\left(\frac{1}{s+250}\right)\left(\frac{4\times 10^7}{s^2+40s+9\times 10^4}\right)$$

The following commands create this plant model and load it into the SISO Design Tool.

```
>> tf1 = tf(1, [1 0]);
>> tf2 = tf(1, [1 250]);
>> tf3 = tf(4e7, [1 40 9e4]);
>> tfplant = tf1 * tf2 * tf3;
>> sisotool('rlocus', tfplant)
```

2. Right-click on the root locus plot and select Design Constraints -> New.... Define the 0.05-second settling time constraint in the New Constraint dialog box. Repeat these steps and define the 0.7 damping ratio constraint.
3. First, determine the plant pole locations by clicking the View menu and selecting the System Data item. The resulting dialog displays the plant poles and zeros. The right-most poles are located at –20 ± 299*i*. Left-click inside the Current Compensator box above the root locus to bring up the Edit Compensator C dialog. In this dialog, add a pair of complex zeros at the plant pole locations. Next, add two real zeros located farther to the left on the real axis, say at –100.
4. One acceptable design places both compensator poles at –600 with a gain of 24. The resulting compensator is

$$C(s) = 24\frac{1+0.00045s+(0.0033s)^2}{(1+0.0017s)^2}\ .$$

Display the step response by going to the Analysis menu and selecting Response to Step Command. Turn off the display of the compensator input-to-output response by right-clicking the step response plot area and selecting the Systems item, then remove the check mark by clicking the item Closed Loop: r to u. Observe that the step response has zero steady-state error. This is because the plant has a pole at the origin.

5. Change the compensator zeros to –22 ± 299*i*. The behavior of the step response should not significantly change. Change the compensator zeros to –22 ± 330*i*. You should begin to see some oscillations on top of the nominal step response. Larger errors in the compensator zero locations will increase the amount of perturbation of the nominal step response.

6. Recall that it is inappropriate to attempt to cancel the unstable plant pole. First, apply the settling time requirement to the root locus diagram. The zero steady-state error requirement necessitates a compensator pole at the origin. One solution places a compensator zero at –1.8 and sets the compensator gain to 16. This satisfies the settling time and steady-state error requirements and has 21 percent overshoot in the step response. The resulting compensator is

$$C(s) = 16\frac{1 + 0.56s}{s}.$$

7. This system has two stable real poles. The compensator must have a pole at the origin to eliminate steady-state error. Canceling the rightmost plant pole and adding a compensator pole farther to the left does not produce a design meeting the requirements. Canceling the second plant pole and placing both compensator poles at –35 with a compensator gain of 134 results in a satisfactory design. The resulting compensator is

$$C(s) = 134\frac{(1 + 0.23s)(1 + 0.085s)}{s(1 + 0.029s)^2}.$$

4.8 References

8. Franklin, Gene F., J. David Powell, and Abbas Emami-Naeini, *Feedback Control of Dynamic Systems* (Reading, MA: Addison Wesley, 1986).

CHAPTER 5

POLE PLACEMENT

5.1 Introduction

In this chapter, I introduce the pole placement design method, which allows the designer to locate the closed-loop system poles at arbitrarily selected points in the complex plane. With an appropriate choice of pole locations, the closed-loop system can exhibit any response speed and damping characteristics desired. This assumes the plant and actuators are capable of producing an approximately linear response and some enabling conditions on the plant are satisfied.

However, this design freedom comes at a small cost. The control algorithm used in pole placement assumes that the full internal state of the plant is known at all times. Most often, this is not the case. In a typical design, perhaps only one of several internal state variables is measured. The values of the unmeasured states must be estimated during controller operation.

An observer (also called a state estimator) performs the task of estimating the complete set of state variables internal to the plant. The observer develops state estimates on the basis of the measured plant outputs and the known plant inputs.

Two restrictions on the structure of the plant model must be satisfied for the pole placement design method to succeed. The first requires that the actuators be capable of driving the system in a manner that allows control of all modes of behavior. This property is called *controllability.* The other restriction is that the sensors must measure sufficient system parameters to enable construction of a complete state estimate. This is called *observability.* Some straightforward tests of the plant model will determine whether it is controllable and observable.

This design approach is applicable to MIMO systems as well as to SISO systems. The same general state-space model form is used for SISO and MIMO systems, and the steps in the design method are applicable in both situations.

The pole placement design method uses some fairly complex matrix algorithms for controller and observer design. The MATLAB Control System Toolbox provides robust implementations of these algorithms. The algorithms themselves will not be discussed here. Instead, I cover the steps necessary to apply the commands in the Control System Toolbox for pole placement design.

5.2 Chapter Objectives

After reading this chapter, you should be able to

- describe the concepts of pole placement design,
- define the terms controllability and observability,
- perform tests to determine the controllability and observability of a linear system model,
- select suitable pole locations to satisfy performance specifications,
- design a controller gain vector (or matrix in the case of a MIMO plant) to place the closed-loop poles at the desired locations,
- design an observer that estimates all system states given a set of sensor measurements, and
- add integral action to a state-space controller design.

5.3 Concepts of Pole Placement

Figure 5.1 shows the basic controller structure considered in this chapter. In this figure, the G_p block represents the plant. The blocks with "–K" and "Observer" labels implement the controller gain and state estimator, respectively. The observer and controller gain together form the compensator. The block labeled "N" is a feedforward gain that scales the reference input to provide zero steady-state error in the absence of modeling errors.

Figure 5.1 assumes that the sensors do not measure the entire state vector and that state estimation is required. In the unusual event that all states are measured accurately, the estimator becomes unnecessary. However, even in systems in which all states are measured, an estimator could still be useful because of the measurement noise filtering it provides.

Note that this compensator resides in the feedback portion of the control loop. Compare this structure to the controller structures described in Chapters 2 and 4, in which the compensator was placed in the forward path of the loop with its output connected to the plant input.

The pole placement compensator consists of three parts designed in separate steps: a controller gain **K**, an observer, and the **N** matrix. Although the notation in Figure 5.1 suggests a SISO system, this design method is equally applicable to MIMO systems.

Figure 5.1 System configuration using pole placement controller design.

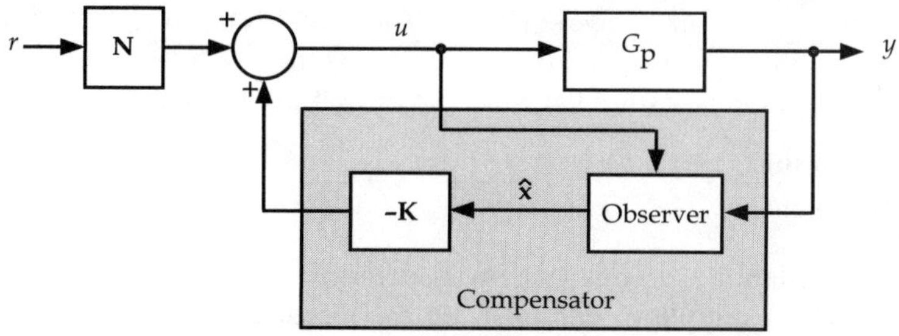

The pole placement design method works only with state-space plant models. If you have a plant model in transfer function format, you can convert it to state-space format with the Control System Toolbox `ss()` command as discussed in Section 3.3.3.

The first steps in the design process are to verify that the actuators are capable of fully controlling the plant and that the sensors measure enough information to enable state estimation. These conditions are called controllability and observability. Some simple tests on the plant model determine whether the plant is controllable and observable.

In the next step, you must determine a set of closed-loop pole locations in the complex plane that satisfy the system performance specifications. Section 5.6 describes a method for selecting suitable closed-loop pole locations.

Given the state-space plant model and the desired pole locations, it takes just one Control System Toolbox command to compute the controller gain **K** vector (or **K** matrix, for a MIMO plant).

The next step is designing the observer. As in the controller gain design procedure, you must first select a set of closed-loop observer pole locations. The dynamic response of the observer must be much faster than that of the closed-loop system. This allows transient errors in the observer estimates to settle out quickly without significantly affecting the behavior of the system. Section 5.7 describes a method for selecting suitable observer pole locations.

The final design step is determining the feedforward gain **N**, which results from a straightforward matrix calculation in MATLAB. This gain is chosen to make the steady-state error zero. Note that this is not the same thing as the use of integral control. Without integral control, errors in the plant modeling will cause the steady-state error to become nonzero. Section 5.10 discusses the addition of an integral control term.

Any linear plant model that passes the tests for controllability and observability can, in principle, produce any desired speed of response. In a real-world implementation, however, effects such as actuator saturation and plant nonlinearities limit the achievable performance of the system. It is important to keep the limitations of real-world systems in mind when using this powerful method to synthesize controller designs.

5.4 Controllability

The pole placement design method begins with a plant model in state-space form. Equation 5.1 shows the state-space equations for a MIMO plant. This discussion is equally applicable to SISO systems, where the **u** and **y** vectors reduce to scalars. In both the SISO and MIMO cases, **x** is a state variable vector containing one or more elements.

$$\begin{aligned} \dot{\mathbf{x}} &= \mathbf{Ax} + \mathbf{Bu} \\ \mathbf{y} &= \mathbf{Cx} + \mathbf{Du} \end{aligned} \qquad \text{Eq. 5.1}$$

The controllability of this system is determined from an analysis of the **A** and **B** matrices. As an example to demonstrate the method, create a second-order state-space model as follows.

```
>> tfplant = tf(100, [1 1.8 100])
>> ssplant = ss(tfplant);
```

Important Point

The following MATLAB statements assess the controllability of the state-space plant model contained in the `ssplant` variable.

```
>> c0 = ctrb(ssplant)
>> controllable = (rank(c0) == length(c0))
```

Following the execution of these statements, the variable `controllable` will have the value 1 if the plant is controllable and 0 if it is not controllable. If the plant is controllable, you can continue on to the next section and test the plant for observability. If it is uncontrollable, it is necessary to identify the plant's uncontrollable behavior modes and determine how to make them controllable, which might require the addition of one or more actuators to drive the uncontrolled modes.

Example 5.1 MIMO plant with an uncontrollable mode.

An example of a MIMO plant with an uncontrollable mode is a linear model of an automobile driving system with an actuator to control the throttle but no actuator to control the steering. If the vehicle's pointing direction is a system state variable and no plant input affects that state, the controllability test shown above will return the value 0, indicating that at least one state variable cannot be controlled.

Advanced Concept

The controllability test computes the plant controllability matrix and tests whether it is of full rank. The controllability matrix rank must equal the number of rows (and columns) it contains for the system to be controllable. The `length()` function returns the number of rows in the square matrix. The controllability matrix is computed from the **A** and **B** matrices of the state-space plant model. See MATLAB help for the `ctrb()` command for more information about the controllability matrix computation.

The rank of a square matrix is the number of linearly independent rows in that matrix. A square matrix is of full rank if all its rows are linearly independent. This condition is satisfied when the rank of the matrix equals the number of rows in the matrix.

The MATLAB `rank()` function returns an estimate of the rank of a matrix. Because MATLAB uses numerical methods to determine this result, it is subject to the limitations of finite-precision floating-point mathematics. In other words, it is possible for the rank function to return an incorrect result for some matrices.

The following example demonstrates this situation. The **a1** matrix has rows that are linearly dependent, so its rank is 1. The **a2** matrix has linearly independent rows and columns, but the rank function returns a value of 1 even though the correct result is 2. This is because the `1e-15` term added to one of the elements in **a2** is truncated during the rank computation.

```
>> a1=[1 1; 2 2] % A matrix with linearly dependent rows
            a1 =
              1     1
              2     2
>> a2=[1 1+1e-15; 2 2] % Linearly independent rows
            a2 =
              1.00000000000000   1.00000000000000
              2.00000000000000   2.00000000000000
>> rank(a1) % Gives correct answer
            ans =
              1
>> rank(a2) % Gives incorrect answer
            ans =
              1
>> a2-a1 % Confirm that the matrices are not identical
            ans =
```

```
    1.0e-014 *
    0    0.11102230246252
    0                   0
>>
```

The relevance of this seemingly abstract topic to control system design is that if your plant model controllability matrix exhibits this type of numerical difficulty, you are unlikely to be able to develop a successful design. This is an indication that additional actuators are required to effectively control the system behavior modes.

Even in cases in which the controllability test returns a value of 1, the plant could still be only weakly controllable. With a weakly controllable plant, it is possible to control all modes of the system dynamics, but it requires excessive actuator effort to do so. One approach for identifying this problem is to complete the design process and thoroughly test the resulting control system by simulation. If the actuator effort turns out to be excessive, it might be necessary to reevaluate the hardware design of the plant and control system.

5.5 Observability

Assuming the plant model passes the controllability test, the remaining test is to determine its observability. A plant is observable if it is possible to form an estimate of all of its internal states using only the plant inputs and measured plant outputs.

The test for observability is similar to the test for controllability. The observability test uses the A and C matrices of the linear plant model.

Important Point

The following MATLAB statements determine the observability of the state-space plant model contained in the `ssplant` variable.

```
>> ob = obsv(ssplant)
>> observable = (rank(ob) == length(ob))
```

Following the execution of these statements, the variable `observable` will have the value 1 if the plant is observable and 0 if it is not observable. If the plant is observable, you can continue on to the next section and begin the controller design. If it is not observable, you will need to assess the plant's unobservable behavior modes and determine the additional sensor measurements needed to make them observable.

Example 5.2 Plant with an unobservable mode.

An example of a plant with an unobservable mode is a linear model of a cruise control system with an actuator to control the throttle but with no sensor for measuring the speed. Because the vehicle speed is a state variable in this example and no output measures that state (directly or indirectly), the observability test shown above will return the value 0, indicating a problem. In other words, you can't implement a speed controller unless you measure the vehicle's speed in some way.

Note that the vehicle speed in this example does not need to be measured directly. For instance, it is possible to measure the vehicle position with an odometer and allow the state estimator to produce a speed estimate by computing the derivative of the position. If the plant model contains vehicle speed as a state and an odometer (but no speedometer), the observability test would return the value 1, assuming the remaining plant states are observable.

Similar to the discussion of weakly controllable plants in the previous section, a plant can be weakly observable. With a weakly observable plant, it is possible for the observer to estimate all system states, but very little information is available for some of the states. In this situation, any noise or bias in the sensor measurements could seriously corrupt the state estimates. One way to identify this problem is to complete the design process and thoroughly test the resulting control system with simulation, including the modeling of realistic measurement errors. If the resulting state estimation errors are excessive, it might be necessary to add one or more sensors to the plant to provide a better state estimate.

5.6 Pole Placement Control Design

After confirming that the plant model is both controllable and observable, the next design step is to select a suitable set of closed-loop pole locations. The number of pole locations that must be selected equals the number of elements in the system state vector. If the system has multiple inputs, it is possible to have multiple poles at the same location in the complex plane. However, the number of poles at any location may not be more than the number of plant inputs. To avoid numerical problems, poles at distinct locations should not be located too close to each other.

Note: The restriction of not allowing more poles than the number of inputs at any location applies to the Control System Toolbox `place()` command, which will be used later in this section. This is not a serious limitation for most control system design purposes.

The `acker()` command in the Control System Toolbox performs the same function as `place()` and does not have this restriction. However, `acker()` is only suitable for use with SISO plants with orders less than approximately 10.

The rules for selecting closed-loop system pole locations with the pole placement method are the same as those used in Chapter 4 for root locus design. First, the closed-loop poles must be located in the region of the complex plane to the left of the origin to ensure stability. They must also be located to the left of a vertical line in the left half of the complex plane to satisfy settling time constraints. Finally, the poles must be located between upper and lower diagonal lines in the left half of the complex plane emanating from the origin to ensure that damping ratio constraints are satisfied. The poles can be placed at points on the negative real axis or in complex conjugate pairs.

To prevent driving the actuators too hard and to avoid the need for an overly fast digital controller sampling rate, the poles should not be located any further to the left in the complex plane than is necessary to satisfy the performance specifications.

As an example, load the `ssplant` model created in the previous section into the SISO Design Tool with the following command.

```
>> sisotool('rlocus',ssplant)
```

Add design constraints for a 1-second settling time and a 0.7 damping ratio. From an examination of the resulting diagram, acceptable real pole locations can be chosen at –6 and –7 on the real axis. Note that it is not possible to place both poles at the same location (with the `place()` function) because this system has only one input. To design the **K** vector, form a vector containing these pole locations and compute the gain with the following two commands.

```
>> p = [-6 -7]
>> K = place(ssplant.a, ssplant.b, p)
```

The `place()` command computes the controller gain given the plant's **A** and **B** matrices and a vector of closed-loop pole locations. See the MATLAB help on the `place()` function for more information about how it works. The resulting controller gain **K** = [5.6000 –0.9062].

Clearly, the difficult part of the controller gain design is the selection of suitable closed-loop pole locations, especially for a high-order plant model. The determination of the controller gain itself requires only one MATLAB function call.

For higher order plants, a more methodical approach for closed-loop pole location selection is desirable. The MATLAB function `select_poles()` is provided on the enclosed CD-ROM to assist in this task.

The `select_poles()` function computes a set of unique closed-loop pole locations given the plant model's order and the closed-loop system's settling time and damping ratio constraints. The poles are equally spaced along an arc in the complex plane centered at the origin and satisfying the design constraints. The online help for this function (viewed with the command `help select_poles`) is displayed here.

```
SELECT_POLES   Determine pole locations for pole placement design.

  P = SELECT_POLES(ORDER, T_SETTLE, DAMP_RATIO)  computes a set of
  pole locations for the system order ORDER, with settling time
  T_SETTLE (in seconds) and a damping ratio of DAMP_RATIO where
  (0 < DAMP_RATIO < 1). The settling percentage error defaults to 1
  percent.

  P = SELECT_POLES(ORDER, T_SETTLE, DAMP_RATIO,
  SETTLING_PCT) allows the settling percentage error SETTLING_PCT
  to be specified.

  The poles are located equidistantly along an arc in the complex
  plane that satisfies the given settling time and damping ratio
  constraints.

  Example: p = select_poles(4, 0.5, 0.8, 0.02)
  This computes the poles for a 4th-order system with a settling
  time of 0.5 seconds, a damping ratio of 0.8, and a settling error
  of 2%. The result is p = (-7.8240 ± 5.8680i, -9.5559 ± 2.0818i).
```

The use of `select_poles()` with the second-order `ssplant` model, a settling time of 1 second, and a damping ratio of 0.7 involves the following steps.

```
>> p = select_poles (2, 1, 0.7)
>> K = place(ssplant.a, ssplant.b, p)
```

The results of these commands are closed-loop poles located at $-4.6052 \pm 4.6982i$ and the controller gain $\mathbf{K} = [3.7052 \;\; -0.8862]$.

This completes the design of the controller gain **K**. If you don't have accurate measurements of all the state variables, the next step is to design a state estimator.

5.7 State Estimation

The observer (or state estimator) is implemented as shown in Eq. 5.2.

$$\dot{\hat{\mathbf{x}}} = \mathbf{A}\hat{\mathbf{x}} + \mathbf{B}\mathbf{u} + \mathbf{L}(\mathbf{y} - \mathbf{C}\hat{\mathbf{x}} - \mathbf{D}\mathbf{u}) \qquad \text{Eq. 5.2}$$

The observer develops an estimate $\hat{\mathbf{x}}$ of the state vector using the plant input vector **u** and the sensor measurements **y** as its input. The term in parentheses in Eq. 5.2 is the observer error, which is the measured output of the plant minus the observer's estimate of the plant output.

The procedure for determining the **L** matrix in Eq. 5.2 is similar to the procedure for determining the controller gain **K** matrix in the previous section. As in the design of the controller gain, it is necessary to select a set of pole locations for the observer. The pole locations must be chosen so that the dynamic response of the observer is significantly faster than that of the closed-loop system. This allows any initial errors in the $\hat{\mathbf{x}}$ estimates to settle out rapidly enough that they do not significantly affect the performance of the closed-loop system.

As a rule of thumb, the real components of the observer pole locations should be approximately three to five times as large as those of the closed-loop system poles. Smaller values of this multiplier cause observer errors to settle out more slowly while performing additional filtering of sensor measurements. Larger multiplier values allow observer errors to settle more rapidly with less filtering of the measurements. Larger multiplier values also increase the sampling rate requirement for a digital implementation of the observer-controller algorithm.

A simple way to develop a suitable set of observer poles is to multiply all of the closed-loop system poles by a factor of 3 to 5. The observer poles resulting from this multiplication have the same damping characteristics as the closed-loop poles and provide the additional settling speed needed for the observer.

The `place()` command is used to design the observer. The usage of this command differs from the controller gain design procedure in that the plant's **C** matrix, rather than the **B** matrix, is used, and the input and result matrices must all be transposed. The following example computes the observer poles from the closed-loop system poles and determines the observer gain matrix **L** with the `place()` command.

```
>> q = 3 * p % Observer pole locations
>> L = place(ssplant.a', ssplant.c', q)'
```

Note: In this example, the MATLAB transpose operator (the single quote) transposes the plant model's **A** and **C** matrices and the result of the `place()` function call.

The results of these commands are observer poles located at $-13.8155 \pm 10.3616i$ and the observer gain matrix

$$\mathrm{L} = \begin{bmatrix} 3.0347 \\ 16.5319 \end{bmatrix}.$$

5.8 Feedforward Gain

The final design step is the computation of the feedforward gain **N**. This scalar (or matrix for MIMO systems) is selected to scale the reference inputs to produce zero steady-state error at the outputs in the absence of modeling errors.

The formula for computing the gain **N** appears in Eq. 5.3.

$$\mathbf{N} = \mathbf{N}_u + \mathbf{K}\mathbf{N}_x \qquad \text{Eq. 5.3}$$

Here, **K** is the controller gain matrix designed previously. The matrices $\mathbf{N}_u$ and $\mathbf{N}_x$ of Eq. 5.3 are determined from the plant model as shown in Eq. 5.4.

$$\begin{bmatrix} \mathbf{N}_x \\ \mathbf{N}_u \end{bmatrix} = \begin{bmatrix} \mathbf{A} & \mathbf{B} \\ \mathbf{C} & \mathbf{D} \end{bmatrix}^{-1} \begin{bmatrix} \mathbf{0} \\ \mathbf{I} \end{bmatrix} \qquad \text{Eq. 5.4}$$

The **0** matrix contains only zeros. **I** is an identity matrix, which has ones along the diagonal (from top left to bottom right) and zeros elsewhere. The MATLAB statements to compute the **N** matrix for the `ssplant` model are shown here; the **K** matrix has already been computed in Section 5.6.

```
>> n = size(ssplant.a, 1); % Number of states
>> m = size(ssplant.c, 1); % Number of outputs
>> Nxu = inv([ssplant.a ssplant.b; ssplant.c ssplant.d]) * ...
       [zeros(n,m); eye(m)];
>> Nx = Nxu(1:n, :);
>> Nu = Nxu(n+1:end, :);
>> N = Nu + K*Nx;
```

5.9 Combined Observer-Controller

The next design step is to combine the observer and controller to form the compensator of Figure 5.1. Equation 5.5 shows the complete computation of the state estimate $\hat{\mathbf{x}}$ and the plant actuator commands **u** using the reference input **r** and sensor measurements **y** as inputs to the algorithm.

$$\begin{aligned} \dot{\hat{\mathbf{x}}} &= \mathbf{A}\hat{\mathbf{x}} + \mathbf{B}\mathbf{u} + \mathbf{L}(\mathbf{y} - \mathbf{C}\hat{\mathbf{x}} - \mathbf{D}\mathbf{u}) \\ &= (\mathbf{A} - \mathbf{L}\mathbf{C})\hat{\mathbf{x}} + \mathbf{L}\mathbf{y} + (\mathbf{B} - \mathbf{L}\mathbf{D})\mathbf{u} \qquad \text{Eq. 5.5} \\ \mathbf{u} &= \mathbf{N}\mathbf{r} - \mathbf{K}\hat{\mathbf{x}} \end{aligned}$$

Note that in the configuration of Figure 5.1, the plant and the observer both receive the actuator commands directly. As a result, assuming the linear plant model ideally represents the real plant, the observer tracks the plant response to changes in the reference input **r** with zero error.

During controller startup, the state estimate vector $\hat{\mathbf{x}}$ should be initialized as accurately as possible. This will minimize transient estimator errors during the initial period of system operation.

Equation 5.5 requires the plant input vector **u** and the measured plant outputs **y** as inputs. In MATLAB state-space models, only the outputs (**y** vector elements) of a state-space component are available as inputs to a subsequent component. The input vector elements are not available to use as outputs, which creates a small problem.

The solution is to form an augmented plant output vector $\tilde{\mathbf{y}}$ by appending the plant inputs to the output vector. This requires modification of the **C** and **D** matrices of the plant model. Equation 5.6 shows the format of the modified matrices.

$$\tilde{\mathbf{y}} = \begin{bmatrix} \mathbf{y} \\ \mathbf{u} \end{bmatrix} = \begin{bmatrix} \mathbf{C} \\ \mathbf{0} \end{bmatrix} \mathbf{x} + \begin{bmatrix} \mathbf{D} \\ \mathbf{I} \end{bmatrix} \mathbf{u} \qquad \text{Eq. 5.6}$$

With the result of Eq. 5.6, the closed-loop system equations consisting of the plant model and the observer-controller are written as follows.

$$\begin{aligned} \dot{\mathbf{x}} &= \mathbf{A}\mathbf{x} + \mathbf{B}\mathbf{u} \\ \tilde{\mathbf{y}} &= \begin{bmatrix} \mathbf{C} \\ \mathbf{0} \end{bmatrix} \mathbf{x} + \begin{bmatrix} \mathbf{D} \\ \mathbf{I} \end{bmatrix} \mathbf{u} \\ \dot{\hat{\mathbf{x}}} &= (\mathbf{A} - \mathbf{L}\mathbf{C})\hat{\mathbf{x}} + \begin{bmatrix} \mathbf{L} & \mathbf{B} - \mathbf{L}\mathbf{D} \end{bmatrix} \tilde{\mathbf{y}} \\ \mathbf{u} &= \mathbf{N}\mathbf{r} - \mathbf{K}\hat{\mathbf{x}} \end{aligned} \qquad \text{Eq. 5.7}$$

Note: In Eqs. 5.6 and 5.7, **0** represents a zero matrix and **I** is an identity matrix. For a system with *r* inputs and *n* states, the **0** matrix in these equations has *r* rows and *n* columns and the **I** matrix has *r* rows and *r* columns.

Equation 5.7 is the mathematical formulation of the closed-loop system shown in Figure 5.1. The top two lines of Eq. 5.7 represent the behavior of the plant. The third line implements the observer, and the fourth line computes the actuator commands. These last two lines form the observer-controller.

The companion CD-ROM contains the MATLAB function `ss_design()`, which develops an observer-controller and feedforward gain for a SISO plant that using the pole placement method. The inputs to this command are the plant model and constraints for the locations of the closed-loop system and the observer poles. The form of `ss_design()` is shown here.

```
>> [n, ssobsctrl, sscl] = ss_design(ssplant, t_settle, ...
                               damp_ratio, obs_pole_mult)
```

The input arguments are `ssplant`, the state-space plant model; `t_settle`, the closed-loop settling time requirement in seconds; `damp_ratio`, the damping ratio requirement; and `obs_pole_mult`, the multiplier used to determine the observer pole locations given the closed-loop pole locations. The `select_poles()` function is used internally to determine the closed-loop pole locations from the given specifications.

The outputs of `ss_design()` are the scalar feedforward gain `n`, the state-space observer-controller `ssobsctrl`, and a state-space model of the closed-loop system `sscl`. The `ssobsctrl` system requires the augmented plant output vector $\tilde{\mathbf{y}}$ as its input and produces the term $-\mathbf{K}\hat{\mathbf{x}}$ as its output. The actuator command must be computed as shown in the last line of Eq. 5.7.

You can use plot_poles() (included on the CD-ROM) to display the pole locations of the closed-loop system sscl and verify that they satisfy the specifications.

```
>> plot_poles(sscl, t_settle, damp_ratio)
```

5.10 Integral Control

The compensation scheme described above produces a generalization of proportional-derivative (PD) feedback control. There is no integral action to eliminate steady-state errors resulting from nonlinearities or modeling errors in the linear plant model.

An integral term can be added to the controller structure to eliminate steady-state errors. Figure 5.2 shows a control system configuration containing an observer and control algorithm similar to those developed previously, along with a term involving the error integral. This diagram represents a SISO system, but the same concept can be extended to MIMO systems as well.

Figure 5.2 Controller configuration with integral term included.

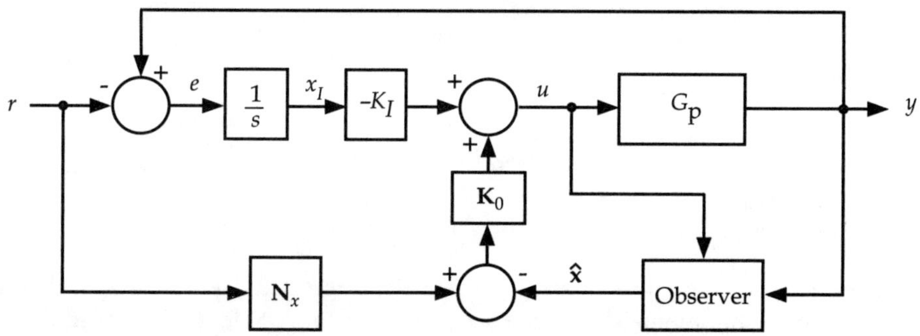

Subtracting the reference input from the output and integrating the result forms the error integral.

$$\dot{x}_I = e = y - r \qquad \text{Eq. 5.8}$$

Multiplying the error integral by the gain $-K_I$ provides the integral control term, which is summed with the output of a control algorithm similar to that developed in the previous section.

With the use of Eq. 5.8 and because $y = \mathbf{Cx} + Du$, the system state equation with the added integral state is shown in Eq. 5.9.

$$\begin{bmatrix} \dot{x}_I \\ \dot{\mathbf{x}} \end{bmatrix} = \begin{bmatrix} \mathbf{0} & \mathbf{C} \\ \mathbf{0} & \mathbf{A} \end{bmatrix} \begin{bmatrix} x_I \\ \mathbf{x} \end{bmatrix} + \begin{bmatrix} D \\ \mathbf{B} \end{bmatrix} u - \begin{bmatrix} 1 \\ 0 \end{bmatrix} r \qquad \text{Eq. 5.9}$$

The control algorithm for this system is given in Eq. 5.10.

$$\mathbf{u} = -\begin{bmatrix} K_I & \mathbf{K}_0 \end{bmatrix} \begin{bmatrix} x_I \\ \hat{\mathbf{x}} \end{bmatrix} + \mathbf{K}_0 \mathbf{N}_x r \qquad \text{Eq. 5.10}$$

The pole placement technique described earlier can be used to design the controller gain for this system. The only difference now is that it is first necessary to form the augmented state equations of Eq. 5.9 and break the resulting gain vector **K** into the two components K_I and $\mathbf{K}_0$ of Eq. 5.10. The $\mathbf{N}_x$ matrix is determined as described in Section 5.8 on the basis of the system model of Eq. 5.9. In designing the controller gain, one additional closed-loop pole location must be specified in the vector **p** to accommodate the added state.

The MATLAB statements that perform these steps for a SISO system are shown here, where `t_settle` is the settling time requirement (in seconds) and `damp_ratio` is the damping ratio requirement.

```
>> n = size(ssplant.a, 1) % Number of states
>> a = [0  ssplant.c; zeros(n, 1) ssplant.a)]
>> b = [ssplant.d; ssplant.b]
>> p = select_poles(n+1, t_settle, damp_ratio)
>> K = place(a, b, p)
>> Ki = K(1)
>> K0 = K(2:end)
>> Nxu = inv([ssplant.a ssplant.b; ssplant.c ssplant.d]) * ...
        [zeros(n,1); 1]
>> Nx = Nxu(1:n, :)
```

The first three statements above create the augmented **A** and **B** matrices of Eq. 5.9. The next two statements develop a set of closed-loop pole locations and determine the controller gain. The next two statements break the **K** vector into the state feedback gain $\mathbf{K}_0$ and the integral gain K_I for implementation in the controller structure shown in Figure 5.2. The final two statements determine the $\mathbf{N}_x$ gain.

The observer for this system is constructed as described in Section 5.7, except that there is one less observer pole than the number of closed-loop poles. This is because there is no need to estimate the error integral state, which is known. The complete equations for the combined observer-controller for this system appear in Eq. 5.11.

$$\begin{aligned} \dot{\hat{\mathbf{x}}} &= \mathbf{A}\hat{\mathbf{x}} + \mathbf{B}u + \mathbf{L}(y - \mathbf{C}\hat{\mathbf{x}} - Du) \\ \dot{x}_I &= y - r \\ u &= -K_I x_I + \mathbf{K}_0(\mathbf{N}_x r - \hat{\mathbf{x}}) \end{aligned} \qquad \text{Eq. 5.11}$$

The controller structure described in this section implements a generalization of the PID controller described in Chapter 2. The closed-loop poles can be placed at arbitrarily selected locations to produce desired performance characteristics. This controller provides zero steady-state error in the presence of minor plant variations from the linear model.

The use of integral control in this structure has the same potential difficulties with actuator saturation and integrator windup as described in Section 2.3. As discussed in that section, the technique of turning off integration when the amplitude of the error signal is above a threshold can reduce the effects of integrator windup to a tolerable level.

5.11 Summary

In this chapter, I discussed the pole placement design approach, which permits the positioning of closed-loop system poles at arbitrarily selected locations in the complex plane. This provides the designer with a great deal of freedom in determining the dynamic behavior of the system.

The feedback control algorithm used in the pole placement method is a gain matrix **K** multiplied by the system state vector **x**. The full state vector is required for this computation, including any state variables that are not directly measured with sensors. Consequently, it is necessary to estimate any unknown states for use in the control algorithm. An observer, also called a state estimator, performs this function.

Some restrictions on the structure of the state-space model must be satisfied for the pole placement design approach to succeed. First, the actuators must be capable of driving the system in a manner that produces the desired response. Second, the sensors must measure sufficient system parameters to enable construction of a complete state estimate. The ability of the actuators to fully control the system is called controllability, and the ability of the sensor measurements to enable complete state estimation is called observability. Performing some straightforward tests on the linear plant model determines whether it is controllable and observable.

Given a controllable and observable state-space plant model along with a set of desired system and observer pole locations, the design of the controller and observer requires only a few MATLAB Control System Toolbox commands. The most difficult part of the design process is the selection of closed-loop system and observer pole locations. The `select_poles()` function, as described in this chapter (provided on the accompanying CD-ROM), determines a suitable set of pole locations from the closed-loop settling time and damping ratio requirements.

The controller resulting from this design approach is a generalization of the PD controller described in Chapter 2. The addition of an error integral to the controller structure enables the elimination of steady-state errors resulting from modeling inaccuracies. Pole placement control with an error integral provides a generalization of the PID control technique discussed in Chapter 2.

The pole placement design approach described in this chapter is applicable to MIMO systems as well as to SISO systems. The same MATLAB commands are used to design the estimator and controller gain in both cases.

5.12 Self-Test

1. An electrohydraulic servomechanism has a control voltage as its input and hydraulic ram position as its output. The transfer function for this plant follows. Enter this transfer function into MATLAB and convert it into a state-space model.

$$G(s) = \frac{4 \times 10^7}{s(s+250)(s^2+40s+9\times 10^4)}$$

2. Determine whether the plant model created in problem 1 is controllable and observable.
3. Select a set of closed-loop poles for the plant of problem 1 that provides a settling time of 0.05 seconds and a damping ratio of 0.8. Use `select_poles()` to determine the locations.
4. Design the gain vector **K** for the controller using the results of problem 3.
5. Design the observer gain vector **L** such that the observer poles are four times the value of the closed-loop poles.
6. Design the feedforward gain **N** to produce zero steady-state error.
7. Assemble the observer-controller into a state-space system in the form of Eq. 5.1.
8. Assemble the closed-loop system consisting of the augmented plant plus controller using the results of problems 1 through 7 and plot the closed-loop pole locations in the complex plane.
9. Rewrite the sequence of MATLAB commands shown in Section 5.10 that computes the $\mathbf{K}_0$, K_I, and $\mathbf{N}_x$ gains so the plant can have an arbitrary but equal number of inputs and outputs. Assume that input number 1 is the command signal for output number 1, input 2 is the command for output 2, and so on.
10. A linear model of a DC electric motor has voltage as its input and motor rotation speed as its output. Consider the motor model below. Design a state-space compensator using integral control with a damping ratio of at least 0.7 and a settling time of 0.5 seconds. Use Simulink to implement the controller structure shown in Figure 5.2. Extract a linear model of the closed-loop system from the Simulink diagram and plot the system pole locations.

$$G(s) = \frac{2}{s^2 + 16s + 50}$$

5.13 Answers

1. The plant transfer function can be rewritten as the product of three simpler transfer functions.

$$G(s) = \left(\frac{1}{s}\right)\left(\frac{1}{s+250}\right)\left(\frac{4\times 10^7}{s^2+40s+9\times 10^4}\right)$$

The following commands create this plant model and convert it into a state-space model.

```
>> tf1 = tf(1, [1 0]);
>> tf2 = tf(1, [1 250]);
>> tf3 = tf(4e7, [1 40 9e4]);
>> tfplant = tf1 * tf2 * tf3;
>> ssplant = ss(tfplant);
```

2. The controllability test is performed with the following commands.

```
>> c0 = ctrb(ssplant)
>> controllable = (rank(c0) == length(c0))
```

The controllability test passes. The observability test is performed with the following commands.

```
>> ob = obsv(ssplant)
>> observable = (rank(ob) == length(ob))
```

The observability test passes.

3.

```
>> p = select_poles(4, 0.05, 0.8)
```

4.

```
>> K = place(ssplant.a, ssplant.b, p)
```

5.

```
>> q = 4 * p
>> L = place(ssplant.a', ssplant.c', q)'
```

6.

```
>> n = size(ssplant.a, 1) % Number of states
>> m = size(ssplant.c, 1) % Number of outputs
>> Nxu = inv([ssplant.a ssplant.b; ssplant.c ssplant.d]) * ...
        [zeros(n,m); eye(m)];
>> Nx = Nxu(1:n, :);
>> Nu = Nxu(n+1:end, :);
>> N = Nu + K*Nx;
```

7. Create the compensator shown in Figure 5.1 with the `ss()` function and the results of Eq. 5.7. The compensator input is the augmented plant output vector $\tilde{\mathbf{y}}$, and its output is $-\mathbf{K}\hat{\mathbf{x}}$.

```
>> ssobsctrl = ss(ssplant.a-L*ssplant.c, ...
               [L ssplant.b-L*ssplant.d], -K, 0);
```

8. Form the augmented plant `ssplant_aug` to pass the plant inputs as additional outputs. Then create a closed-loop system model `sscl` consisting of the augmented plant plus compensator using positive feedback and multiply it by **N**. The `plot_poles()` function on the accompanying CDROM displays the closed-loop pole locations and the damping ratio and settling time constraints in the complex plane. The resulting plot appears in Figure 5.3. The four poles near the origin are the system poles and the four to the left are the observer poles.

```
>> ssplant_aug = ss(ssplant.a, ssplant.b, ...
                 [ssplant.c; zeros(m, n)], [ssplant.d; eye(m)]);
>> sscl = N * feedback(ssplant_aug, ssobsctrl, +1);
>> plot_poles(sscl, 0.05, 0.8)
```

9. The following sequence of commands produces the $\mathbf{K}_0$, K_I, and $\mathbf{N}_x$ gains for SISO and MIMO plants assuming each input element is the command for the corresponding output element. The error integral states become the first m elements in the $\mathbf{x}$ vector, which will have length $n + m$.

```
>> a = [zeros(m) ssplant.c; zeros(n, m) ssplant.a)]
>> b = [ssplant.d; ssplant.b]
>> p = select_poles(n+m, t_settle, damp_ratio)
>> K = place(a, b, p)
>> Ki = K(1:m)
>> K0 = K(m+1:end)
>> Nxu = inv([ssplant.a ssplant.b; ssplant.c ssplant.d]) * ...
        [zeros(n,m); eye(m)];
>> Nx = Nxu(1:n, :);
```

Figure 5.3 Closed-loop pole locations (circles) and design constraints (solid lines).

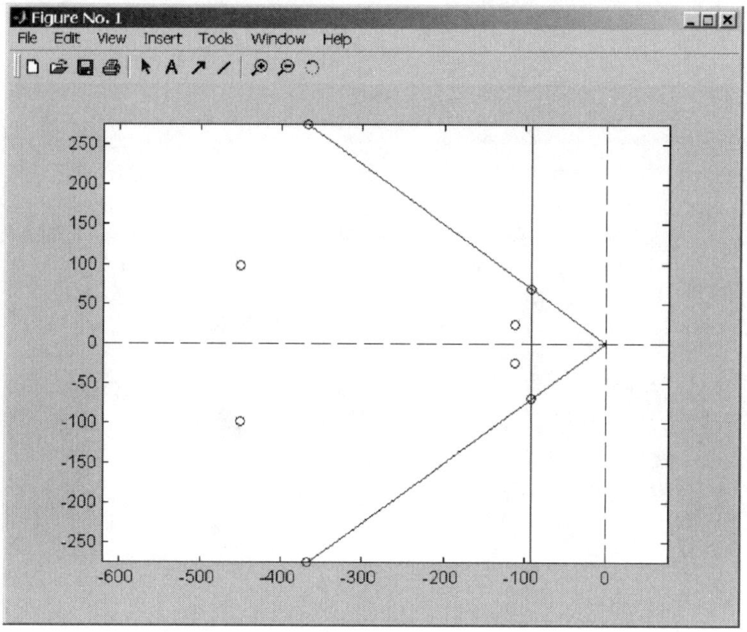

10. The sequence of commands to create the DC motor plant model; design the **L**, $\mathbf{K}_0$, K_I, and $\mathbf{N}_x$ gains; and create the augmented plant and observer are shown below. These commands were entered into the file `question_10.m` in the `Self-Test/Ch05` directory of the CD-ROM, so the command line prompt (>>) is not shown.

```
% Create the plant model
tfplant = tf(2, [1 16 50])
ssplant = ss(tfplant);

% Controller performance specifications
t_settle = 0.5; % Seconds
damp_ratio = 0.7;
obs_pole_mult = 4; % Multiplies closed loop poles to place observer
                   % poles

% Check controllability
c0 = ctrb(ssplant);
controllable = (rank(c0) == length(c0))
if ~controllable
```

```
    error('Plant is not controllable');
end

% Check observability
ob = obsv(ssplant);
observable = (rank(ob) == length(ob))
if ~observable
    error('Plant is not observable');
end

n = size(ssplant.a, 1); % Number of states
m = size(ssplant.c, 1); % Number of outputs

% Augment the plant with the error integral
a = [zeros(m) ssplant.c; zeros(n, m) ssplant.a];
b = [ssplant.d; ssplant.b];

% Design the controller gain
p = select_poles(n+1, t_settle, damp_ratio);
K = place(a, b, p);
Ki = K(1);
K0 = K(2:end);

% Design the observer gain
q = obs_pole_mult * select_poles(n, t_settle, damp_ratio);
L = place(ssplant.a', ssplant.c', q)'

% Create a state-space observer
ssobs = ss(ssplant.a-L*ssplant.c,
           [L ssplant.b-L*ssplant.d], eye(n), 0);

% Compute the feedforward gain
Nxu = inv([ssplant.a ssplant.b; ssplant.c ssplant.d]) *
        [zeros(n,m); eye(m)];
```

```
Nx = Nxu(1:n, :);

% Augment the plant model to pass the inputs as additional outputs
ssplant_aug = ss(ssplant.a, ssplant.b, [ssplant.c; zeros(m, n)],
              [ssplant.d; eye(m)]);
```

These gains and state-space components are used in the Simulink model contained in the `ss_pid.mdl` file in the `Self-Test/Ch05` directory of the CD-ROM. The Simulink diagram for this model is shown in Figure 5.4.

Figure 5.4 **Simulink model of state-space controller with integral term.**

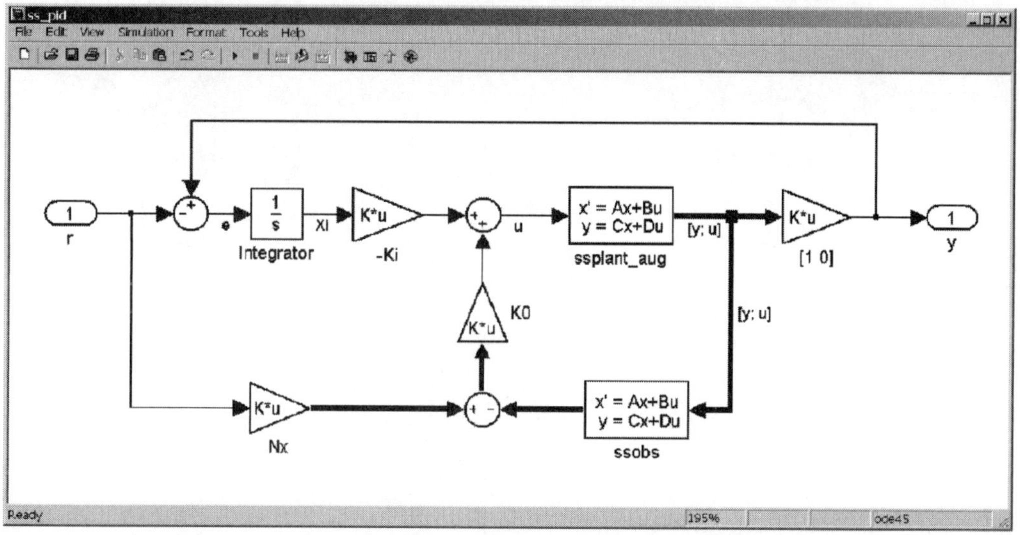

You can extract the state-space model for the closed-loop system from this diagram with `linmod()`. Plot the poles along with settling time and damping ratio constraints using `plot_poles()`. The result is shown in Figure 5.5; the three poles near the origin are the system poles and the two further to the left are the observer poles.

```
% Extract the linear model from the ss_pid.mdl Simulink diagram
[a,b,c,d] = linmod('ss_pid');
sscl = ss(a,b,c,d);

% Display closed loop poles
plot_poles(sscl, t_settle, damp_ratio);
```

Figure 5.5 Closed-loop pole locations (circles) and design constraints (solid lines).

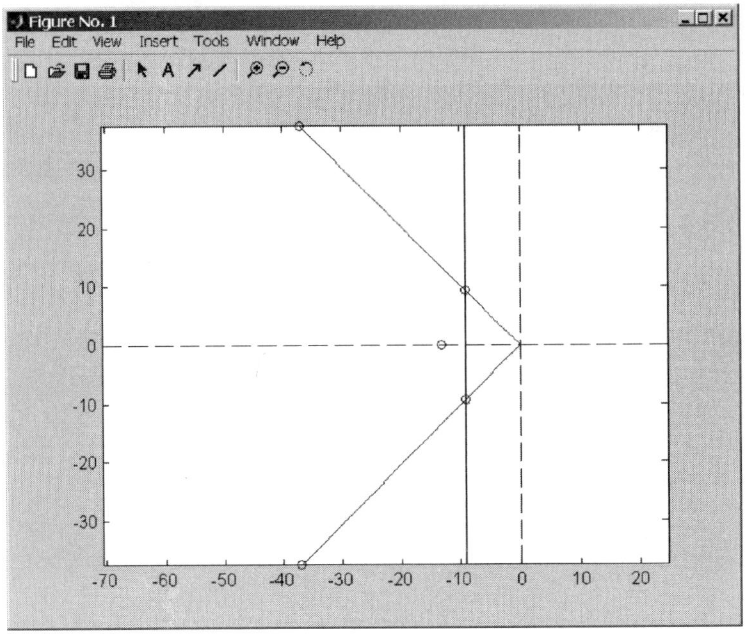

CHAPTER 6

OPTIMAL CONTROL

6.1 Introduction

In Chapters 2 (PID control), 4 (classical control system design), and 5 (pole placement), I described techniques for designing control systems that satisfy a given set of performance specifications. In those approaches, the controller design effort proceeds until it is "good enough" in terms of satisfying performance requirements. There has been no attempt to design the "best" controller possible for a given application.

In this chapter, I introduce techniques that produce the best, or optimal, controller design for a given plant model and associated weighting criteria. As a first step, it is necessary to precisely define what is meant by "optimal" and describe it in mathematical terms. The MATLAB Control System Toolbox commands for selecting controller and observer gains on the basis of the optimality criteria will then be discussed. As in the preceding chapters, I will not address the complex algorithms used by the Toolbox to perform the computations. Only the necessary steps to make effective use of the commands and their results will be covered.

In Chapter 5, I identified an ad hoc approach (using the `select_poles()` function) for choosing closed-loop system and observer pole locations that satisfy a set of performance specifications. The techniques introduced in this chapter determine the pole locations for the closed-loop system and the observer on the basis of optimality criteria described below. The resulting controller designs are optimal in the sense that no other set of pole locations could do a better job of satisfying the optimality criteria for the given plant model and weighting criteria.

The methods I discuss in this chapter work only with state-space plant models and use the controller structures described in Chapter 5. I will not repeat the descriptions of the controller structures here, so familiarity with Chapter 5 is assumed. In fact, the only differences between the design approaches of Chapter 5 and of this chapter are the techniques used for determining the controller **K** matrix and the observer **L** matrix.

The optimality criterion for the controller is based on a weighted trade-off between speed of system response and actuator effort. Two matrices (**Q** and **R**) specify the weighting function applied to the states and actuator commands. The designer must develop these matrices and provide them, along with the plant model, to a Control System Toolbox command that computes the optimal controller gain **K**. It is seldom obvious what weighting matrices to use to produce satisfactory controller performance, so some iteration on the contents of the **Q** and **R** matrices is usually necessary.

The observer optimality criterion is based on the *measurement noise* of the sensors and the "noise" of the plant itself, called *process noise*. Measurement noise is the result of errors in the measurement of plant outputs. Process noise models how the actual plant output varies from the expected output resulting from driving the linear plant model with known plant inputs. The process noise is modeled as a state-space system driven by *white noise* inputs.

Two matrices, called covariance matrices, describe the measurement noise and process noise properties. A single Control System Toolbox command determines the optimal observer gain matrix **L** on the basis of the plant model, the process noise model, and covariance matrices. This observer minimizes the mean-squared state estimation error for the plant given its process noise model and the measurement noise and process noise characteristics.

The optimal controller and observer gains are placed in a controller structure as described in Chapter 5 to provide generalized forms of proportional derivative (PD) control and proportional integral derivative (PID) control. As in Chapter 5, these techniques are applicable to both SISO and MIMO plants.

The techniques I describe in this chapter are widely used in applications in which incremental improvements in control system performance can provide substantial benefits. One example of such an application is an electrical power generation plant, in which significant fuel cost reductions can be realized from small control system improvements.

6.2 Chapter Objectives

After reading this chapter, you should be able to

- describe the differences between optimal control system design approaches and those discussed in Chapters 2, 4, and 5;
- describe the optimality criterion for the linear quadratic regulator (LQR) controller;
- develop appropriate weighting matrices for use in LQR controller design;
- use the MATLAB Control System Toolbox to develop an LQR controller gain **K**;
- describe the optimality criterion for the Kalman filter;
- understand how to determine the process noise model and covariance matrices given a plant model and its related noise characteristics;

- use the MATLAB Control System Toolbox to develop a Kalman observer gain **L**; and
- use the approaches described in Chapter 5 to form an observer-controller and connect it to the plant to form a closed-loop system.

6.3 Concepts of Optimal Control

The design process for optimal control uses a sequence of high-level steps similar to those of pole placement design described in Chapter 5. The differences are in the methods used to select the controller and observer gain matrices **K** and **L**. In optimal control, instead of directly selecting the pole locations, the designer must develop optimality criteria for the controller and observer gains. Mathematical algorithms then compute the pole locations and, hence, the **K** and **L** gains that produce the compensator optimally satisfying the criteria.

As with the pole placement method described in Chapter 5, the controller and observer gains are designed in separate steps. In the first step, the designer must verify that the plant model is both observable and controllable. It must pass the controllability and observability tests described in Sections 5.4 and 5.5.

As in pole placement, the design of the controller begins with an assumption that the full system state is known. The optimality criterion for the controller is to minimize the scalar cost function J shown in Eq. 6.1.

$$J(\mathbf{u}) = \int_0^{\infty} \mathbf{x}^T\mathbf{Q}\mathbf{x} + \mathbf{u}^T\mathbf{R}\mathbf{u}\, dt \qquad \text{Eq. 6.1}$$

In this formula, $\mathbf{x}$ is the plant state vector with length n, and $\mathbf{u}$ is the input vector with length r. **Q** is an $n \times n$ matrix and **R** is an $r \times r$ matrix. The elements of **Q** and **R** must be chosen so the scalar terms $\mathbf{x}^T\mathbf{Q}\mathbf{x}$ and $\mathbf{u}^T\mathbf{R}\mathbf{u}$ are greater than or equal to zero for all possible values of $\mathbf{x}$ and $\mathbf{u}$. A simple way to ensure this is to make **Q** and **R** diagonal matrices with the elements along the diagonal all greater than or equal to zero.

Think of Eq. 6.1 as describing the behavior of a system starting at an arbitrary initial condition $\mathbf{x}(0)$ with the control system attempting to drive all the states to zero (in other words, functioning as a regulator with a zero reference input). The cost function J is minimized when the states go to zero as rapidly as possible with the smallest possible control input $\mathbf{u}$, in accordance with the constant weighting matrices **Q** and **R**. The weighting matrices must be selected by the designer to provide satisfactory system response speed and damping characteristics. You'll see how to determine the contents of these matrices later in this chapter.

When **Q** and **R** are diagonal matrices, Eq. 6.1 can be written as shown in Eq. 6.2. Here, q_{ii} and r_{ii} represent the diagonal elements of **Q** and **R**, and x_i and u_i are the ith elements of the $\mathbf{x}$ and $\mathbf{u}$ vectors, respectively. In this formulation, the cost function is the integral of the weighted sum of the squared magnitudes of the plant states and input signals.

$$J(\mathbf{u}) = \int_0^{\infty} \sum_{i=1}^{n} q_{ii}x_i^2 + \sum_{i=1}^{r} r_{ii}u_i^2\, dt \qquad \text{Eq. 6.2}$$

Given the plant model and the **Q** and **R** matrices, a single MATLAB Control System Toolbox command computes the optimal controller gain **K**. However, because it is seldom obvious what values to select for the elements of **Q** and **R**, iterative adjustment of these matrices is usually needed to provide a satisfactory trade-off between closed-loop performance and system limitations, such as actuator saturation.

The next step is to design an optimal observer gain **L**. The optimality criterion for the observer is to minimize the mean-squared error in the state estimate. The observer that provides an optimal estimation of the system state in the presence of process noise and measurement noise is called the *Kalman filter.*

A Kalman filter can be time varying or steady state. A time-varying Kalman filter computes a new value of the observer gain **L** each time the filter is updated. This results in an optimal estimate of the system state at every step, which minimizes transient errors during system start-up. This approach also enables the filter to adapt if the noise properties of the plant vary during operation. However, the time-varying filter is fairly complex and computationally intensive and will not be described here. Instead, I discuss the steady-state Kalman filter. This filter uses the **L** matrix to which the time-varying filter converges after a number of iterations, assuming the system noise properties remain fixed.

Process noise models the deviation of the actual plant behavior from its linear model. These deviations could result from unmodeled disturbance inputs the plant receives or could be caused by nonlinearities within the plant itself. It is possible to develop a process noise model analytically, or a simplified model can be employed that assumes some noise is added to each plant input signal. I describe this simplified process noise model later.

The modeling of sensor noise is more straightforward and typically relies on manufacturers' data describing the accuracy of sensor measurements. One example of measurement error is the quantization of analog-to-digital converter (ADC) samples.

Some error sources contained in the process noise and measurement noise are truly random (such as thermal noise on an analog electrical signal), whereas others result from systematic errors (such as ADC quantization). In developing the Kalman filter, all of the error sources must be described in terms of truly random white noise passed through a filter. Most sources of process and measurement noise can be modeled reasonably using this approach, though doing it well requires a degree of skill and persistence.

The designer must develop two covariance matrices describing the properties of the white noise inputs to the process noise and measurement noise models. Given the plant model, the process noise model, and the covariance matrices, a single MATLAB Control System Toolbox function computes the optimal steady-state Kalman gain **L**.

The **K** and **L** matrices resulting from the optimal design procedures described above must be placed in controller structures identical to those described in Chapter 5. The remaining design steps described in Chapter 5 are applicable as well. These steps include the determination of the feedforward gain **N** and the optional use of integral control.

It is important to understand that the optimal design approach does not eliminate the need for iteration in control system design. Rather, optimal design moves the iteration from the selection of pole locations as described in Chapter 5 to the development of cost function weighting matrices, the selection of a process noise model, and the determination of process and measurement noise covariance matrices.

When using optimal design, you must test the resulting controller and iteratively adjust design parameters to produce a final design meeting all specifications. The optimal design approach requires more work, but the payoff of an optimal controller design is often worth the additional effort.

6.4 Linear Quadratic Regulator Design

The controller gain **K** that minimizes the cost function J shown in Eq. 6.1 is called a *linear quadratic regulator.* It has this name because the system is linear, the cost function J contains quadratic terms (seen in Eqs. 6.1 and 6.2), and the minimization procedure assumes the control system functions as a regulator. However, note that it is not necessary to restrict the use of the resulting controller to regulator applications. I will use the controller structure of Figure 5.1, which includes a reference input.

The MATLAB Control System Toolbox provides the `lqr()` command for LQR design in continuous-time systems. With this command, the work is mainly in the selection of appropriate **Q** and **R** weighting matrices. As discussed in the previous section, it is often best to set up these matrices so that only elements along the diagonal are nonzero and none of the diagonal elements are negative. This results in a cost function of the form shown in Eq. 6.2.

If you have no idea what values to use for **Q** and **R** (which is not unusual), a reasonable starting point is to set both to identity matrices. This arrangement weights each input signal and state equally. With this initial condition for the matrices, the steps of LQR controller design follow.

1. Initialize the **Q** and **R** matrices as identity matrices.
2. Compute a controller gain **K** with `lqr()`. The inputs to `lqr()` are the linear plant model and the **Q** and **R** matrices.
3. Evaluate the performance of the resulting controller assuming perfect state estimation. If the performance is acceptable, you are done. Otherwise, continue with step 4.
4. If necessary, increase the weights of specific diagonal elements of the **Q** matrix for states that must respond more rapidly. For plant input signals that are being driven too hard, increase the corresponding element of the **R** matrix. For input and output signals that are of less concern, the corresponding matrix elements can be reduced in magnitude. For initial design iterations, increase and decrease the weights by a factor of 10.
5. Return to step 2.

Example 6.1 Second-order SISO system.

Consider the following plant model. The control system design requirements are a 1-second settling time with a damping ratio of at least 0.7.

$$G = \frac{100}{s^2 + 1.8s + 100}$$

This is a second-order SISO system, so **Q** is a 2×2 matrix and R is a scalar. Because only the relative values of the elements are significant in minimizing the cost function, I will fix the value $R = 1$ and vary the diagonal elements of **Q** during the design process.

As a first attempt, set **Q** as the identity matrix and design a controller gain with `lqr()`.

```
>> tfplant = tf(100, [1 1.8 100])
>> ssplant = ss(tfplant);
>> Q = diag([1 1]);
>> R = 1;
>> K = lqr(ssplant, Q, R)
```

This sequence of commands produces the controller gain **K** = [2.44 0.29].

For the moment, assume that all states are available as outputs. Setting the plant's **C** matrix to a 2×2 identity matrix will accomplish this.

```
>> ssplant.c = eye(2);
```

Form a closed-loop system with the controller gain and plot the closed-loop pole locations with 1-second settling time and 0.7 damping ratio constraints.

```
>> cl_sys = feedback(ssplant, -K, +1);
>> t_settle = 1;
>> damp_ratio = 0.7;
>> plot_poles(cl_sys, t_settle, damp_ratio)
```

The resulting plot appears in Figure 6.1.

The initial design moves the open-loop pole locations only a small amount. Significantly more weight in one or more of the **Q** matrix diagonal terms will be required. Try increasing the first element of **Q** by a factor of 10.

```
>> Q = diag([10 1]);
```

Repeat the steps to compute the controller gain, form a closed-loop system, and plot the closed-loop pole locations. As the new plot will show, the pole locations have moved to the left to a real component of –4.5. This is better, but still not good enough. After a few more iterations, the following **Q** matrix is found to produce a response satisfying the damping ratio requirement.

```
>> Q = diag([50 1]);
```

Figure 6.1 Closed-loop pole locations of initial controller design.

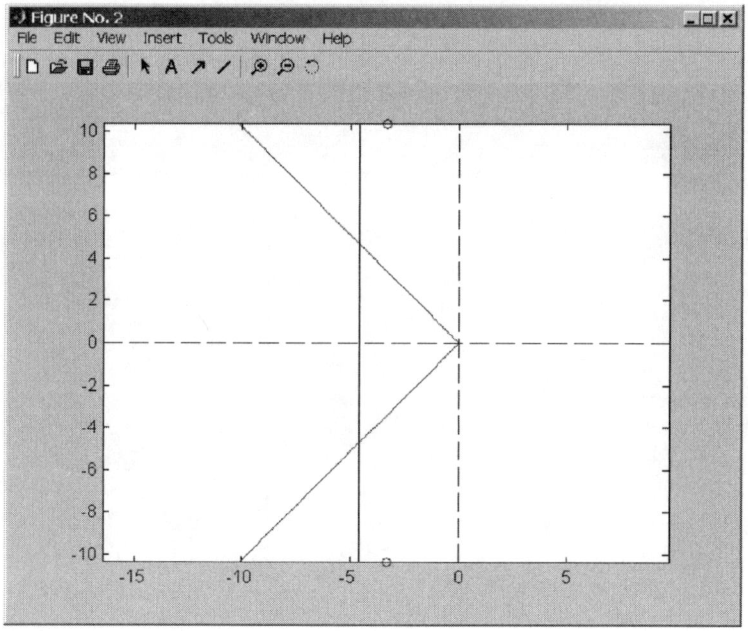

This results in the gain vector **K** = [6.86 0.29]. The closed-loop poles of this system, along with the 1-second settling time and 0.7 damping ratio constraints, appear in Figure 6.2.

Observe in Figure 6.2 that the poles are much faster (with a real part of –7.8) than required to meet the settling time constraint. These pole locations are approximately the same distance from the origin as the open-loop poles. This occurs because the LQR design process simultaneously minimizes the state responses and the control effort. In this example, it would take *more* control effort (as represented in Eq. 6.1) to produce a *slower* closed-loop response!

To get a feel for how the design process works, try repeating the above steps with several different values for the **Q** matrix diagonal elements. Observe how changes to the **Q** matrix affect the closed-loop pole locations. See if you can find any slower closed-loop poles than those shown in Figure 6.2 that also satisfy the damping ratio constraint.

Figure 6.2 Closed-loop pole locations with settling time and damping ratio constraints.

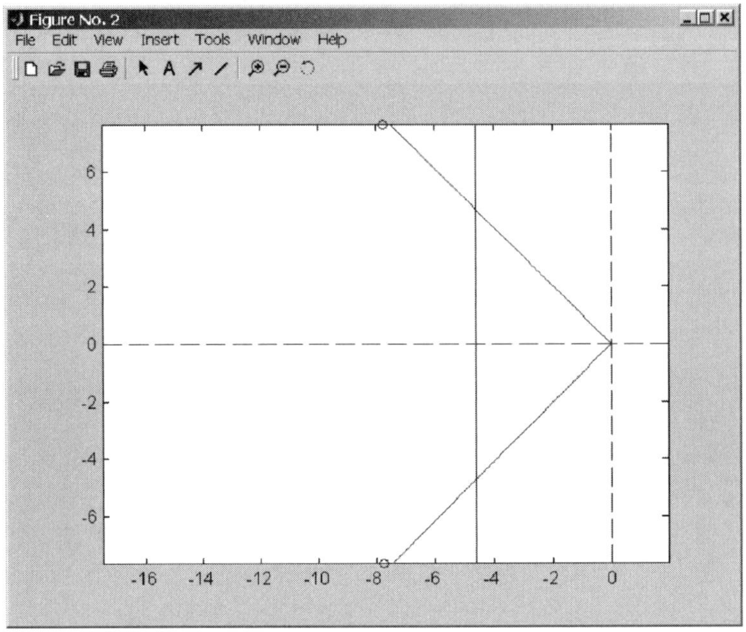

6.5 Kalman State Estimation

The Kalman filter forms an optimal state estimate for a state-space plant model in the presence of process and measurement noise. The optimality criterion for the steady-state Kalman filter is the minimization of the steady-state error covariance matrix **P** shown in Eq. 6.3.

$$\mathbf{P} = \lim_{t \to \infty} E(\{\hat{\mathbf{x}} - \mathbf{x}\}\{\hat{\mathbf{x}} - \mathbf{x}\}^T) \qquad \text{Eq. 6.3}$$

In Eq. 6.3, E represents the expectation (or mean) of the of the parenthesized expression, $\hat{\mathbf{x}}$ is the state estimate, and $\mathbf{x}$ is the true state vector. The term $\{\hat{\mathbf{x}} - \mathbf{x}\}$ is the state estimation error. The diagonal elements of **P** contain the variance (the square of the standard deviation) of the state estimation error. The off-diagonal terms represent the correlation between the errors of the state vector elements.

The Kalman filter minimizes the **P** matrix, which minimizes the mean-squared error in the state estimates. For this reason, Kalman filtering is also called minimum mean-squared error filtering.

Example 6.2 Practical application of the Kalman filter.

The Kalman filter provides an elegant solution to many engineering problems involving noisy measurements of dynamic system behavior. One such application is the combination of Global Positioning System (GPS) measurements with the output of an inertial navigation system (INS).

A GPS receiver provides position and velocity measurements with very small long-term errors. In other words, a stationary GPS receiver that averages position measurements over a long time (hours or days) has an expected position error measured in centimeters. However, GPS receivers tend to have a slow update rate (typically 1Hz) and a single position measurement can contain a significant amount of error (perhaps 10 meters).

Inertial navigation systems, on the other hand, have good short-term error performance and can provide high-speed updates (typically hundreds of hertz) but are subject to drift that degrades their accuracy over time.

A Kalman filter navigation system combining a GPS and an INS uses the INS as a high-speed measurement device, while the GPS measurements remove the bias and drift that would otherwise corrupt the INS measurements over time. This filter combines the best attributes of both sensor types while compensating for the drawbacks of each. The result is an exceptionally accurate navigation system that maintains its accuracy even when operating over long periods of time.

I will not explore the full depth and subtlety of Kalman filtering in this chapter. Additional information can be found in Brown (1983) [1] and in many other excellent books on the topic. Instead, our goal will be to determine the constant observer gain **L** that minimizes the steady-state error covariance matrix **P** shown in Eq. 6.3. This is the steady-state Kalman filter.

The filter development begins with a state-space plant model incorporating process and measurement noise effects. This model has the form shown in Eq. 6.4.

$$\begin{aligned} \dot{\mathbf{x}} &= \mathbf{Ax} + \mathbf{Bu} + \mathbf{Gw} \\ \mathbf{y} &= \mathbf{Cx} + \mathbf{Du} + \mathbf{Hw} + \mathbf{v} \end{aligned} \qquad \text{Eq. 6.4}$$

The matrices **G** and **H** describe how the process noise **w** enters the system. The measurement noise appears in **v**. The vectors **w** and **v** consist of zero-mean white noise with the following properties.

$$\begin{aligned} E(\mathbf{w}) &= E(\mathbf{v}) = 0 \\ E(\mathbf{w}\mathbf{w}^T) &= \mathbf{Q}_N \\ E(\mathbf{v}\mathbf{v}^T) &= \mathbf{R}_N \end{aligned} \qquad \text{Eq. 6.5}$$

Equation 6.5 states that the means of the elements of **w** and **v** are zero and the constant matrices $\mathbf{Q}_N$ and $\mathbf{R}_N$ describe the covariances of **w** and **v**. In this discussion, **w** and **v** are assumed to be uncorrelated.

In addition to the **A**, **B**, **C**, and **D** matrices describing the linear plant model, four additional matrices will be required to design the steady-state Kalman filter. These are the **G** and **H** matrices, which describe the process noise dynamics, and the $\mathbf{Q}_N$ and $\mathbf{R}_N$ matrices, which describe the process and measurement noise covariances. Once all the matrices have been determined, a call to `kalman()` in the Control System Toolbox computes the optimal observer gain **L**.

The **G**, **H**, and $\mathbf{Q}_N$ matrices describe the process noise model. These matrices can be determined from knowledge of the noiselike properties of the disturbance inputs and plant dynamics. For example, in an aircraft autopilot design, the noise inputs might represent random wind gusts. The **G** and **H** matrices model the effects of these gusts on the system states and outputs by using white noise as the driving input. The expected variances of the noise inputs are contained in the diagonal elements of $\mathbf{Q}_N$.

Sometimes insufficient information is available to develop a realistic process noise model for a given system. In this situation, a simplified default model assumes that noise is added to each element of the input vector **u**. In this model, $\mathbf{G} = \mathbf{B}$ and $\mathbf{H} = \mathbf{D}$. The diagonal elements of $\mathbf{Q}_N$, corresponding to the noise variance on each input, can be adjusted iteratively to produce an observer with satisfactory performance.

The remaining matrix required for Kalman filter design is the measurement noise covariance $\mathbf{R}_N$. This matrix is usually diagonal, with each element along the diagonal containing the variance of the error in the corresponding sensor measurement. This error term can be determined from manufacturer-provided data describing the sensor error characteristics. The error variance is computed by squaring the root mean square jitter error specification (or equivalent specification with a different name) from the sensor manufacturer's data sheet. Note that the units of each diagonal term of $\mathbf{R}_N$ must be the square of the units of the corresponding plant output.

Example 6.3 ADC quantization.

A common example of measurement noise is ADC quantization. An ADC measures an analog voltage and converts it to a digital value, which contains some error because the digital value has limited precision. This is called the quantization error.

Assume an ADC samples its (assumed error-free) analog input at a frequency well above the Nyquist frequency and that the input voltage change equivalent to the least significant bit (LSB) of the ADC measurement is small relative to input signal variations. These assumptions lead to quantization errors that are uncorrelated with the input signal. Under these conditions, the measurement error variance for a SISO system can be approximated as shown in Eq. 6.6, where Δ is the size of the ADC's LSB in the units of the plant output y [2].

$$\mathbf{R}_N = \frac{1}{12}\Delta^2 \qquad \text{Eq. 6.6}$$

Having specified the linear plant model matrices, the process noise model, and the noise covariance matrices, the design of the steady-state Kalman filter is performed with the following commands.

```
>> obs_plant = ss(A, [B G], C, [D H])
>> [kest, L] = kalman(obs_plant, QN , RN)
```

The first command above forms a state-space plant model combining the linear plant model and the process noise model. The second command designs the Kalman filter. The `kest` output from the `kalman()` command is a state-space model of the Kalman filter observer. The **L** matrix is the optimal steady-state Kalman observer gain.

Example 6.4 Second-order plant with nonlinearities.

Consider again the second-order plant

$$G = \frac{100}{s^2 + 1.8s + 100}.$$

Assume the system contains nonlinearities such as friction and is affected by random, externally generated disturbances. A simplified model of these combined effects is a random value added to the plant input. In this model, the **G** matrix equals the plant **B** matrix, and the **H** matrix is the plant **D** matrix. Let the standard deviation of this random input be 0.1. The process noise variance is then $\mathbf{Q}_N = 0.1^2$.

The plant output is measured with a sensor that provides quantized samples with an LSB of 0.1 units. This results in the measurement noise variance $\mathbf{R}_N = 0.1^2/12$.

With this information, the steady-state Kalman observer gain is computed with the following MATLAB commands, and the resulting matrix is

$$\mathbf{L} = \begin{bmatrix} 4.45 \\ 13.50 \end{bmatrix}.$$

```
>> tfplant = tf(100, [1 1.8 100])
>> ssplant = ss(tfplant);

>> QN = 0.1^2;
>> RN = 0.1^2/12;

>> G = ssplant.b;
>> H = ssplant.d;

>> obs_plant = ss(ssplant.a, [ssplant.b G], ssplant.c, [ssplant.d H]);
>> [kest, L] = kalman(obs_plant, QN, RN);
```

6.6 Combined Observer-Controller

The previous sections described the LQR controller gain design and Kalman observer gain design procedures. The results are **K** and **L** matrices in the same format as was used in the pole placement technique described in Chapter 5. The combined observer-controller with the optimal controller and observer gain matrices is assembled exactly as was shown in Section 5.9.

Example 6.5 Observer–controller.

Continuing the previous example with the **K** and **L** gain vectors developed previously, the closed-loop system containing this observer-controller has the pole constellation shown in Figure 6.3.

Figure 6.3 Closed-loop pole locations with settling time and damping ratio constraints.

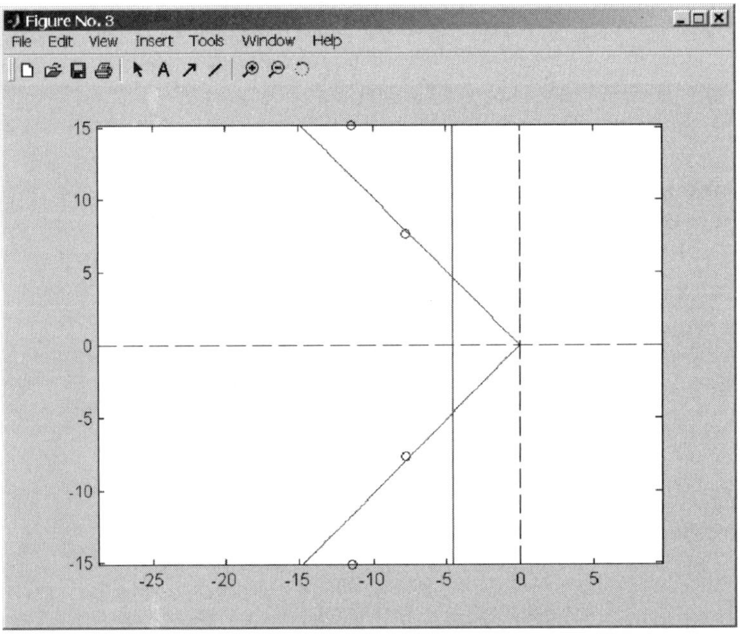

In Figure 6.3, the leftmost two poles are the observer poles. These pole locations result from the minimization of the state estimation error for the given process and measurement noise covariances and the assumed model of the process noise as an additive term to the plant input.

Note that in this design approach, there is no inherent requirement that the observer poles be faster than the closed-loop system poles. If the measurements are very noisy (i.e., $\mathbf{R}_N$ is large), the observer poles can be slower than the system poles, which could result in undesired coupling of the observer dynamics into the system dynamics and indicates a need for reduction in the measurement noise.

6.7 Summary

In this chapter, I discussed how to use the MATLAB Control System Toolbox to design optimal controller and observer gains. The LQR controller minimizes the performance index J shown in Eq. 6.1, which depends on the weighting matrices **Q** and **R** supplied by the designer. In most cases, these matrices will be diagonal, with appropriate positive weighting factors applied to each state variable and output signal. Because it is rarely obvious what values to use in the **Q** and **R** matrices, the design process generally involves iteratively tuning these matrices and testing the resulting controller. The product of the LQR design process is a controller gain **K** in the same format as was developed with the pole placement technique in Chapter 5.

The optimal observer described in this chapter is the steady-state Kalman filter. This filter minimizes the steady-state mean-squared state estimation error in the presence of process noise and measurement noise. In the development of the Kalman filter, a process noise model is required. This model represents the dynamic response of the system states and outputs to random inputs modeled by white noise. The process noise model is contained in the **G** and **H** matrices of Eq. 6.4. A simplified model of process noise assumes that noise terms are added to each plant input. In this model, **G** = **B** and **H** = **D**.

The variances of the process noise inputs are contained in the diagonal terms of the process noise covariance matrix $\mathbf{Q}_N$. The measurement noise is also modeled as white noise with variances in the diagonal terms of $\mathbf{R}_N$. The linear plant model (**A**, **B**, **C**, and **D** matrices), the process noise model (**G** and **H** matrices), and the noise covariance matrices ($\mathbf{Q}_N$ and $\mathbf{R}_N$) are supplied to the `kalman()` command, which computes the optimal observer gain **L**. As with the controller gain **K**, this gain is in the same format as was used in the pole placement technique.

It is not mandatory that the optimal controller gain be combined with the optimal observer gain. For example, it might make sense to develop an optimal controller gain for a given system and use the pole placement technique to develop the observer. Although this approach results in an observer with less than optimal error characteristics, it also avoids the work of developing the process noise model and the noise covariance matrices. It is up to the designer to select the most appropriate techniques to use for designing controller and observer gains.

6.8 Self-Test

1. An electrohydraulic servomechanism has a control voltage as its input and hydraulic ram position as its output. Enter the following transfer function for this plant into MATLAB and convert it into a state-space model.

$$G(s) = \frac{4 \times 10^7}{s(s+250)(s^2+40s+9\times 10^4)}$$

2. Copy the model from problem 1 to a new model and modify it so that the outputs become the system states. This model will be used to plot closed-loop pole locations.
3. Develop **Q** and **R** weighting matrices for LQR design with the plant of problem 1. Initialize both as identity matrices.
4. Design an LQR gain with the plant model from problem 1 and the **Q** and **R** matrices from problem 3.
5. Form a closed-loop system with the modified plant model from problem 2 and the controller gain from problem 4. Plot the closed-loop pole locations for this system along with 0.05-second settling time and 0.7 damping ratio constraints.
6. Multiply the **Q** matrix by 10^5 and repeat problems 4 and 5.
7. Iteratively increase the gains on the first two diagonal elements of **Q** until the design requirements are satisfied. Hint: Satisfactory values for both terms can be found between 10^5 and 10^6.
8. Develop a process noise model assuming noise is added to the plant input with a standard deviation of 0.5.
9. Develop a measurement noise variance estimate for an ADC measurement with an LSB of 0.01.
10. Design a steady-state Kalman observer gain with the results of problems 8 and 9.
11. Using the techniques of Chapter 5, compute the feedforward gain, form a combined observer-controller, and create a state-space model of the complete system.
12. Plot the closed-loop system pole locations. Comment on the pole locations in comparison to the pole locations developed for this plant in the Chapter 5 self-test, problem 8.

6.9 Answers

1. The plant transfer function can be rewritten as the product of three simpler transfer functions (Eq. 6.7). The following commands create this plant model and convert it into a state-space model.

$$G(s) = \left(\frac{1}{s}\right)\left(\frac{1}{s+250}\right)\left(\frac{4\times 10^7}{s^2+40s+9\times 10^4}\right) \qquad \text{Eq. 6.7}$$

```
>> tf1 = tf(1, [1 0]);
>> tf2 = tf(1, [1 250]);
>> tf3 = tf(4e7, [1 40 9e4]);
>> tfplant = tf1 * tf2 * tf3;
>> ssplant = ss(tfplant);
```

2. An assignment statement copies the model. Setting the **C** matrix to an identity matrix causes the states to become the outputs. MATLAB automatically adjusts the size of the **D** matrix (containing only zeros) to compensate for this change.

```
>> ssplant2 = ssplant;
>> ssplant2.c = eye(4);
```

3.

```
>> Q = eye(4);
>> R = 1;
```

4.

```
>> K = lqr(ssplant, Q, R);
```

5. The design constraints and closed-loop pole locations appear in Figure 6.4.

```
>> cl_sys = feedback(ssplant2, -K, +1);
>> t_settle = 0.05;
>> damp_ratio = 0.7;
>> plot_poles(cl_sys, t_settle, damp_ratio);
```

Observe that the resulting pole locations are not close to meeting the design constraints.

6. The design constraints and closed-loop pole locations appear in Figure 6.5.

```
>> Q = 1e5*eye(4);
>> K = lqr(ssplant, Q, R);
>> cl_sys = feedback(ssplant2, -K, +1);
>> plot_poles(cl_sys, t_settle, damp_ratio);
```

The pole locations are closer to meeting the specifications but are still not there.

Figure 6.4 Closed-loop pole locations using identity **Q** and **R** matrices.

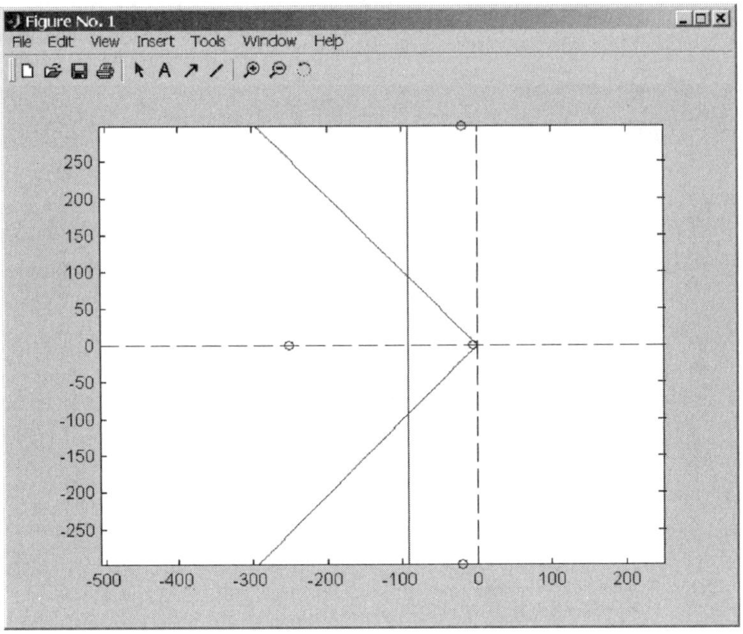

Figure 6.5 Closed-loop pole locations after multiplying **Q** by 10^5.

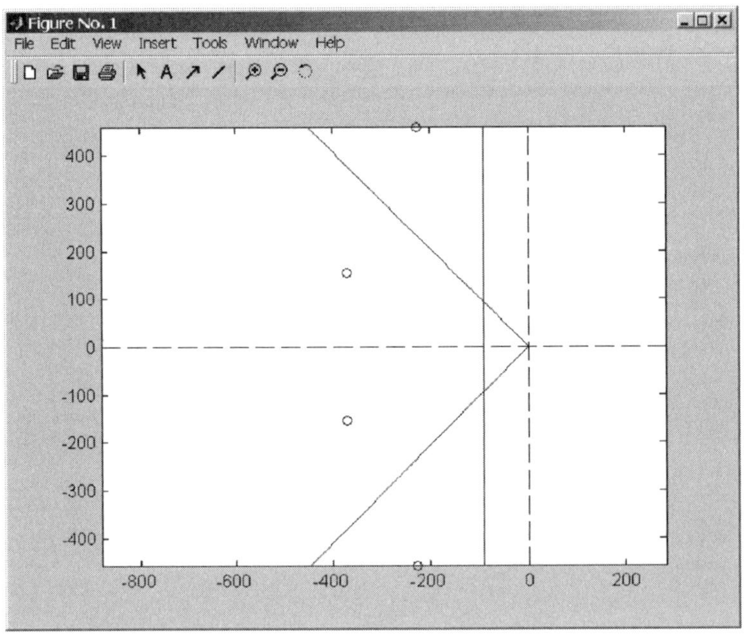

7. One solution is shown here.

```
>> Q = 1e5*diag([8 5 1 1]);
```

The resulting pole locations are shown in Figure 6.6.

Figure 6.6 **Closed-loop pole locations after iteratively tuning Q.**

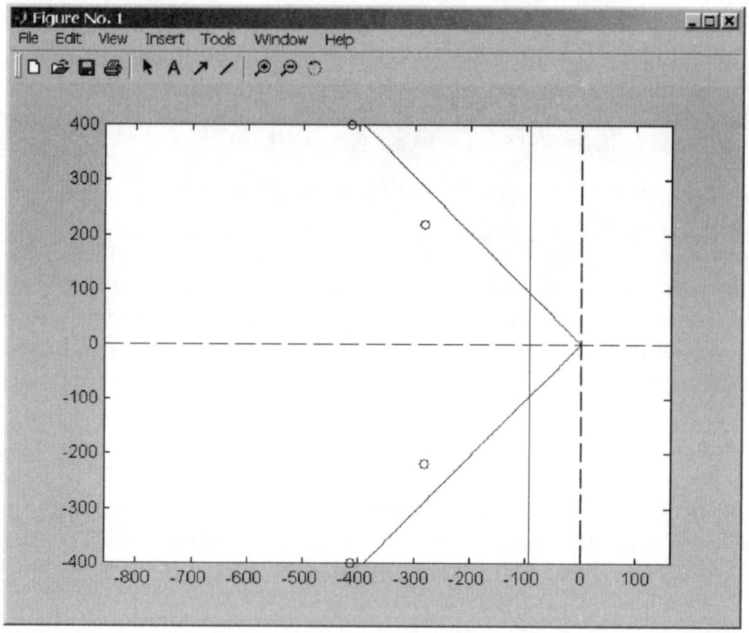

8.

```
>> G = ssplant.b;
>> H = ssplant.d;
>> QN = 0.5^2;
```

9.

```
>> RN = 0.01^2/12;
```

10.

```
>> obs_plant = ss(ssplant.a, [ssplant.b G], ssplant.c, [ssplant.d H]);
>> [kest, L] = kalman(obs_plant, QN, RN)
```

11. Create a state-space observer-controller.

```
>> ssobsctrl = ss(ssplant.a-L*ssplant.c, ...
   [L ssplant.b-L*ssplant.d], -K, 0);
```

Compute the feedforward gain.

```
>> Nxu = inv([ssplant.a ssplant.b; ssplant.c ssplant.d]) ...
   * [zeros(n,1); 1];
>> Nx = Nxu(1:n, :);
>> Nu = Nxu(n+1:end, :);
>> N = Nu + K*Nx;
```

Augment the plant model to pass the inputs as additional outputs.

```
>> ssplant_aug = ss(ssplant.a, ssplant.b, ...
   [ssplant.c; zeros(1, n)], [ssplant.d; 1]);
```

Form the closed-loop system with positive feedback.

```
>> sscl = N * feedback(ssplant_aug, ssobsctrl, +1);
```

12. The closed-loop pole locations appear in Figure 6.7. The observer pole locations are all slower than (to the right of) the closed-loop system pole locations shown in Figure 6.6. In addition, two of the observer poles are very lightly damped. Nevertheless, this observer produces the minimum mean-square estimation errors for the given plant and process noise models and noise covariance matrices. The system response is significantly faster than the controller developed in the Chapter 5 self-test because the LQR optimization criterion of Eq. 6.1 with the weighting matrices from problem 7 results in a faster response compared with the pole locations arbitrarily selected for the problem in the Chapter 5 self-test.

Figure 6.7 Closed-loop system and observer pole locations.

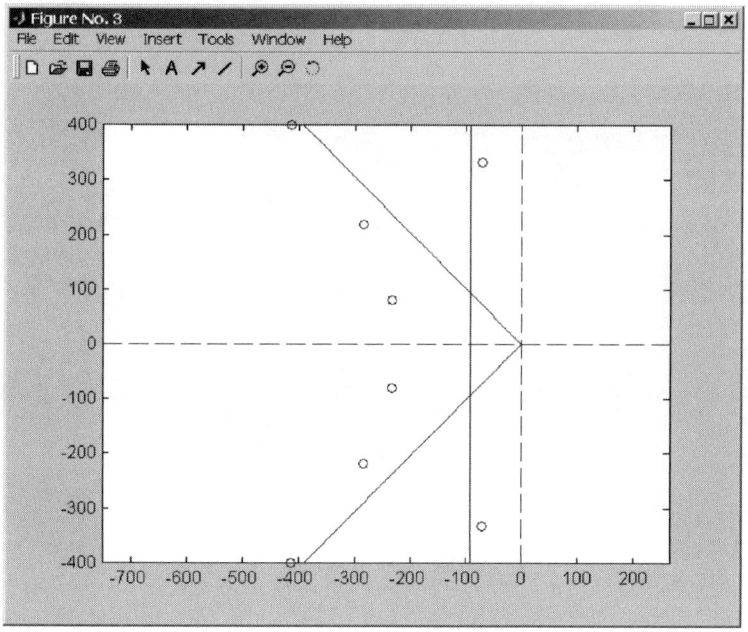

6.10 References

1. Brown, Robert G., *Introduction to Random Signal Analysis and Kalman Filtering* (New York, NY: John Wiley & Sons, 1983).
2. Oppenheim, Alan V., and Ronald W. Schafer, *Discrete-Time Signal Processing* (Englewood Cliffs, NJ: Prentice Hall, 1989), §3.7.3.

Chapter 7

MIMO Systems

7.1 Introduction

A SISO plant has exactly one input signal and one output signal, whereas a MIMO plant has multiple inputs, multiple outputs, or both. Although the design methods of Chapters 2 (PID control) and 4 (root locus and Bode design) are directly applicable only to SISO plants, the state-space design techniques described in Chapters 5 (pole placement) and 6 (optimal control) work with both SISO and MIMO plants.

In cases where each MIMO plant input primarily affects only one output, it could make sense to think of the plant as a collection of SISO plants. When this assumption is reasonable, each of the SISO plants requires a separate controller design. This approach is valid when the cross-coupling between the SISO systems is small. However, when cross-coupling is significant, MIMO design techniques will generally produce superior control system performance.

In this chapter, I present two example MIMO plants and develop controllers for them with the pole placement and optimal design techniques described in Chapters 5 and 6. With these state-space design methods, the steps for designing the controller gains are essentially identical to those used when working with SISO systems.

In this chapter, I do not introduce any new control system design concepts. Instead, the intent is to demonstrate the application of techniques developed in earlier chapters to the design of control systems for MIMO plants. In designing controllers for these typically complex systems, it is more important than ever that the linear plant model faithfully represent the actual system. See Chapter 3 (plant models) for more information on developing valid plant models.

7.2 Chapter Objectives

After reading this chapter, you should be able to

- identify control system design techniques suitable for MIMO systems,
- develop performance specifications for a MIMO controller,
- specify a MIMO controller structure,
- use pole placement techniques to develop MIMO controller and observer gains, and
- use optimal design techniques to develop MIMO controller and observer gains.

7.3 Difficulties of MIMO Control Design

The fundamental reason MIMO controller design is more difficult than SISO controller design is the presence of cross-coupling between plant inputs and outputs. If there were no cross-coupling (i.e., if each plant input influenced only one plant output), it would be perfectly correct to assume the MIMO system consists of a group of independent SISO systems and deal with them separately.

MIMO systems in the real world often are more complicated than this. In many everyday systems, each plant input primarily affects one output but also has a smaller influence on other outputs. In the most complex case, each plant input significantly affects all of the outputs.

Example 7.1 Helicopter control cross-coupling.

One example of control cross-coupling occurs in a helicopter. A helicopter has three primary flight controls.

Collective This control changes the simultaneous tilt of all the rotor blades. Pulling the collective up causes the blade leading edges to tilt up, causing the helicopter to move upward.

Cyclic This controls the varying tilt of the rotor blades as they rotate. Moving the cyclic to the left alters the blade tilt so that the helicopter responds by tilting left. Rightward cyclic motion tilts the helicopter to the right. Similar motion controls the front–back tilt of the helicopter.

Tail Rotor The foot pedals control the tilt of the tail rotor blades. The functions of the tail rotor are to cancel out the torque on the helicopter body produced by the main rotor and to allow the nose of the helicopter to be pointed in the desired direction.

Each of the three controls has one primary effect on helicopter flight behavior. However, changes to any of the control inputs cause additional effects that the control system (usually a pilot) must counteract.

For example, the primary effect of pulling up on the collective is increased upward force. However, this control input also causes the torque from the main rotor to increase, which causes the helicopter body to begin turning about the main rotor axis. This body rotation is usually undesirable and can be prevented by adjusting the tail rotor tilt to balance out the additional main rotor torque. The result of this cross-coupling is that a desired change in one plant output (helicopter altitude) requires manipulation of (at least) two of the control inputs: the collective and the tail rotor.

The need to simultaneously adjust multiple control inputs to produce a desired system response is a typical attribute of MIMO systems. Obviously, this makes the control system development procedure more difficult. Although it is often possible to apply techniques such as PID controller design (Chapter 2) and root locus design (Chapter 4) in these situations, the results are seldom satisfactory. Because the SISO design techniques do not account for cross-coupling within the plant, the resulting controllers might be unable to satisfy the design requirements.

The pole placement (Chapter 5) and optimal (Chapter 6) state-space design techniques are inherently capable of designing MIMO controllers. These approaches create controllers that are tuned to deal effectively with the cross-coupling within the plant.

The remainder of this chapter consists of two MIMO controller design examples. Because these systems are more complex than the plant models used in previous chapters, the linear model development process will be discussed in some detail before the controller design work begins. I will then determine performance specifications and proceed with development of the control systems. Both pole placement and optimal design techniques will be demonstrated.

Example 7.2 Aircraft glideslope control.

Consider a large passenger jet aircraft on approach to landing. By sensing radio signals transmitted from the ground-based instrument landing system (ILS), the aircraft is able to determine how far it is above or below the desired flight path, which is called the glideslope. The design task is to develop an autopilot control system to fly the aircraft in the vertical plane along the glideslope while maintaining its speed at a desired constant setting. I will ignore the side-to-side motion and roll orientation of the aircraft and assume those flight aspects are handled adequately by other control systems. I will also ignore the effects of wind and the actions required to initially position the aircraft on the glideslope and to land the aircraft when it reaches the runway.

The system configuration is shown in Figure 7.1, where x is the forward direction in aircraft body coordinates. The engine thrust T (in units of newtons) acts in the x direction. The angle of attack α (radians) is the angle between the aircraft velocity vector V (m/s) and the body x-axis. The flight path angle γ (radians) is the angle between the horizontal and the velocity vector V. As drawn in Figure 7.1, γ has a negative value. The drag force D (newtons) acts in the negative direction of the velocity vector. The lift force L (newtons) acts in an upward direction perpendicular to the velocity vector.

Figure 7.1 Aircraft and glideslope.

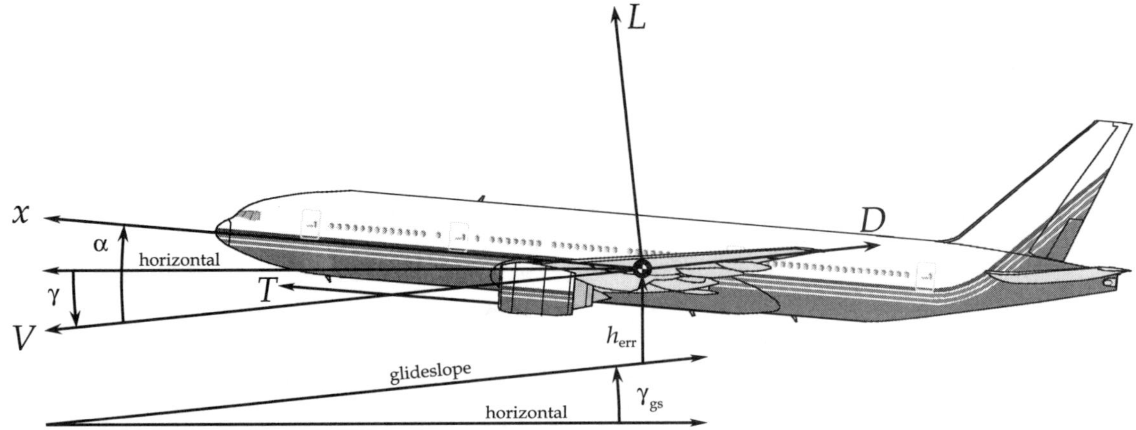

The glideslope is a fixed line in space radiating upward from the runway at an angle of γ_{gs} (radians) relative to the horizontal. The vertical distance from the aircraft to the glideslope is the height error, h_{err} (meters). The goal of the autopilot is to drive h_{err} to zero and simultaneously maintain the commanded velocity V_c (m/s).

This plant has three outputs: the measured aircraft speed V, the measured flight path angle γ, and the measured distance of the aircraft above or below the glideslope h_{err}. The plant inputs are the throttle setting and the elevator command. The elevator is the moveable surface along the back edge of the horizontal tail that controls the aircraft angle of attack. These two plant inputs enable control of the aircraft speed and vertical motion.

However, there is significant cross-coupling between the two inputs and the three outputs. An increase in the throttle setting causes the speed to increase but also causes the aircraft to climb in altitude. An upward deflection of the elevator causes the aircraft to climb but also results in a decrease in speed. The use of multiple SISO systems in the design process would not account for this cross-coupling, so a MIMO design approach is preferable.

The response time of the engines to throttle commands and the airframe to elevator commands is fast compared with changes in the aircraft speed and altitude rate. To keep the model simple, those effects will be ignored. Instead, I will change the assumed plant inputs to be the engine thrust T and the angle of attack α.

This simplified system is described by the nonlinear equations shown in Eq. 7.1 [1]. The first row of Eq. 7.1 is Newton's law applied along the direction of the velocity vector. The second row uses the forces perpendicular to the velocity vector to determine the rate of change of the flight path angle. The third row describes the rate of change of the altitude error on the basis of the aircraft velocity, flight path angle, and glideslope angle.

$$\begin{bmatrix} m\dot{V} \\ mV\dot{\gamma} \\ \dot{h}_{err} \end{bmatrix} = \begin{bmatrix} -D(\alpha, V) + T\cos\alpha - mg\sin\gamma \\ L(\alpha, V) + T\sin\alpha - mg\cos\gamma \\ V(\sin\gamma + \cos\gamma\tan\lambda_{gs}) \end{bmatrix} \qquad \text{Eq. 7.1}$$

The lift and drag force terms ($L(\alpha, V)$ and $D(\alpha, V)$, in newtons) of Eq. 7.1 are shown in Eq. 7.2, in which ρ is the air density and S is the aircraft reference area.

$$\begin{aligned} C_L(\alpha) &= C_{L_0} + C_{L_\alpha}\alpha \\ C_D(\alpha) &= C_{D_0} + KC_L^2(\alpha) \\ L(\alpha, V) &= C_L(\alpha)\frac{1}{2}\rho V^2 S \\ D(\alpha, V) &= C_D(\alpha)\frac{1}{2}\rho V^2 S \end{aligned} \qquad \text{Eq. 7.2}$$

The parameters appearing in Eqs. 7.1 and 7.2 are defined in Table 7.1. These values represent a nominal flight condition during approach for a landing.

Table 7.1 Aircraft and glideslope model parameters.

Parameter	Description	Value	Units
m	Aircraft mass	190,000	kg
g	Gravitational acceleration	9.81	m/s^2
γ_{gs}	Glideslope angle	3 0.052359	degrees radians
C_{L_0}	Zero-angle of attack lift coefficient	0.8212	Dimensionless
C_{L_α}	Lift coefficient due to angle of attack	5.105	1/rad
C_L	Zero-angle of attack drag coefficient	0.025455	Dimensionless
K	Drag coefficient due to lift	0.04831	Dimensionless
ρ	Air density	1.225	kg/m^3
S	Aircraft reference area	427.8	m^2

I begin the control system design procedure by creating a linear model of the system. Because the plant model of Eqs. 7.1 and 7.2 is nonlinear, I must linearize the model about an appropriate equilibrium point. Recall that the equilibrium condition occurs when all the derivatives in Eq. 7.1 are zero.

The equilibrium of interest occurs when the aircraft is trimmed on the glideslope ($\gamma = -3°$ (–0.05236 radians), $h_{err} = 0$) and moving at the commanded velocity $V = V_c = 81.8$ m/s. The values of α and T at the equilibrium condition can be found by setting the left-hand side of Eq. 7.1 to zero and performing an iterative search to solve the first two rows for the two unknowns α and T. This equilibrium solution occurs when $\alpha = 2.6857°$ (0.04688 radians) and $T = 42{,}387$ newtons.

For this example, the equilibrium solution was obtained from a Simulink model of the nonlinear system. The `trim()` command was used at the MATLAB command line to determine the equilibrium conditions. See `Glideslope.mdl` in the `Examples\Ch07` directory of the accompanying CD-ROM for the nonlinear Simulink model and `dotrim.m` for the trim procedure.

With the equilibrium conditions determined, the next step is to develop a linear plant model. A standard engineering approach is to use calculus techniques to linearize the nonlinear plant model about the equilibrium point. An alternative is to execute `linmod()` at the MATLAB command prompt to derive the linearized model from the Simulink diagram. The latter approach was used in this case. In addition to determining the equilibrium solution, the `dotrim.m` script extracts the linear plant model from the diagram. The resulting model appears in Eq. 7.3, where $\mathbf{x} = [V \ \ \gamma \ \ h_{err}]^T$ and $\mathbf{u} = [\alpha \ \ T]^T$.

$$\dot{\mathbf{x}} = \begin{bmatrix} -0.018001 & -9.7966 & 0 \\ 0.0029251 & -0.0062765 & 0 \\ -2.0817e{-}017 & 81.912 & 0 \end{bmatrix} \mathbf{x} + \begin{bmatrix} -4.8374 & 5.2574e{-}006 \\ 0.57862 & 3.0149e{-}009 \\ 0 & 0 \end{bmatrix} \mathbf{u} \qquad \text{Eq. 7.3}$$

I should mention a couple of points of numerical interest regarding Eq. 7.3. First, the lower left element of the **A** matrix is extremely small and probably should be zero. It is not exactly zero because finite-precision floating-point mathematics is subject to small errors such as this. Second, the two upper elements in the right column of the **B** matrix are quite small as well but should *not* be assumed to be zero. These elements are much smaller than the others because the magnitude of variations in T is about six orders of magnitude larger than the variations in α. It's usually best to use the models produced by `linmod()` directly and not try to tweak them by setting apparently insignificant matrix elements to zero.

I will use the pole placement design technique to develop a MIMO observer-controller for the linear plant model of Eq. 7.3. The control system will use the configuration shown in Figure 5.1, except that the reference inputs are zero. With no reference input, the controller functions as a regulator and attempts to maintain all the states at zero deviation from the equilibrium values.

Note: It is important to remember that the inputs and states for the model of Eq. 7.3 are defined as *deviations* from the equilibrium values. For instance, if the instantaneous thrust is 42,400 N, the T input to Eq. 7.3 would be (42,400 – 42,387) = 13 N. Similarly, if the state $V = 0.2$, the actual velocity represented by that value is (81.8 + 0.2) = 82.0 m/s.

The design specifications for the controller are given as a settling time of 2 seconds and a damping ratio of 0.8. The output of the design process will be the controller gain matrix **K** and the observer gain matrix **L**, which will be used in the controller structure of Figure 5.1.

The first step is to create a state-space plant model.

```
>> a = [-0.018001   -9.7966     0; ...
        0.0029251  -0.0062765  0; ...
        0           81.912     0];
>> b = [-4.8374   5.2573e-6; ...
        0.57862  3.0149e-9; ...
        0        0];
>> c = eye(3);
>> d = 0;

>> ssplant = ss(a, b, c, d);
```

The plant's controllability and observability must be checked as described in Chapter 5. Those tests will not be repeated here. This plant model passes both of the tests.

This is a third-order plant, so three closed-loop pole locations must be selected. The `select_poles()` function performs this task.

```
>> n = 3;
>> t_settle = 2;
>> damp_ratio = 0.8;
>> p = select_poles(n, t_settle, damp_ratio);
```

The controller gain is computed with a call to `place()`.

```
>> K = place(ssplant.a, ssplant.b, p)
```

Next, the observer poles must be selected. I will multiply the closed-loop poles by 3 to locate the observer poles. A second call to `place()` determines the observer gain matrix **L**.

```
>> obs_pole_mult = 3;
>> q = obs_pole_mult * p;
>> L = place(ssplant.a', ssplant.c', q)'
```

The design of the controller and observer gains is now complete. The next step is to form the state-space observer-controller.

```
>> ssobsctrl = ss(ssplant.a-L*ssplant.c,
                  [L ssplant.b-L*ssplant.d], -K, 0);
```

Form an augmented plant model that passes the plant inputs as additional outputs. This modified model is needed because the observer-controller requires the plant inputs in addition to the plant outputs. In the following statements, n is the number of plant states (3 in this case)and r is the number of inputs (2 in this case).

```
>> r = size(b, 2); % Number of inputs
>> n = size(a, 1); % Number of states
>> ssplant_aug = ss(ssplant.a, ssplant.b, [ssplant.c; zeros(r, n)], ...
      [ssplant.d; eye(r)]);
```

Form a closed-loop system consisting of the augmented plant model and the observer-controller.

```
>> sscl = feedback(ssplant_aug, ssobsctrl, +1);
```

Plot the pole locations along with the design specifications. The resulting plot appears in Figure 7.2.

```
>> plot_poles(sscl, t_settle, damp_ratio);
```

Figure 7.2 Closed-loop pole locations.

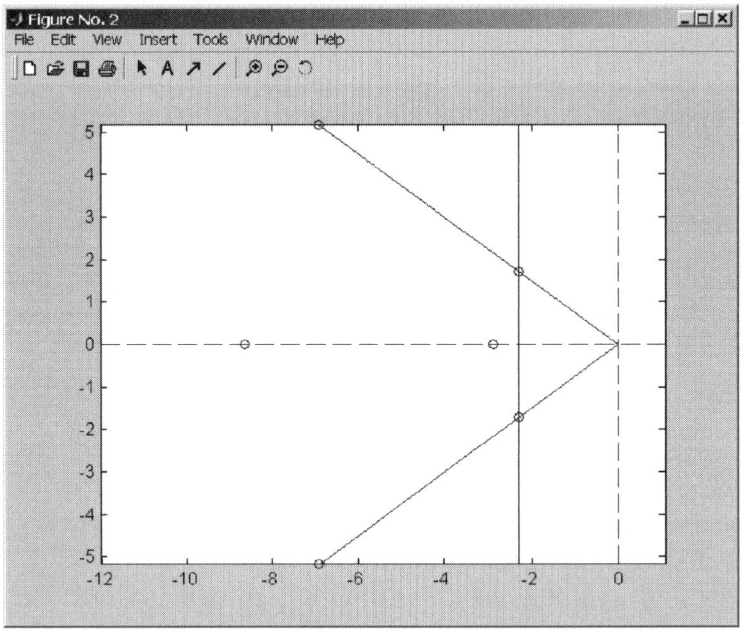

This controller functions as a regulator: All the states, inputs, and outputs are defined as deviations from their equilibrium values. Because of this, it is not necessary to develop a feedforward gain matrix **N** as was described in Chapter 5.

Because the controller is based on a linearized model about nonzero equilibrium states and inputs, it is important to remember to adjust the inputs and outputs accordingly. All inputs to the observer-controller must first have the equilibrium values subtracted from them, and all outputs must have the equilibrium values added back.

Example 7.3 Inverted pendulum on a cart.

This example involves a plant with one input and two outputs. I use optimal control design techniques (Chapter 6) to develop the observer-controller.

An inverted pendulum on a cart is shown in Figure 7.3. The input to this plant is the cart driving force F (newtons). An electric motor provides the force. The motor is assumed to have a fast response compared with the cart and pendulum, so I do not model it.

This is a fourth-order plant. Two of the system states are the cart's horizontal position x (meters) and the angle of the pendulum θ (radians) with respect to the vertical. The two remaining states are the cart velocity $\dot{x}$ (m/s) and the pendulum angular velocity $\dot{\theta}$ (rad/s).

The pendulum is a thin cylindrical rod with length l = 1 meter and mass m_p = 2.5 kilograms. It pivots freely about the pin attaching it to the cart. The cart mass m_c = 5 kilograms. The dynamics of the wheels will be ignored.

Figure 7.3 Inverted pendulum on a cart.

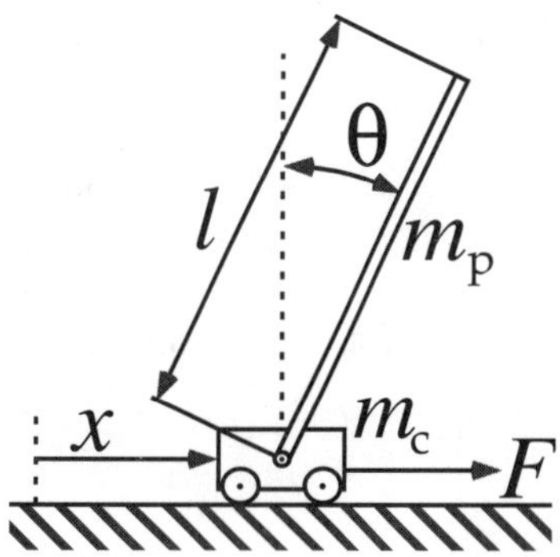

The control system must keep the pendulum inverted by balancing it by moving the cart and simultaneously driving the cart to a commanded position. These objectives conflict to some degree, so this presents an interesting control design problem. The controller design goal is to provide a cart position settling time of 1.5 seconds with satisfactory damping characteristics.

The first step is to develop a plant model for this system. One approach is to use the equations of motion of rigid bodies to analyze the system and produce a set of nonlinear system equations. An alternative is to use software tools to perform this analysis for you. I take the latter approach.

SimMechanics is an add-on product for Simulink from The MathWorks, Inc., that supports the modeling of mechanical systems such as the inverted pendulum and cart. The user constructs block diagrams of a mechanical system, in which the blocks define the properties of rigid bodies and the joints that connect them.

The inverted pendulum system contains two bodies: the cart and the pendulum. For modeling purposes, we assume the cart is connected to the ground by a sliding joint. The pendulum is connected to the cart by a pivot joint. The Simulink/SimMechanics block diagram of the inverted pendulum appears in Figure 7.4.

Figure 7.4 Simulink/SimMechanics model of the inverted pendulum on a cart.

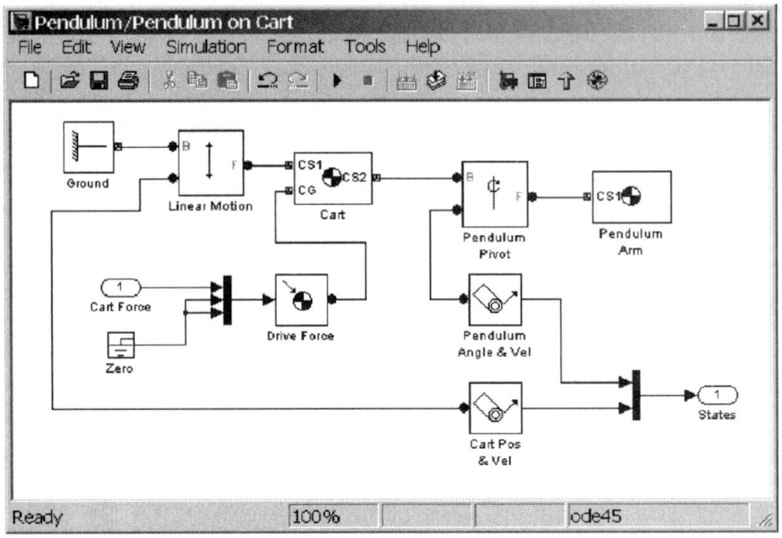

The diagram of Figure 7.4 is contained in the file `Pendulum.mdl` in the `Examples\Ch07` directory of the accompanying CD-ROM. The input to this model is the cart force F and the outputs are $\mathbf{y} = [\theta \quad \dot{\theta} \quad x \quad \dot{x}]^T$. This model is nonlinear, so to design a controller, I must select an equilibrium point and linearize the system about it. The equilibrium point of interest is when all of the states are zero, which occurs when the cart is stopped at the origin of the x-axis and the pendulum is straight up and stationary.

The `linmod()` command extracts the linear model from the Simulink diagram. The following commands extract the model matrices and create a state-space plant model.

```
>> [a,b,c,d] = linmod('Pendulum');
>> ssplant = ss(a,b,c,d);
```

The resulting linear model is shown in Eq. 7.4. The states are $\mathbf{x} = [\theta \; x \; \dot{\theta} \; \dot{x}]^T$, the outputs are $\mathbf{y} = [\theta \; \dot{\theta} \; x \; \dot{x}]^T$, and the input is $\mathbf{u} = F$.

$$\dot{\mathbf{x}} = \begin{bmatrix} 0 & 0 & 1 & 0 \\ 0 & 0 & 0 & 1 \\ 19.59 & 0 & 0 & 0 \\ -3.256 & 0 & 0 & 0 \end{bmatrix} \mathbf{x} + \begin{bmatrix} 0 \\ 0 \\ -0.2666 \\ 0.1778 \end{bmatrix} \mathbf{u} \qquad \mathbf{y} = \begin{bmatrix} 1 & 0 & 0 & 0 \\ 0 & 0 & 1 & 0 \\ 0 & 1 & 0 & 0 \\ 0 & 0 & 0 & 1 \end{bmatrix} \mathbf{x} \qquad \text{Eq. 7.4}$$

The controller reference input is the desired cart position (meters), and the output is the commanded cart drive force F (newtons). As mentioned previously, the dynamics of the power amplifier and drive motor are assumed to be fast relative to the plant dynamics and will be ignored.

I will use optimal design techniques to develop controller and observer gains for this system. The control system structure is shown in Figure 5.1. I will develop the controller gain **K** by the LQR method, and the observer will function as a steady-state Kalman filter.

I begin with the controller gain design. This is a fourth-order system with one input, so the **Q** weighting matrix is 4 × 4 and **R**is a scalar. Because only the relative values of **Q** and **R** affect the results, I fix **R** = 1 and vary the diagonal elements of **Q** during the design process.

As a first attempt, create a linear plant model, set **Q** to be the identity matrix, and design a controller gain with `lqr()`.

```
>> Q = eye(4);
>> R = 1;
>> K = lqr(ssplant, Q, R)
```

This sequence of commands produces the controller gain **K** = [–165.9 –1 –38.2 –4.5].

Form a closed-loop system using the controller gain.

```
>> cl_sys = feedback(ssplant, -K*inv(ssplant.c), +1);
```

Note: In the previous statement, the inverse of the plant **C** matrix was used to recover the states from the plant outputs. This is possible in this example because the output equation $\mathbf{y} = \mathbf{Cx}$ can be rewritten as $\mathbf{x} = \mathbf{C}^{-1}\mathbf{y}$ since **C** is a square and invertible matrix. This simplification is not generally available because **C** does not usually possess these properties.

Plot the closed-loop pole locations.

```
>> t_settle = 1.5;
>> damp_ratio = 0.7;
>> plot_poles(cl_sys, t_settle, damp_ratio);
```

The resulting plot appears in Figure 7.5. As the figure shows, two of the poles are much slower than the design specifications.

Try increasing the element of **Q** corresponding to the x state by a factor of 10.

```
>> Q = diag([1 10 1 1]);
```

Repeat the steps to compute the controller gain, form a closed-loop system, and plot the closed-loop pole locations. As the new plot will show, the slowest pole locations have moved to the left, but not far enough. After a few more iterations, the following **Q** matrix is found to produce a response satisfying the design requirement.

```
>> Q = diag([1 1e6 1 1]);
```

Figure 7.5 Closed-loop pole locations for initial controller design.

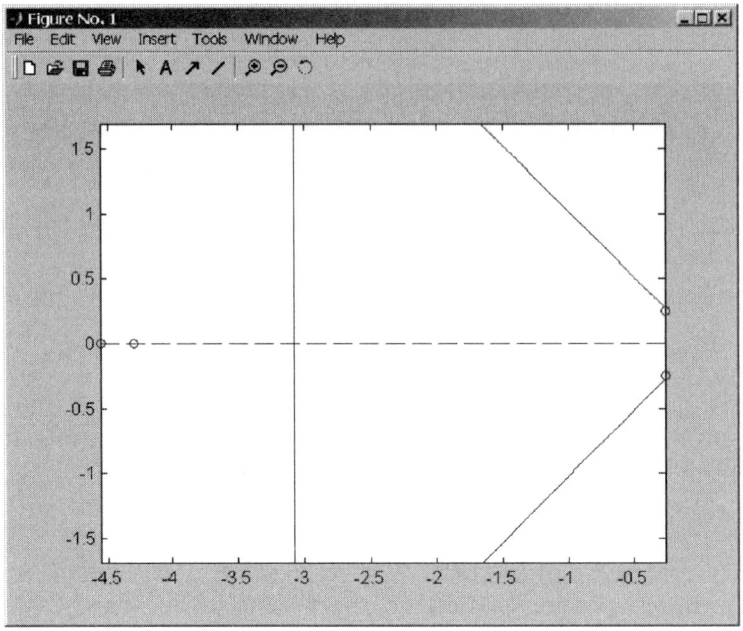

This system has the gain vector **K** = [–2012 –1000 –520 –629]. The closed-loop poles, along with 1.5-second settling time and 0.7 damping ratio constraints, appear in Figure 7.6.

Observe in Figure 7.6 that two of the poles are much faster (with a real part of –9.55) than the other two poles (which have a real part of –3.84). The faster poles correspond to motion of the pendulum relative to the cart. The slower poles relate to moving the cart to the commanded position.

The next step is to design the observer gain. Assume that the cart position x and pendulum angle θ are measured with sensors that provide quantized samples. It will be necessary to estimate the cart velocity $\dot{x}$ and pendulum angular rate $\dot{\theta}$ from those measurements. This linear system model is shown in Eq. 7.5, where $\mathbf{x} = [\theta \; x \; \dot{\theta} \; \dot{x}]^T$, $\mathbf{y} = [\theta \; x]^T$, and $\mathbf{u} = F$.

$$\dot{\mathbf{x}} = \begin{bmatrix} 0 & 0 & 1 & 0 \\ 0 & 0 & 0 & 1 \\ 19.59 & 0 & 0 & 0 \\ -3.256 & 0 & 0 & 0 \end{bmatrix} \mathbf{x} + \begin{bmatrix} 0 \\ 0 \\ -0.2666 \\ 0.1778 \end{bmatrix} \mathbf{u} \qquad \mathbf{y} = \begin{bmatrix} 1 & 0 & 0 & 0 \\ 0 & 1 & 0 & 0 \end{bmatrix} \mathbf{x} \qquad \text{Eq. 7.5}$$

Figure 7.6 Closed-loop pole locations with settling time and damping ratio constraints.

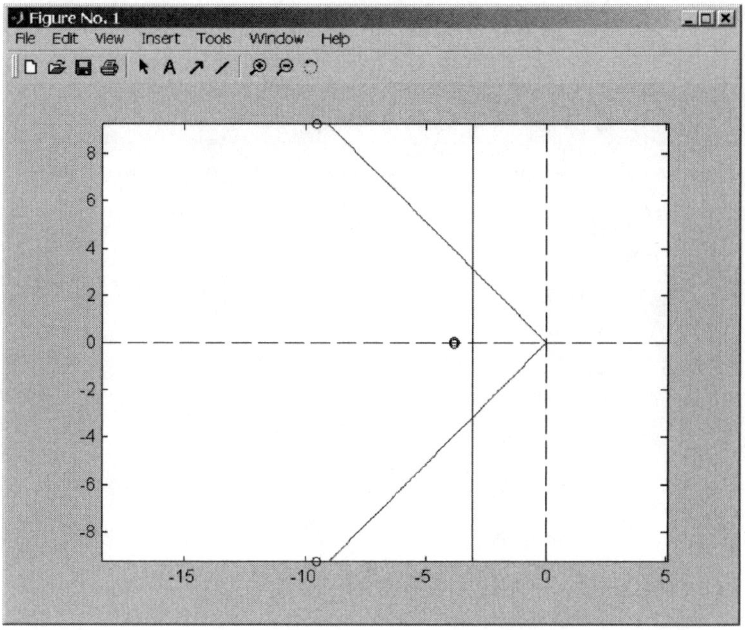

Assume the system contains nonlinearities, such as friction and random disturbances applied to the cart and pendulum. A simplified model of these combined effects is a random force applied to the cart in addition to the force generated by the drive motor. In this model, the **G** matrix equals the **B** matrix shown in Eq. 7.5, and the **H** matrix is zero. Let the standard deviation of this random force be 0.1 newtons. The process noise covariance is then $\mathbf{Q}_N = 0.1^2$.

Assume the quantization least significant bit (LSB) for the cart position is 0.01 meters and the quantization of θ is 0.0044 radians (0.25°). This results in measurement noise covariance

$$\mathbf{R}_N = \begin{bmatrix} \frac{0.01^2}{12} & 0 \\ 0 & \frac{0.0044^2}{12} \end{bmatrix}.$$

With this information, the steady-state Kalman observer gain is computed with the following MATLAB commands.

```
>> a = ssplant.a; b = ssplant.b;
>> c = [1 0 0 0; 0 1 0 0]; d = [0; 0];
>> g = b;
>> h = d;
```

```
>> obs_plant = ss(a, [b g], c, [d h]);

>> QN = 0.1^2;
>> RN = [0.01^2/12 0; 0 0.0044^2/12];

>> [kest, L] = kalman(obs_plant, QN, RN);
```

The resulting gain matrix is

$$\mathbf{L} = \begin{bmatrix} 8.63 & -4.03 \\ -0.78 & 5.04 \\ 38.80 & -22.70 \\ -6.27 & 14.28 \end{bmatrix}.$$

Form a state-space observer-controller.

```
>> ssobsctrl = ss(a-L*c, [L b-L*d], -K, 0);
```

Augment the plant model to pass its inputs as additional outputs.

```
>> r = size(b, 2); % Number of inputs
>> n = size(a, 1); % Number of states
>> ssplant_aug = ss(a, b, [c; zeros(r, n)], [d; eye(r)]);
```

The reference input provides a commanded value for the x state. The next step is to determine the feedforward gain **N** that results in zero steady-state error to a step input. To do this, form the state-space model of Eq. 7.5 and extract from it a SISO system that describes the transfer function between the plant input and the x output. Note that the x state is the second element of the **y** vector.

```
>> ssplant2 = ss(a, b, c, d);
>> sys_r_to_x = ssplant2(2,1);
```

Compute the feedforward gain with the technique described in Section 5.8.

```
>> Nxu = inv([sys_r_to_x.a sys_r_to_x.b; ...
             sys_r_to_x.c sys_r_to_x.d]) * [zeros(n,1); 1];
>> Nx = Nxu(1:n);
>> Nu = Nxu(end);
>> N = Nu + K*Nx;
```

The value of **N** resulting from this computation is –1000.

Form a closed-loop system with positive feedback.

```
>> sscl = N*feedback(ssplant_aug, ssobsctrl, +1);
```

Plot the pole locations of the closed-loop system (Figure 7.7).

```
>> plot_poles(sscl, t_settle, damp_ratio);
```

Figure 7.7 Closed-loop pole locations including the observer-controller.

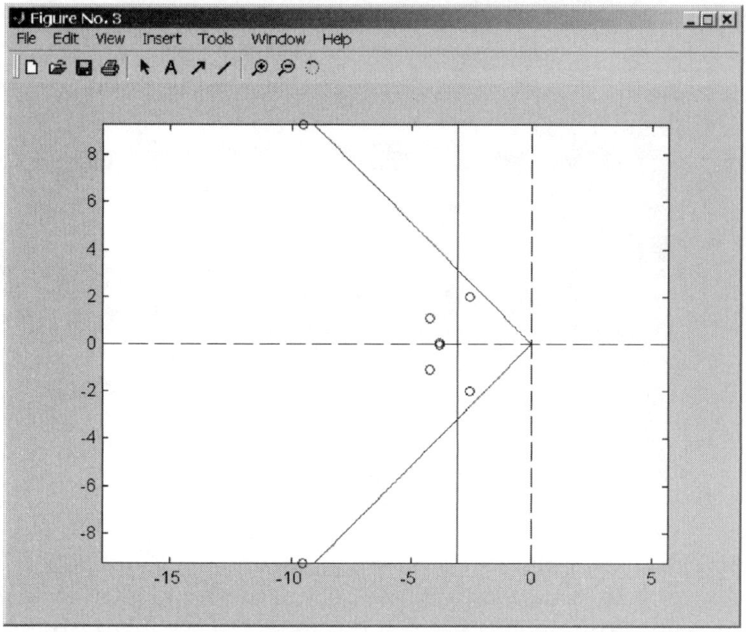

Notice that two of the observer poles in Figure 7.7 are slower than the settling time requirement, though all of them satisfy the damping ratio requirement.

Finally, display the step response of the linear closed-loop system, which is the response to a step of 1 meter in the x cart position command. The first command shown below specifies names for the `sscl` model inputs and outputs. The second command plots the step response, including input and output names. The resulting plot appears in Figure 7.8.

```
>> set(sscl,'InputName','R (m)', 'OutputName', {'Theta (rad)', ...
       'X (m)', 'Force (N)'});
>> step(sscl)
```

As you can see from Figure 7.8, a step command of 1 meter in r results in an initial cart force of 1,000 N in the $-x$ direction. This motion deflects the pendulum in the $+\theta$ direction before the cart begins moving in the $+x$ direction. The cart then moves to the $x = 1$ position in a manner that brings the pendulum back into vertical balance just as the cart arrives at its destination.

Figure 7.8 Closed-loop step response.

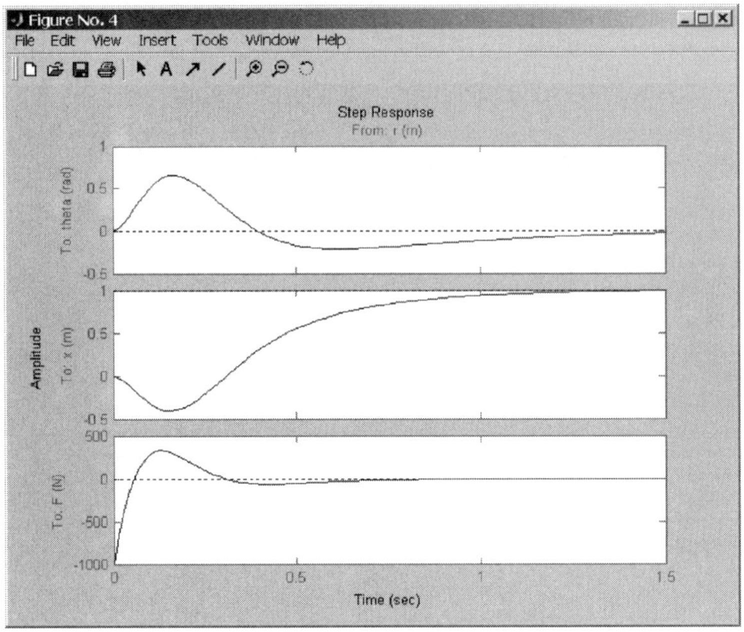

Observe that the θ plot (the top trace in Figure 7.8) shows a peak amplitude of 37° (0.65 radians) at 0.16 seconds after the `step()` command. This large angular deflection could violate the assumptions of the linear model to such a degree that the control system would fail to function properly with the nonlinear plant. The linear model assumes the angle θ is small enough that $\sin\theta \approx \theta$ and $\cos\theta \approx 1$, which might not be reasonable for this large of a deflection. In Chapter 9 (control system implementation and testing), I explore testing strategies for determining whether a controller will behave appropriately under all anticipated operating conditions.

7.4 Summary

In this chapter, I presented two MIMO control design examples. The first (Example 7.2) was an aircraft control problem in which the plant had two inputs (aircraft angle of attack α and engine thrust T) and three outputs (the measured aircraft speed V, the measured flight path angle γ, and the measured distance of the aircraft above or below the glideslope h_{err}). This plant has significant cross-coupling between the inputs and outputs, so breaking the model into separate SISO systems would not be a satisfactory approach. I used the pole placement design method to develop an observer-controller for this system that provides satisfactory performance.

The second example (Example 7.3) was an inverted pendulum on a cart. This system has one input (the cart driving force F) and two outputs (the cart position x and the pendulum angle θ). I used optimal design techniques to develop an observer-controller for this system.

These examples demonstrate the application of the state-space design techniques introduced in Chapters 5 (pole placement) and 6 (optimal design) to MIMO plants. As demonstrated by these examples, the basic design approach does not change very much in moving from a SISO plant to a MIMO plant. The state-space design approaches are ideal for use with complex MIMO plants as well as with simpler SISO systems.

7.5 Self-Test

1. Consider again the inverted pendulum of Figure 7.3. This time, the pendulum is a thin cylindrical rod with length l = 0.2 meters and mass = 0.1 kilograms. The cart mass = 0.3 kilograms. A linear model for this system (with the same inputs, states, and outputs as Eq. 7.4) is shown below. Create a state-space model of this system in MATLAB.

$$\dot{\mathbf{x}} = \begin{bmatrix} 0 & 0 & 1 & 0 \\ 0 & 0 & 0 & 1 \\ 90.55 & 0 & 0 & 0 \\ -2.26 & 0 & 0 & 0 \end{bmatrix}\mathbf{x} + \begin{bmatrix} 0 \\ 0 \\ -23.08 \\ 3.08 \end{bmatrix}\mathbf{u} \qquad \mathbf{y} = \begin{bmatrix} 1 & 0 & 0 & 0 \\ 0 & 0 & 1 & 0 \\ 0 & 1 & 0 & 0 \\ 0 & 0 & 0 & 1 \end{bmatrix}\mathbf{x}$$

2. The performance specifications for this controller are a settling time of 0.5 seconds and a damping ratio of 0.7. Set the weight matrix **Q** to a 4 × 4 identity matrix and let R = 1. Determine the optimal controller gain using these weighting matrices and plot the pole locations along with the performance constraints. Is this design acceptable?
3. Iterate on the **Q** matrix diagonal elements and repeat the steps of problem 2 until you find a solution that satisfies the performance specifications.
4. Now assume that only the cart position and pendulum angle are available as measurements, as shown in Eq. 7.5. Modify the plant model created in problem 1 to reflect this.
5. Use pole placement to design an observer gain with pole locations three times the values of the closed-loop pole locations.
6. Create a state-space observer-controller with the gains computed in the previous steps.
7. Augment the plant model to pass the inputs as additional outputs.
8. Form the closed-loop system consisting of the augmented plant plus the observer-controller, and plot the pole locations for the system.
9. Extract the SISO linear system from the plant model that gives the response from the reference input to the cart position output.

10. Determine the feedforward gain **N** that will provide zero steady-state error to a step input.
11. Append the feedforward gain to the closed-loop model and plot the 1-meter step response of the system. Do you see any potential problems with the 1-meter step response? How would you prevent the occurrence of those problems?
12. In this chapter, I developed a feedforward gain **N** for the inverted pendulum, but not for the aircraft flight controller. Identify the conditions under which it is appropriate to include a controller feedforward gain as shown in Figure 5.1.

7.6 Answers

1.

```
>> a =  [0 0 1 0; 0 0 0 1; 90.55 0 0 0; -2.26 0 0 0];
>> b = [0; 0; -23.08; 3.08];
>> c = [1 0 0 0; 0 0 1 0; 0 1 0 0; 0 0 0 1];
>> d = 0;
>> ssplant = ss(a, b, c, d);
```

2. The pole locations are shown in Figure 7.9. This design is clearly not acceptable.

```
>> Q = eye(4);
>> R = 1;
>> K = lqr(ssplant, Q, R)
>> cl_sys = feedback(ssplant, -K*inv(ssplant.c), +1);
>> t_settle = 0.5;
>> damp_ratio = 0.7;
>> plot_poles(cl_sys, t_settle, damp_ratio);
```

3. One solution is `Q = diag([1 5e4 1 1])`. The closed-loop pole locations appear in Figure 7.10. The resulting gain matrix is

$$K = [-97.7366\ \ -223.6068\ \ -11.3490\ \ -65.3583].$$

4.

```
>> c = [1 0 0 0; 0 1 0 0];
>> ssplant = ss(a, b, c, d);
```

Figure 7.9 Closed-loop pole locations for initial design iteration.

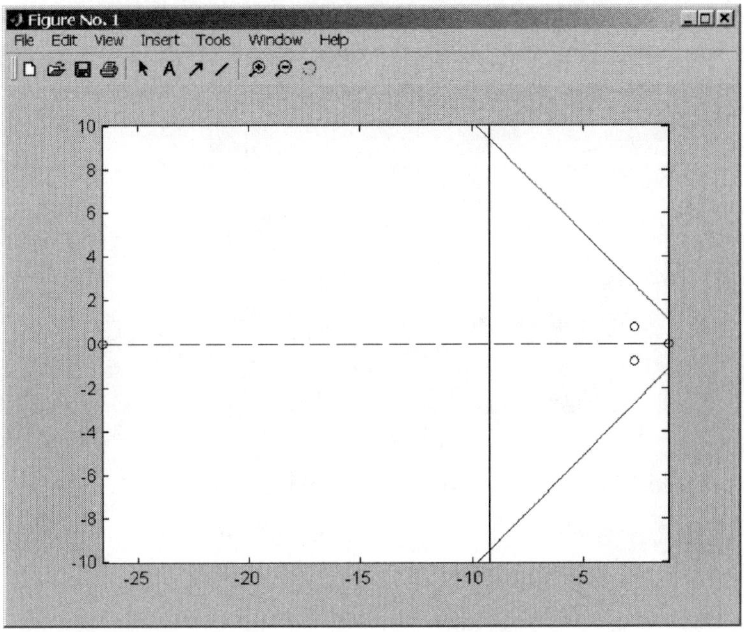

Figure 7.10 Example closed-loop pole locations for final design iteration.

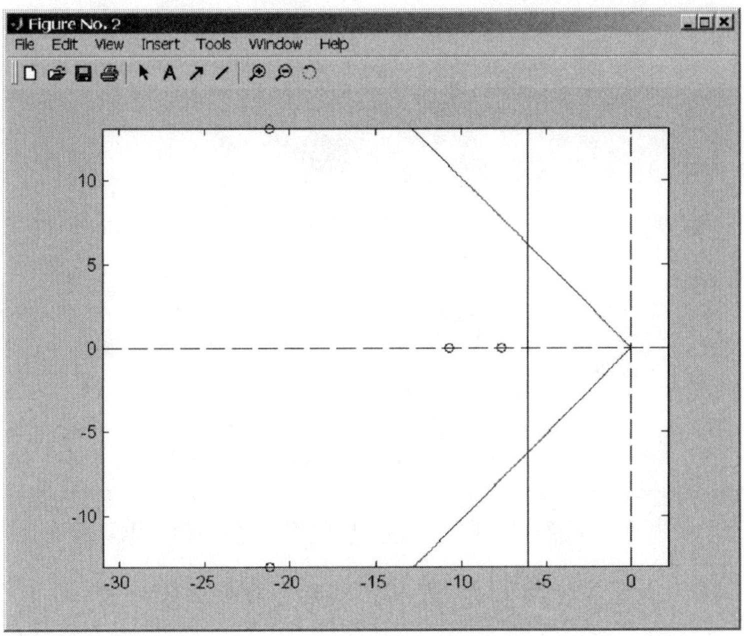

5. The resulting observer gain is **L** = [126.8 0; 0 55.1; 5657 0; –2.3 737.8].

```
>> obs_pole_mult  = 3;
>> q = obs_pole_mult * p;
>> L = place(ssplant.a', ssplant.c', q)';
```

6.

```
>> ssobsctrl = ss(ssplant.a-L*ssplant.c, ...
                  [L ssplant.b-L*ssplant.d], -K, 0);
```

7.

```
>> r = size(ssplant.b, 2); % Number of inputs
>> n = size(ssplant.a, 1); % Number of states
>> ssplant_aug = ss(ssplant.a, ssplant.b, ...
                    [ssplant.c; zeros(r, n)], [ssplant.d; eye(r)]);
```

8. The closed-loop pole locations are shown in Figure 7.11.

```
>> sscl = feedback(ssplant_aug, ssobsctrl, +1);
```

9.

```
>> sys_r_to_x = ssplant(2,1);
```

10. The feedforward gain that results from this computation is **N** = –223.6.

```
>> Nxu = inv([sys_r_to_x.a sys_r_to_x.b; ...
              sys_r_to_x.c sys_r_to_x.d]) * [zeros(n,1); 1];
>> Nx = Nxu(1:n);
>> Nu = Nxu(end);
>> N = Nu + K*Nx;
```

11. The resulting step response to a 1-meter `step()` command appears in Figure 7.12.

```
>> sscl = N*sscl;
>> set(sscl,'InputName','r (m)', 'OutputName', ...
      {'theta (rad)', 'x (m)', 'F (N)'});
>> step(sscl)
```

The problem here is that the pendulum deflection has a peak of 2.8 radians (160°), which is clearly a violation of the assumption of linear behavior. If the step command amplitude is limited to a much smaller value (say, a few centimeters) it would be possible to maintain approximately linear operation.

Figure 7.11 Closed-loop pole locations for plant plus observer-controller.

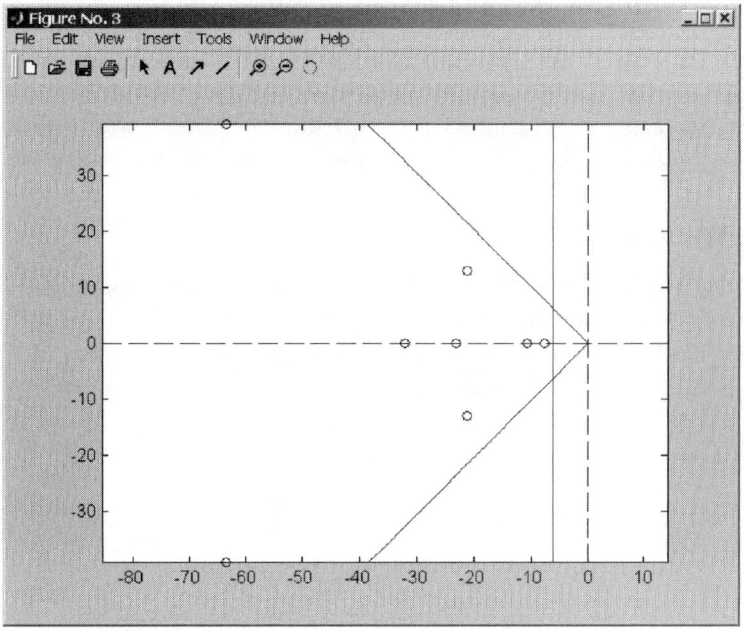

Figure 7.12 Closed-loop of the inverted pendulum on cart.

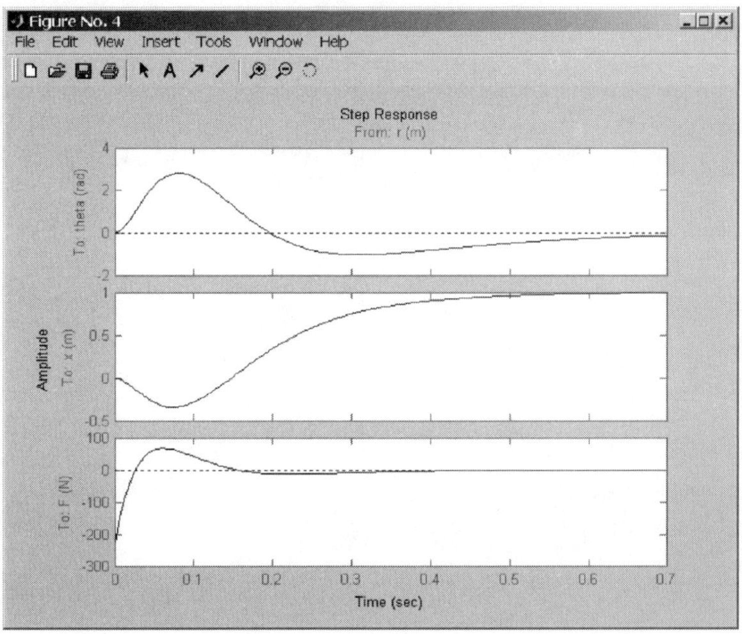

12. A feedforward gain only makes sense in a system with one or more reference inputs. In a regulator (such as the aircraft controller Example 7.2), the reference input is zero, so no feedforward gain is needed. In addition, each reference input should be a command for a corresponding output. This was the case for the inverted pendulum, in which the reference input was the command for the cart's x position. In this situation, we can extract a SISO system from the MIMO model and use the technique shown in Section 5.8 to determine the feedforward gain.

7.7 References

1. Oishi, M., I. Mitchell, A. Bayen, C. Tomlin, and A. Degani, *Hybrid Verification of an Interface for an Automatic Landing*. Proceedings of the 41st IEEE Conference on Decision and Control, Las Vegas, NV, December 2002.

CHAPTER 8

DISCRETE-TIME SYSTEMS AND FIXED-POINT MATHEMATICS

8.1 Introduction

In the preceding chapters, I performed modeling and control design procedures in the continuous-time domain and implemented those designs in MATLAB with floating-point mathematics. It is now time to make the transition from continuous-time to discrete-time controller implementations. This step is necessary because software-based controllers are generally implemented as discrete-time systems. In addition, because of requirements to use low-cost, low-power microprocessors in many applications, it is often necessary to use fixed-point, rather than floating-point, mathematics.

A discrete-time control system samples its inputs and updates its outputs at equally spaced points in time. The values of the input signals between sampling instants are unknown to the controller. The output signals are normally held constant following each update until the next update. As an example, a SISO controller might sample its input signal with an ADC at 100Hz and update its output through a DAC at the same rate.

The time between input samples (and between output updates) is called the *sampling period,* T_s. The *sampling frequency,* f_s, is the reciprocal of T_s. The selection of a sampling period is a critical step in the conversion of a continuous-time controller to a discrete-time implementation. The smaller the value of T_s, the more closely the behavior of the discrete-time controller approximates that of the continuous-time system from which it was derived. However, as the value of T_s becomes smaller, additional computing power is required to perform the more frequent controller updates. Taken to extremes, reductions in the sampling period could result in excessive I/O hardware performance requirements and higher controller cost and power usage.

On the other hand, making T_s too large has serious negative consequences as well. As the value of T_s increases, the performance of the discrete-time controller diverges from that of the continuous-time system. If T_s becomes too large, a point can be reached in which the closed-loop system becomes oscillatory or even unstable. By the Nyquist Sampling Theorem [1], the sampling frequency f_s must be at least twice the highest significant frequency in the controller input signal to enable processing by the controller.

The selection of the value of T_s for a discrete-time controller implementation is clearly a critical design decision. Section 8.5 of this chapter is devoted to selecting an appropriate value for this parameter and ensuring that the resulting controller meets its performance and stability requirements.

You might wonder why I didn't perform all the controller design work in the discrete-time domain in the earlier chapters. It is certainly possible to do so; however, there is a good reason for delaying the conversion to discrete-time as long as possible. One of the first steps in creating a discrete-time model is the selection of a sampling period for the model. Once you've selected a value for T_s, all subsequent representations of the model are dependent on it. Changing the value of T_s requires that all manipulations of the model be repeated with the new sampling period. This can result in a significant amount of repeated work if the initial choice for T_s turns out to be inappropriate.

Because of this, I have deferred the conversion to discrete time until now. I assume here that a continuous-time control system design has been completed with the techniques described in earlier chapters. In this chapter, I discuss techniques for discretizing the continuous-time model and implementing the linear portion of the controller with the use of fixed-point mathematics in the C and C++ programming languages.

Except for the integrator windup reduction technique discussed in Section 2.3, the controllers and observer-controllers discussed in previous chapters have been linear systems. Even when windup reduction is employed, the controller can be separated into linear and nonlinear sections. In this chapter, I describe how to convert the continuous-time linear section of the controller (or observer-controller) into an approximately equivalent discrete-time system suitable for implementation in a real-time computer system with the use of either integer or floating-point mathematics.

Many low-cost embedded processors do not provide support for floating-point mathematical operations. Even for those that do, an algorithm that uses floating-point math typically requires significantly more memory and execution time than a corresponding algorithm that uses only integer mathematics. For these reasons, it is often desirable to implement a control algorithm in fixed-point mathematics with integer operations.

Fixed-point mathematics represents real numbers as scaled integer values. The integer word length and scale factor used to convert real-valued parameters to fixed-point equivalents must be chosen carefully to provide sufficient range and resolution in the integer representation.

Range limits and quantization levels represent significant limitations of fixed-point mathematical models compared with the double-precision floating-point format I used in previous chapters. The conversion of a floating-point mathematical model to a fixed-point representation must ensure that these limitations do not significantly degrade the control system performance. In this chapter, I provide a set of automated tools for converting linear control system elements from the MATLAB representation to C or C++ source code in floating-point or fixed-point format.

8.2 Chapter Objectives

After reading this chapter, you should be able to

- describe why discrete-time modeling is necessary for embedded controller development,
- describe why fixed-point algorithm implementation is often needed for embedded controllers,
- select an appropriate sampling period for a discrete-time implementation of a given continuous control system,
- choose an appropriate discretization method for converting the continuous-time model to discrete time,
- convert a MATLAB state-space system to floating-point C or C++ source code that produces essentially identical results to the MATLAB version, and
- convert a MATLAB state-space system to fixed-point C or C++ source code suitable for implementation on a microprocessor with stringent limitations on processor speed and memory use.

8.3 Difference Equations

A discrete-time system is implemented as a set of *difference equations*. A difference equation is a recursive algebraic equation that computes the next value of a discrete output given the current and previous values of the equation input, output, and state variables. Updates to a discrete-time system occur at equally spaced points in time. Each update involves evaluation of the equations to compute the new values of the states and the outputs.

In a general discrete-time system, the output at any time is a function of the current system input, the input at previous time steps, and previous output values. As with continuous-time systems described by differential equations, difference equations can be linear or nonlinear and time invariant or time varying.

An example linear difference equation appears in Eq. 8.1. This equation represents the continuous-time transfer function $Y/X = 1/(s^2 + 2s + 1)$ after conversion to discrete time by use of the zero-order hold method and with a sampling interval of 0.1 seconds. The zero-order hold and other discretization methods will be discussed in the next section. I discuss the selection of appropriate discrete system step times in Section 8.5.

$$y_{n+1} = 0.004679x_n + 0.004377x_{n-1} + 1.81y_n - 0.8187y_{n-1} \qquad \text{Eq. 8.1}$$

The subscripts in Eq. 8.1 represent the sample number in the discrete system's input and output sequences as follows.

- x_n is the current input value.
- x_{n-1} is the input value from the previous time step.
- y_{n+1} is the output value for the next time step.
- y_n is the output value computed for the current time step.
- y_{n-1} is the output value computed for the previous time step.

In the example of Eq. 8.1, the equation must be updated at precise time intervals of 0.1 seconds.

The order of a difference equation is determined by the oldest previous output value that appears in the equation. Equation 8.1 is a second-order difference equation because y_{n-1} appears on the right-hand side, which is two steps older than the equation output y_{n+1}. If no previous output values appear in the equation, the order of the difference equation is determined by the oldest previous input value.

As with continuous-time systems, discrete-time systems can appear in transfer function, state-space, and frequency domain formats. The state-space format is suitable for representing both SISO and MIMO discrete-time systems and will be the primary format discussed in this chapter. The general form of a state-space discrete-time system model is shown in Eq. 8.2.

$$\begin{aligned} \mathbf{x}_{n+1} &= \mathbf{A}\mathbf{x}_n + \mathbf{B}\mathbf{u}_n \\ \mathbf{y}_n &= \mathbf{C}\mathbf{x}_n + \mathbf{D}\mathbf{u}_n \end{aligned} \qquad \text{Eq. 8.2}$$

The state-space format will be used in the conversion of control system models in MATLAB to C and C++ implementations.

8.4 Discretization Methods

Continuous-time model discretization is performed in MATLAB by the `c2d()` command provided in the Control System Toolbox. The `c2d()` command takes three arguments: a continuous linear time-invariant model, the sampling period for the discrete-time model, and the name of the discretization method to use for the conversion.

```
>> sysd = c2d(sysc, Ts, method)
```

In the statement above, `sysc` is the continuous-time system, `Ts` is the sampling period (usually in units of seconds), and `method` is a character string giving the name of the discretization method to be used. The discrete-time system `sysd` is the result of the discretization process.

The discretization methods available in MATLAB are described below. For each discretization method, comparison results are displayed in the time domain (as the unit step response) and in the frequency domain (as Bode diagrams). In these examples, the continuous-time model to be discretized is $Y/X = 1/(s^2 + 2s + 1)$ and the sampling period is

1.0 second. The sampling period has been intentionally set to a large value to emphasize the differences among the discretization methods.

`method = 'zoh'` Zero-order hold. This method assumes the input is held constant between sampling instants. The output of the discrete-time model matches that of the continuous system at the sampling instants. The zero-order hold introduces a one-half sample time delay into the model. Figure 8.1 shows the time response and frequency response of the continuous and discretized versions of this system.

Figure 8.1 Zero-order hold discretization.

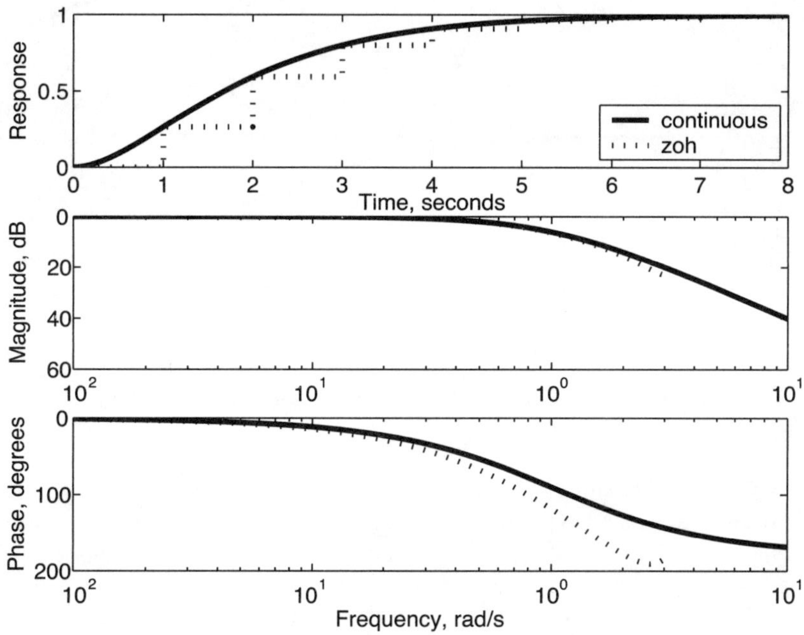

Note that the discrete-time system response terminates at a frequency of π rad/s (0.5Hz in this example), which is the Nyquist frequency for a 1.0-second sampling period. Also note the phase response discrepancy between the continuous-time and discrete-time responses, even at low frequencies. This is primarily a result of the one-half sample time delay introduced by the zero-order hold.

`method = 'foh'` First-order hold. This method uses linear interpolation between the input samples rather than holding the input constant as in the zero-order hold method. This method does not introduce additional delay into the model. Figure 8.2 shows the time response and frequency response of the continuous and discretized versions of this system.

Figure 8.2 First-order hold discretization.

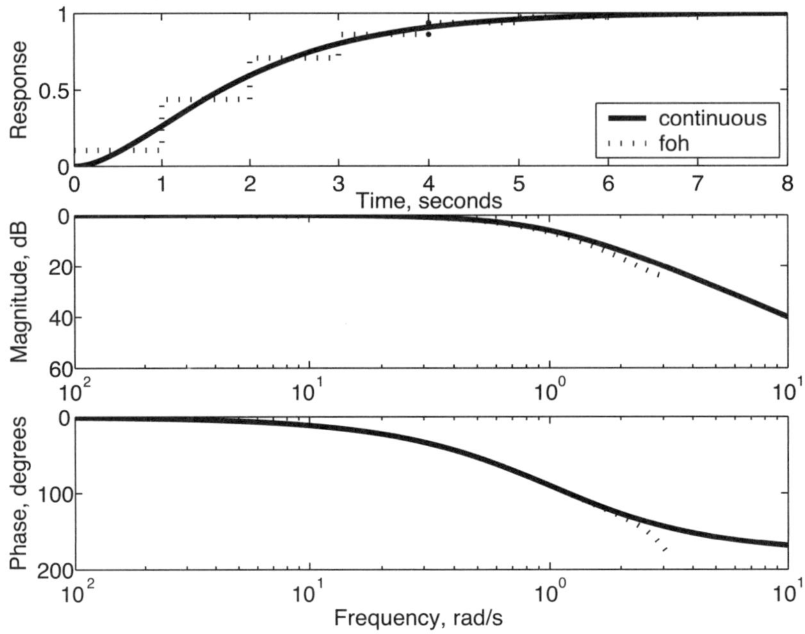

Note that the phase response error at lower frequencies has been essentially eliminated in comparison to Figure 8.1.

`method = 'imp'` Impulse-invariant discretization. This method guarantees matching continuous-time and discrete-time responses to single-sample pulse input signals (Figure 8.3).

`method = 'tustin'` Bilinear (Tustin) approximation. This method uses an approximation of the exponential function to relate the continuous-time and discrete-time domains (Figure 8.4).

`method = 'prewarp'` Tustin approximation with frequency prewarping. In this method, an additional parameter is required for the `c2d()` command following the `method` argument. This parameter gives a prewarp frequency (in rad/s) at which the continuous-time and discrete-time frequency responses must match (Figure 8.5). This method should be used when there is a specific frequency at which accurate discrete-time system performance is critical. This method is similar to the Tustin method, except a change of variable is performed to ensure that matching performance occurs at the prewarp frequency.

Note that the continuous-time and discrete-time magnitude and phase responses match at the prewarp frequency of 1 rad/s selected for this example.

Figure 8.3 Impulse-invariant discretization.

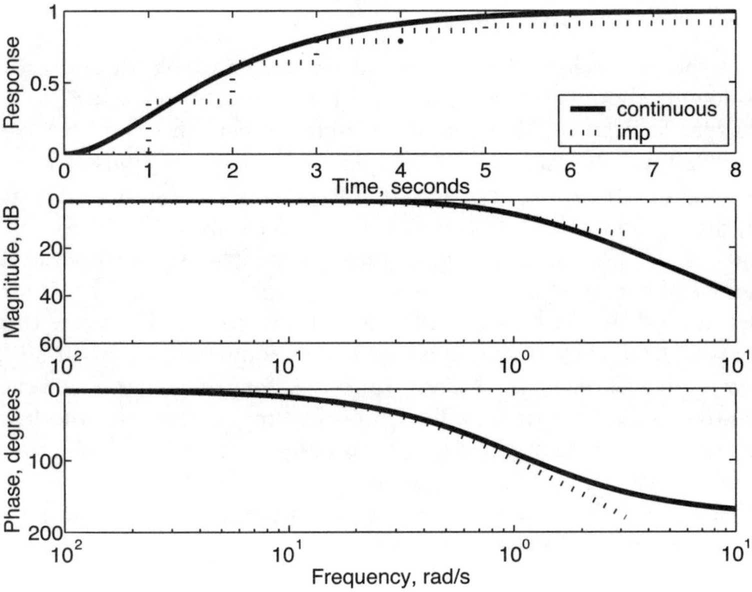

Figure 8.4 Bilinear (Tustin) discretization.

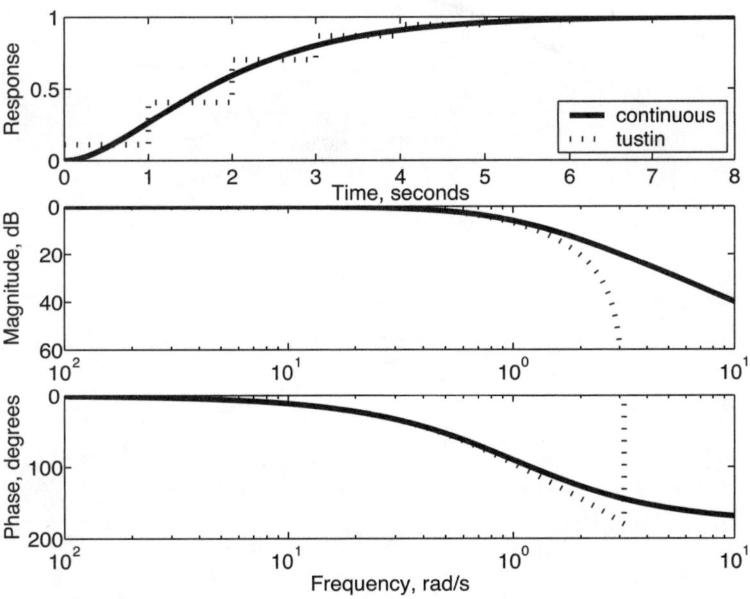

`method = 'matched'` Matched pole-zero method (for SISO systems only). In this method, the continuous-time and discrete-time systems have identical DC gains and their poles and zeros have equivalent locations (Figure 8.6).

Given the above information describing the available discretization methods, how should one go about selecting a method for a given application? Some of the methods provide specific features that might be useful in certain circumstances. For example, if the system input consists of single-sample pulses, the impulse-invariant discretization method might be the most appropriate. Or, if accurate response at a specific frequency is critical, the Tustin method with frequency prewarping might be the best choice.

If no special performance characteristics such as those described above exist, the first-order hold method is a good general-purpose choice. This discretization method provides a good match between the continuous-time and discrete-time models in both the time and frequency domains up to a fairly high frequency. In addition, even at frequencies approaching the discrete-time system's Nyquist frequency, the deviation between the continuous-time and discrete-time models remains modest.

The zero-order hold method is conceptually simpler than the first-order hold, but the half-sample time delay it introduces is a significant drawback. For these reasons, the first-order hold is the preferred discretization method unless specific requirements dictate the use of one of the other methods.

Figure 8.5 Tustin discretization with frequency prewarping at 1 rad/s.

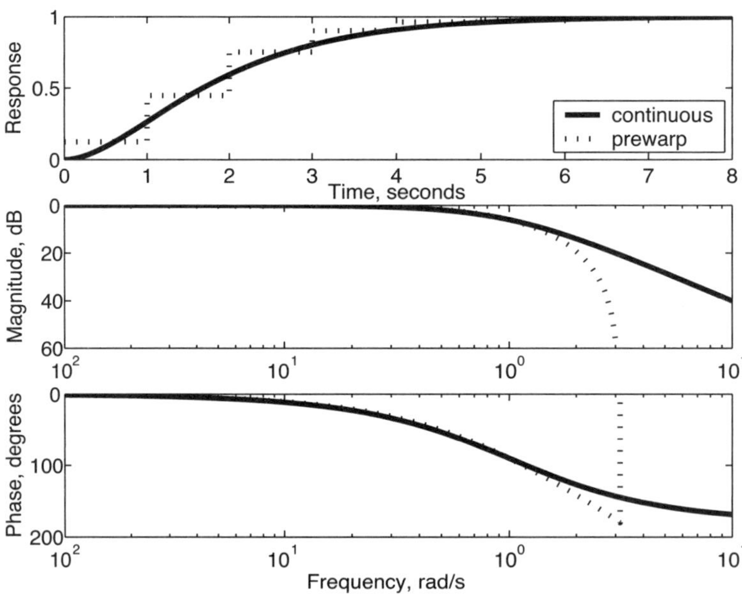

Figure 8.6 Matched pole-zero discretization.

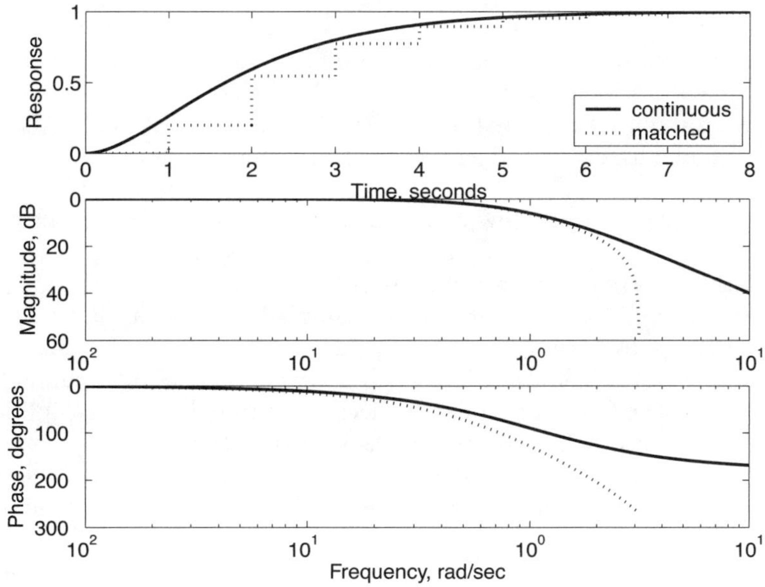

8.5 Choosing a Sampling Period

Sometimes the sampling period of a discrete-time controller is dictated by external factors, such as a preexisting hardware design. When such constraints do not exist, the control system designer must select a suitable sampling period. Some considerations for sampling period selection are listed below.

- The shorter the sampling period, the more closely the behavior of the discrete-time system resembles that of the continuous-time system. In the limit as the sampling period approaches zero, the responses of the discrete-time and continuous-time systems become indistinguishable.
- If the sampling period is too large, the closed-loop system can experience excessive overshoot, oscillation, or even instability.
- The sampling period must result in a Nyquist frequency (half the sampling rate) greater than the highest input signal frequency of interest.
- The sampling period must be compatible with the update rate specifications of the I/O devices (such as DACs and ADCs) used in the system design.
- The sampling period must be long enough that sufficient time is available for the execution of the controller algorithm and I/O operations during each discrete time step. Additional free time should be available to allow for future enhancements to the controller algorithm.

It is critical that input signal components with frequencies above the Nyquist frequency (which equals half the sampling frequency) have small amplitudes compared with lower frequency components. If an input signal at a frequency above the Nyquist frequency is presented to an ADC, the sampled signal will be aliased to a lower frequency, which can result in erroneous controller behavior.

When an input signal contains undesired frequencies above the Nyquist frequency, the addition of a hardware lowpass filter can attenuate the higher frequencies while leaving the desired lower frequencies essentially unchanged. In this approach, the controller input signal feeds into the lowpass filter input and the filter output goes to the ADC input. The lowpass filter cutoff frequency must be selected to block frequencies above the Nyquist frequency while passing lower frequencies.

Alternatively, the input signal can be sampled at a much higher rate that places all significant input frequency components below the Nyquist frequency. This high-rate stream of samples is then passed through a digital lowpass filter running on the embedded processor. The filter output can be decimated to reduce the sampling frequency to a rate suitable for use by the controller. Decimation consists of keeping every *N*th sample in the sequence and discarding the remaining samples. This approach avoids the additional hardware cost of a separate lowpass filter, although it requires additional I/O operations and processing resources.

When selecting a controller sampling frequency, a methodical approach should be employed. The following steps provide an iterative procedure for selecting a sampling period.

1. Develop a linear plant model and design a continuous-time controller with the methods of the previous chapters. Plot the step response and frequency response of the closed-loop system.
2. Choose a very short sampling period that provides a good discrete-time system approximation to the continuous-time system performance.
3. Discretize the controller algorithm with the `c2d()` command and an appropriate discretization method.
4. Plot the step response and frequency response of the closed-loop system using the discretized controller in place of the continuous-time controller.
5. Increase the sampling period and repeat steps 3 and 4. Continue until the step response or frequency response of the system with the discrete time controller diverges unacceptably from that of the continuous-time system.

The preceding steps give you an idea of the maximum sampling period the closed-loop system can tolerate. However, remember that this approach uses the linear plant model. When the controller is interfaced with the actual plant (or a more realistic plant model), other factors could come into play that reduce the maximum allowable sampling period.

8.6 Fixed-Point Mathematics

The development and implementation of controller designs up to this point have been based on double-precision floating-point mathematics in the MATLAB environment. Although it is sometimes possible to implement embedded controllers with floating-point math, many lower cost embedded processors do not support floating-point operations. Even on those that do, the execution of floating-point operations can be much slower and more memory intensive than similar computations that use fixed-point mathematics.

Fixed-point math uses integers to represent continuous values. The fixed-point representation has two differences from the continuous representation of a value.

- The range (from minimum value to maximum value) of a fixed-point integer is extremely limited compared to a floating-point representation.
- Fixed-point integers are quantized with a resolution dependent on the number of bits in the integer representation.

Although both of these limitations also apply to MATLAB's double-precision floating-point values, they are negligible in most circumstances of interest to us. In fixed-point mathematics, however, these limitations can cause serious degradation or outright failure of a control system algorithm.

Fixed-point representations of continuous variables employ a scale factor to adjust the range of the integer representation so that it matches the expected range of the continuous value. This helps to minimize quantization errors. However, it is important to ensure that the continuous value does not exceed the range of the integer representation. This typically results in wraparound (erroneously jumping from positive full-scale to negative full-scale, or vice versa) in the fixed-point computation. To prevent these errors, you must usually add some extra range in the integer representation to allow for extraordinary situations where the continuous value exceeds its expected range. However, adding this extra range also has the negative effect of increasing the quantization step size of the integer values.

In addition to selecting a scale factor for each fixed-point variable, it is also necessary for the developer to choose the number of bits in the integer representation. Increasing the number of bits in the integer reduces the quantization error. However, larger numbers of integer bits also increase the memory and execution time requirements for the controller implementation.

Controller inputs and outputs might already be in the form of scaled integers, such as values received from ADCs and sent to DACs. An efficient fixed-point controller implementation accepts integer inputs directly (without further conversion) and produces integer outputs that can be fed directly to output hardware devices.

The steps in converting a floating-point control system implementation to use fixed-point mathematics are as follows.

- Determine the scale factors for scaled integer controller input and output signals.
- Determine the maximum expected magnitude of all internal variables in the control system algorithms under all expected operating conditions.
- Determine the number of bits required to represent each input, state, and output variable in fixed-point mathematics.
- Modify the controller implementation to use inputs, outputs, and intermediate variables in the fixed-point format.
- Implement the controller algorithm with integer variables and math operations.

Simulink and the Fixed-Point Blockset provide several tools for converting a floating-point controller model to a fixed-point representation in a semiautomated manner. Once the controller has been converted to fixed-point representation, the code to implement it can be automatically generated from a Simulink diagram with the Real-Time Workshop® product. This process will not be covered here, although it is described in detail in the documentation for those products. Instead, I will discuss an approach that does not require these additional products.

8.6.1 Converting a Discrete-Time Model to Fixed-Point Math

The goal in this section is to develop an automated procedure for converting a state-space floating-point SISO or MIMO control system model to use fixed-point mathematics. I will assume that the fixed-point model will be implemented using the two's complement number representation. Two's complement is the signed number representation most commonly employed in embedded processors. In the two's complement representation, positive numbers are expressed in the usual binary format. To negate a positive number in the two's complement representation, invert all the bits then add one to the result.

I also assume that a discrete-time floating-point state-space model exists that must be converted to fixed-point math. The first important concept to apply in the conversion to fixed-point math is that it is useful to scale the inputs, states, and outputs of the model so that all these values are real numbers between +1 and –1. This approach is useful because all bits in the binary representation of each number lie to the right of the radix point. The precision of the results can be adjusted by merely truncating the binary representation at the desired point.

The input and output signal scaling is often determined by factors such as the hardware design of an ADC or DAC interface. For the state variables, it is necessary to estimate the required range of values or use simulation techniques to determine the range. It is also necessary to allow some extra range in the state scaling to permit operation in extraordinary situations. It is generally unacceptable for a variable in two's complement to exceed its scaled limit. This results in wraparound to a full-scale value with the opposite sign, which can be expected to cause the control system to fail immediately.

Advanced Concept

The result of the above analysis is the set of vectors $\mathbf{u}_s$, $\mathbf{x}_s$, and $\mathbf{y}_s$ containing the maximum expected magnitudes (in engineering units) of the input ($\mathbf{u}$), state ($\mathbf{x}$), and output ($\mathbf{y}$) vectors. To begin the model conversion to fixed-point math, first define the vectors $\tilde{\mathbf{u}}$, $\tilde{\mathbf{x}}$, and $\tilde{\mathbf{y}}$ to be the input, state, and output vectors after scaling to the range [–1, +1]. Define square matrices $\mathbf{U}_s$, $\mathbf{X}_s$, and $\mathbf{Y}_s$ to contain the elements of $\mathbf{u}_s$, $\mathbf{x}_s$, and $\mathbf{y}_s$, respectively, along the diagonals, with zeros everywhere else. These matrices and vectors are related by the following equations, where the subscript n indicates the current time step.

$$\begin{aligned} \mathbf{u}_n &= \mathbf{U}_s\tilde{\mathbf{u}}_n \\ \mathbf{x}_n &= \mathbf{X}_s\tilde{\mathbf{x}}_n \\ \mathbf{y}_n &= \mathbf{Y}_s\tilde{\mathbf{y}}_n \end{aligned} \qquad \text{Eq. 8.3}$$

Substitute Eq. 8.3 into the discrete-time state-space model of Eq. 8.2 as shown in Eq. 8.4.

$$\begin{aligned} \tilde{\mathbf{x}}_{n+1} &= (\mathbf{X}_s^{-1}\mathbf{A}\mathbf{X}_s)\tilde{\mathbf{x}}_n + (\mathbf{X}_s^{-1}\mathbf{B}\mathbf{U}_s)\tilde{\mathbf{u}}_n \\ \tilde{\mathbf{y}}_n &= (\mathbf{Y}_s^{-1}\mathbf{C}\mathbf{X}_s)\tilde{\mathbf{x}}_n + (\mathbf{Y}_s^{-1}\mathbf{D}\mathbf{U}_s)\tilde{\mathbf{u}}_n \end{aligned} \qquad \text{Eq. 8.4}$$

The next step is to scale the four constant matrices contained in parentheses in Eq. 8.4 so that the results of evaluating the equation right-hand sides lie in the range [–1, +1]. I will perform this scaling separately for the state equation (the top equation in Eq. 8.4) and for the output equation (the bottom equation in Eq. 8.4). The scaling will be performed so that the largest possible magnitude in the result for each equation is 1.

The result of this scaling appears in Eq. 8.5, where a_s is the scaling factor for the state equation matrices and c_s is the scaling factor for the output equation matrices. a_s is the inverse of the maximum absolute value of the row sums of the combined elements in the $(\mathbf{X}_s^{-1}\mathbf{A}\mathbf{X}_s)$ and $(\mathbf{X}_s^{-1}\mathbf{B}\mathbf{U}_s)$ matrices, and c_s is the corresponding value for the $(\mathbf{Y}_s^{-1}\mathbf{C}\mathbf{X}_s)$ and $(\mathbf{Y}_s^{-1}\mathbf{D}\mathbf{U}_s)$matrices.

$$\begin{aligned} a_s\tilde{\mathbf{x}}_{n+1} &= a_s(\mathbf{X}_s^{-1}\mathbf{A}\mathbf{X}_s)\tilde{\mathbf{x}}_n + a_s(\mathbf{X}_s^{-1}\mathbf{B}\mathbf{U}_s)\tilde{\mathbf{u}}_n \\ c_s\tilde{\mathbf{y}}_n &= c_s(\mathbf{Y}_s^{-1}\mathbf{C}\mathbf{X}_s)\tilde{\mathbf{x}}_n + c_s(\mathbf{Y}_s^{-1}\mathbf{D}\mathbf{U}_s)\tilde{\mathbf{u}}_n \end{aligned} \qquad \text{Eq. 8.5}$$

You can rewrite Eq. 8.5 as shown in Eq. 8.6, in which all elements of the $\tilde{\mathbf{A}}$, $\tilde{\mathbf{B}}$, $\tilde{\mathbf{C}}$, and $\tilde{\mathbf{D}}$ matrices and the $\tilde{\mathbf{u}}$, $\tilde{\mathbf{x}}$, and $\tilde{\mathbf{y}}$ vectors have magnitudes in the range [–1, +1]. In Eq. 8.6, $\tilde{\mathbf{A}} = a_s(\mathbf{X}_s^{-1}\mathbf{A}\mathbf{X}_s)$, $\tilde{\mathbf{B}} = a_s(\mathbf{X}_s^{-1}\mathbf{B}\mathbf{U}_s)$, $\tilde{\mathbf{C}} = c_s(\mathbf{Y}_s^{-1}\mathbf{C}\mathbf{X}_s)$, and $\tilde{\mathbf{D}} = c_s(\mathbf{Y}_s^{-1}\mathbf{D}\mathbf{U}_s)$.

$$\begin{aligned} \tilde{\mathbf{x}}_{n+1} &= \frac{1}{a_s}(\tilde{\mathbf{A}}\tilde{\mathbf{x}}_n + \tilde{\mathbf{B}}\tilde{\mathbf{u}}_n) \\ \tilde{\mathbf{y}}_n &= \frac{1}{c_s}(\tilde{\mathbf{C}}\tilde{\mathbf{x}}_n + \tilde{\mathbf{D}}\tilde{\mathbf{u}}_n) \end{aligned} \qquad \text{Eq. 8.6}$$

On each update of Eq. 8.6, the input vector must be scaled from engineering units to the [–1, +1] range with the formula $\tilde{\mathbf{u}}_n = \mathbf{U}_S^{-1}\mathbf{u}_n$. The state and output vectors produced by Eq. 8.6 can be converted to engineering units with Eq. 8.3.

[redacted]

After the equations have been scaled, the next step is to convert Eq. 8.6 to an integer representation. You must first select appropriate integer word sizes to use in the computations. The word size determines the precision of the numerical values that can be represented by a variable of that size. Table 8.1 shows the range and precision in terms of decimal digits of some common two's complement integer word sizes.

Table 8.1 Range and precision of common two's complement word sizes.

Word Size (bits)	Minimum Value	Maximum Value	Decimal Digits of Precision
8	–128	127	2.1
16	–32,768	32,767	4.5
32	–2,147,483,648	2,147,483,647	9.3

To avoid introducing excessive error into the computations, the word size used should be at least as large as the word sizes of the input and output devices. In many control system implementations, a 16-bit word size is sufficient. For low-resolution systems, 8-bit words might be acceptable.

The computation of Eq. 8.6 consists of a series of multiply-and-accumulate operations followed by multiplication by the $1/a_s$ and $1/c_s$ terms. In general, when two n-bit integers are multiplied, the result is a $2n$-bit integer, which means that as the parenthesized terms in Eq. 8.6 are evaluated, assuming each element of the matrices and vectors is an n-bit integer, the result should be accumulated in a $2n$-bit integer. The resulting sums must then be scaled (by the $1/a_s$ and $1/c_s$ terms) and truncated to n-bit integers to provide the integer results of Eq. 8.6.

Equation 8.6 converts to an integer representation by multiplying each of the $\tilde{\mathbf{A}}, \tilde{\mathbf{B}}, \tilde{\mathbf{C}}$, and $\tilde{\mathbf{D}}$ matrices by the full-scale value of the integer word size that will contain them. As Table 8.1 indicates, the two's complement representation has a slight asymmetry. The negative full-scale value is 1 LSB larger in magnitude than the positive full-scale value. For this reason, the magnitude of the positive full-scale value is used in the conversion of the matrices to integer format. Each element in the resulting matrices should be rounded to the nearest integer value. This results in a maximum error of 0.5 LSB in the resulting matrices.

The results of evaluating Eq. 8.6 in integer format are the vectors $\tilde{\mathbf{x}}_{n+1}$ and $\tilde{\mathbf{y}}_n$ in integer representation. The $\tilde{\mathbf{y}}_n$ vector might need to be scaled before passing it along to the plant actuators. To recover the floating-point values of inputs, states, and outputs in engineering units (e.g., for display to an operator), use the formulas of Eq. 8.3.

8.7 C/C++ Control System Implementation

If sufficient processing power and execution time are available, it might be appropriate to implement an embedded controller with floating-point mathematics. When possible, this approach minimizes the effects of quantization and essentially eliminates the possibility of errors due to overflow in the controller calculations. For processors containing dedicated floating-point hardware units or sufficiently fast software implementations of floating-point operations, the use of floating-point math is often the preferred approach.

Converting a MATLAB discrete-time control system model to a fixed-point C or C++ source code implementation consists of a straightforward series of steps. This conversion process has been mechanized in two MATLAB M-files, `write_c_model.m` and `write_cpp_model.m`. The help text for each is shown here.

```
WRITE_C_MODEL Write a C model of a discrete-time system using
floating-point math.

  WRITE_C_MODEL(MODEL) generates a C language implementation of
  the discrete-time model MODEL using double-precision math and
  displays it on the screen.

  WRITE_C_MODEL(MODEL, DEST) directs the C language output to the
  file indicated by DEST. DEST is a character string name of a file
  to be created or the integer handle of an already-open output
  file. If DEST is an integer, the output file remains open after
  this function completes.

  WRITE_C_MODEL(MODEL, DEST, DATATYPE) uses the character string
  typename indicated by DATATYPE instead of the 'double' type.

WRITE_CPP_MODEL Write a C++ model of a discrete-time system using
floating-point math.

  WRITE_CPP_MODEL(MODEL) generates a C++ language implementation
  of the discrete-time model MODEL using double-precision math and
  displays it on the screen.

  WRITE_CPP_MODEL(MODEL, DEST) directs the C++ language output to
  the file indicated by DEST. DEST is a character string name of a
  file to be created or the integer handle of an already-open
  output file. If DEST is an integer, the output file remains open
  after this function completes.

  WRITE_CPP_MODEL(MODEL, DEST, DATATYPE) uses the character string
  typename indicated by DATATYPE instead of the 'double' type.
```

Each of these functions requires a discrete-time model as its first parameter and outputs the generated C or C++ source code to the screen or to a file specified by the second parameter. The default data type used in the implementations is `double`, but a third parameter can be provided to specify an alternative data type, such as `float`.

A single source file is created for each model processed by one of these functions. The resulting file can be included directly in another source file that uses the discrete-time model, or the file can be separated into header and implementation files for compilation separately from other modules in the control system implementation.

The C implementation created by `write_c_model.m` provides two functions for initializing and updating the discrete-time model. Additional functions are provided for accessing the state vector and output vector. The initialization function is named `Initialize_`*`sysname`*`()` (where *`sysname`* is replaced by the name of the MATLAB discrete-time model) and has two array arguments: the initial state vector and the initial input vector. The `Update_`*`sysname`*`()` function has one array argument: the current input vector. Following each call to the initialization or update functions, the output vector can be accessed with `Output_`*`sysname`*`()`. The state vector can be accessed with `State_`*`sysname`*`()`.

An example will demonstrate the use of this function and the resulting C source code (Listing 8.1). Consider again the transfer function

$$\frac{Y}{X} = \frac{1}{s^2 + 2s + 1}.$$

The following MATLAB commands develop a continuous-time model of this system, convert it to a discrete-time state-space model with a first-order hold and a 0.1-second step time, and generate a floating-point C implementation.

```
>> num = 1;
>> den = [1 2 1];
>> sys = ss(tf(num, den));
>> dsys = c2d(sys, 0.1, 'foh');
>> write_c_model(dsys, 'dsys.c')
```

The resulting source code is placed in the output file `dsys.c` and appears in Listing 8.1.

Listing 8.1 C implementation of discrete-time floating-point model.

```
/* Model: dsys  */
/* Sampling period =  0.100000 seconds */
/* Generated at 19:17:17 on 26-Feb-2003 */

/* n = #states, m = #outputs, r = #inputs */
enum {n_dsys = 2, m_dsys = 1, r_dsys = 1};
```

```
void Initialize_dsys(const double* x0);
void Update_dsys(const double* u);
const double *Output_dsys();
const double *State_dsys();

static const double a[n_dsys*n_dsys] =
{
    8.143536762e-001, -2.262093545e-002,
    3.619349672e-001,  9.953211598e-001
};

static const double b[n_dsys*r_dsys] =
{
    4.524187090e-002,
    9.357680321e-003
};

static const double c[m_dsys*n_dsys] =
{
    0.000000000e+000,  5.000000000e-001
};

static const double d[m_dsys*r_dsys] =
{
    0.000000000e+000
};

static double x[n_dsys], y[m_dsys];

void Initialize_dsys(const double* x0)
{
   int i;

   /* Initialize x */
   for (i=0; i<n_dsys; i++)
       x[i] = x0[i];
```

```
}

void Update_dsys(const double* u)
{
    int i, j;
    double x_next[n_dsys];

    /* Evaluate x_next = A*x + B*u */
    for (i=0; i<n_dsys; i++)
    {
        x_next[i] = 0;
        for (j=0; j<n_dsys; j++)
            x_next[i] += a[i*n_dsys+j]*x[j];

        for (j=0; j<r_dsys; j++)
            x_next[i] += b[i*r_dsys+j]*u[j];
    }

    /* Evaluate y = C*x + D*u */
    for (i=0; i<m_dsys; i++)
    {
        y[i] = 0;
        for (j=0; j<n_dsys; j++)
            y[i] += c[i*n_dsys+j]*x[j];

        for (j=0; j<r_dsys; j++)
            y[i] += d[i*r_dsys+j]*u[j];
    }

    /* Update x to its next value */
    for (i=0; i<n_dsys; i++)
        x[i] = x_next[i];
}

const double *Output_dsys()
{
    return y;
```

```
}

const double *State_dsys()
{
    return x;
}
```

The C implementation of the discrete-time system directly supports only a single instance of the model. This is acceptable in many cases, but sometimes a control system contains multiple identical controllers. This occurs, for example, when a plant contains multiple identical channels that must be controlled in the same way.

The C implementation can support multiple identical controllers if a separate copy of the state vector is maintained for each of the controllers. To do this, prior to each call to `Update_`*`sysname`*`()`, the contents of the state vector for the controller being updated must be copied to the `x[]` state vector (which is accessible by means of `State_`*`sysname`*`()`). After `Update_`*`sysname`*`()` completes, the updated contents of `x[]` must be copied out and saved for use on the next update call. To perform these steps, the pointer to the state vector returned by `State_dsys()` must be coerced from a pointer to `const double` to a pointer to `double`. This works, but it is not a very elegant solution.

The C++ version of this discrete-time system (Listing 8.2) is generated with a command of the form `write_cpp_model(dsys, 'dsys.cpp')`. The generated code contains a C++ class that implements the controller model. Any number of instances of this class can be declared without restriction. The four constant matrices describing the discrete-time system are declared as `static` class members, which means that only one copy of them exists in memory regardless of the number of objects of the class type.

Listing 8.2 C++ implementation of discrete-time floating-point model.

```
// Model: dsys
// Sampling period = 0.100000 seconds
// Generated at 19:17:17 on 26-Feb-2003

class dsys
{
public:
    // n = #states, m = #outputs, r = #inputs
    enum {n = 2, m = 1, r = 1};

    void Initialize(const double x0[n]);
    void Update(const double u[r]);
    const double* Output(void) { return y; }
```

```
    const double* State(void) { return x; }

private:
    static const double a[n*n], b[n*r], c[m*n], d[m*r];
    double x[n], y[m];
};

const double dsys::a[n*n] =
{
    8.143536762e-001, -2.262093545e-002,
    3.619349672e-001,  9.953211598e-001
};

const double dsys::b[n*r] =
{
    4.524187090e-002,
    9.357680321e-003
};

const double dsys::c[m*n] =
{
    0.000000000e+000,  5.000000000e-001
};

const double dsys::d[m*r] =
{
    0.000000000e+000
};

void dsys::Initialize(const double x0[n])
{
    int i;

    // Initialize x
    for (i=0; i<n; i++)
        x[i] = x0[i];
}
```

```
void dsys::Update(const double u[r])
{
    int i, j;
    double x_next[n];

    // Evaluate x_next = A*x + B*u
    for (i=0; i<n; i++)
    {
        x_next[i] = 0;
        for (j=0; j<n; j++)
            x_next[i] += a[i*n+j]*x[j];

        for (j=0; j<r; j++)
            x_next[i] += b[i*r+j]*u[j];
    }

    // Evaluate y = C*x + D*u
    for (i=0; i<m; i++)
    {
        y[i] = 0;
        for (j=0; j<n; j++)
            y[i] += c[i*n+j]*x[j];

        for (j=0; j<r; j++)
            y[i] += d[i*r+j]*u[j];
    }

    // Update x to its next value
    for (i=0; i<n; i++)
        x[i] = x_next[i];
}
```

The example C and C++ source code generated above from discrete-time models is suitable for use in applications where floating-point capability exists in the execution environment and sufficient time and memory are available to perform the calculations. In more restricted situations, such as on an 8-bit processor with no floating-point capability, it is necessary to implement the model with fixed-point mathematics.

The MATLAB M-files `write_c_fixpt_model.m` and `write_cpp_fixpt_model.m` are provided to generate C and C++ source code suitable for use in the most restricted environments. These functions require additional inputs to describe the scale factors for the input, state, and output vectors. The generated code makes the following assumptions about the discrete-time model and the C or C++ compiler that will be used with the generated code.

- Two's complement arithmetic will be used.
- The `short` data type is 16 bits wide and the `long` data type is 32 bits wide. If necessary, these assumed lengths could be modified near the top of the `write_c_fixpt_model.m` or `write_cpp_fixpt_model.m` file.
- The `short` type contains sufficient resolution to hold the system input, state, and output variables.
- The elements of the input, output, and state vectors will never exceed the given scale factors.
- Right-shifts of signed quantities (via the >> operator) propagate the sign bit into the vacated bit positions. This is called an arithmetic shift. The alternative is filling the vacated bits with zeros, which is called a logical shift. The use of the arithmetic or logical shift for right-shifting signed quantities is compiler dependent, although the arithmetic shift is most common.

If your compiler right-shifts signed quantities with the logical shift technique, the generated C and C++ source code will not work properly. You must modify the generated code to employ an alternative method of dividing signed integers by powers of 2. One approach, although probably not very efficient, is to use the division operation instead of shifting. For example, you could replace the expression `accum >> 15` with `accum/32768`.

You must carefully determine the full-scale value to use for each input, output, and state vector element. This information can be derived by a variety of approaches, such as examination of the specifications of system components, analysis of the system operational requirements, and simulation tests of the closed-loop system. It is critical that the full-scale values are sufficiently large that they will never be exceeded during operation of the controller. If any variable exceeds its range limits, you can expect the controller to fail immediately and catastrophically.

Because of the extreme consequences of an overflow, it is prudent to allow some extra range for worst-case situations. You do not want the control system to cause a complete system failure if, for example, a component failure causes a perturbation that could be managed if integer overflow did not occur. However, you should not allow too much extra range because this results in increased quantization errors in the control system. Like many of the other procedures discussed in this book, the selection of optimum full-scale values for fixed-point implementations usually involves some iteration.

The following example demonstrates how to generate a C fixed-point implementation of the $Y/X = 1/(s^2 + 2s + 1)$ transfer function. The input and output are expected to lie in the approximate range [–1, +1], so scale factors of 2 will be chosen for both of them. Examination of the state trajectories in response to a unit step input results in the selection of the state scale factors 0.5 and 4.

The `write_c_fixpt_model()` function converts this model to C source code. The arguments to `write_c_fixpt_model()` are similar to those of `write_c_model()`, except that the three scaling vectors also must be included. The `dsys` model (created earlier in this chapter) is assumed to already exist in the MATLAB workspace. The generated source code is written to a file named `dsys_fixpt.c`.

```
>> us = 2; % Input scale factor
>> xs = [0.5 4]; % State scale factors
>> ys = 2; % Output scale factor
>> write_c_fixpt_model(dsys, us, xs, ys, 'dsys_fixpt.c');
```

The resulting C source code is shown in Listing 8.3.

Listing 8.3 C implementation of discrete-time fixed-point model.

```
/* Model: dsys
 * Sampling period =  0.100000 seconds
 *
 * Input scaling:  [2]
 * State scaling:  [0.5           4]
 * Output scaling: [2]
 *
 * Generated at 19:17:18 on 26-Feb-2003
 */

/* n = #states, m = #outputs, r = #inputs */
enum {n_dsys = 2, m_dsys = 1, r_dsys = 1};

void Initialize_dsys(const short* x0);
void Update_dsys(const short* u);
const short *Output_dsys();
const short *State_dsys();

static const short a[n_dsys*n_dsys] =
{
     22685,  -5041,
      1260,  27726
```

```
};

static const short b[n_dsys*r_dsys] =
{
     5041,
      130
};

static const short c[m_dsys*n_dsys] =
{
        0,  32767
};

static const short d[m_dsys*r_dsys] =
{
        0
};

static short x[n_dsys], y[m_dsys];

void Initialize_dsys(const short* x0)
{
    int i;

    /* Initialize x */
    for (i=0; i<n_dsys; i++)
        x[i] = x0[i];
}

void Update_dsys(const short* u)
{
    int i, j, n_offset = 0, r_offset = 0;
    short x_next[n_dsys];
    long accum;

    /* Evaluate x_next = A*x + B*u */
    for (i=0; i<n_dsys; i++)
```

```
    {
        accum = 0;

        for (j=0; j<n_dsys; j++)
            accum += (long) a[n_offset+j]*x[j];

        for (j=0; j<r_dsys; j++)
            accum += (long) b[r_offset+j]*u[j];

        accum = (accum >> 15) * 38543;
        x_next[i] = (short) (accum >> 15);

        n_offset += n_dsys;
        r_offset += r_dsys;
    }

    n_offset = 0;
    r_offset = 0;

    /* Evaluate y = C*x + D*u */
    for (i=0; i<m_dsys; i++)
    {
        accum = 0;

        for (j=0; j<n_dsys; j++)
            accum += (long) c[n_offset+j]*x[j];

        for (j=0; j<r_dsys; j++)
            accum += (long) d[r_offset+j]*u[j];

        accum = (accum >> 15) * 32767;
        y[i] = (short) (accum >> 15);

        n_offset += n_dsys;
        r_offset += r_dsys;

    /* Update x to its next value */
```

```
    for (i=0; i<n_dsys; i++)
        x[i] = x_next[i];
    }
}

const short *Output_dsys()
{
    return y;
}

const short *State_dsys()
{
    return x;
}
```

The C++ fixed-point implementation of this model is generated with the command `write_cpp_fixpt_model(dsys, us, xs, ys, 'dsys_fixpt.cpp')`. The resulting code appears in Listing 8.4.

Listing 8.4 C++ implementation of discrete-time fixed-point model.

```
// Model: dsys
// Sampling period = 0.100000 seconds
//
// Input scaling:  [2]
// State scaling:  [0.5          4]
// Output scaling: [2]
//
// Generated at 19:17:18 on 26-Feb-2003

class dsys
{
public:
    // n = #states, m = #outputs, r = #inputs
    enum {n = 2, m = 1, r = 1};

    void Initialize(const short x0[n]);
    void Update(const short u[r]);
```

```
    const short* Output(void) const { return y; }
    const short* State(void) const { return x; }

private:
    static const short a[n*n], b[n*r], c[m*n], d[m*r];
    short x[n], y[m];
};

const short dsys::a[n*n] =
{
     22685,  -5041,
      1260,  27726
};

const short dsys::b[n*r] =
{
      5041,
       130
};

const short dsys::c[m*n] =
{
         0,  32767
};

const short dsys::d[m*r] =
{
         0
};

void dsys::Initialize(const short x0[n])
{
    int i;

    // Initialize x
    for (i=0; i<n; i++)
        x[i] = x0[i];
```

```
}

void dsys::Update(const short u[r])
{
    int i, j, n_offset = 0, r_offset = 0;
    short x_next[n];
    long accum;

    // Evaluate x_next = A*x + B*u
    for (i=0; i<n; i++)
    {
        accum = 0;

        for (j=0; j<n; j++)
            accum += (long) a[n_offset+j]*x[j];

        for (j=0; j<r; j++)
            accum += (long) b[r_offset+j]*u[j];

        accum = (accum >> 15) * 38543;
        x_next[i] = (short) (accum >> 15);

        n_offset += n;
        r_offset += r;
    }

    n_offset = 0;
    r_offset = 0;

    // Evaluate y = C*x + D*u
    for (i=0; i<m; i++)
    {
        accum = 0;

        for (j=0; j<n; j++)
            accum += (long) c[n_offset+j]*x[j];
```

```
        for (j=0; j<r; j++)
            accum += (long) d[r_offset+j]*u[j];

        accum = (accum >> 15) * 32767;
        y[i] = (short) (accum >> 15);

        n_offset += n;
        r_offset += r;
    }

    // Update x to its next value
    for (i=0; i<n; i++)
        x[i] = x_next[i];
}
```

The discrete-time implementations shown in Listings 8.3 and 8.4 should be reasonably efficient on processors with the capability to perform addition and multiplication operations on 16- and 32-bit integer data types. The number of multiplications is kept to a minimum, and the remaining operations consist primarily of loop iterations, additions, and shifts. The `Update()` operations consume the bulk of the execution time during controller operation and are the place to look if performance optimization is required.

Some obvious improvements could be made in cases such as SISO systems in which the loops over the `m` and `r` parameters can be eliminated. However, because these parameters are compile-time constants, a decent compiler optimizer should be able to do this for you automatically. It might also be helpful to unroll the inner loops. This consists of eliminating the inner `for` statements and replacing the loop body with a sequence of statements performing the same steps. Again, your compiler optimizer might be able to do this for you.

The fixed-point models are necessarily less accurate than the floating-point implementations because of quantization. For the system modeled in the examples above, the fixed-point implementation's response to a unit step input remains within 0.5 percent of the continuous-time system's response at all times. You can expect a similar degradation of accuracy when moving your controller design to a fixed-point implementation.

Keep in mind that the state-space format is suitable for both SISO and MIMO systems. The four MATLAB functions described in this chapter are able to generate code for arbitrarily complex state-space observer-controllers with any number of inputs and outputs. The results of executing the floating-point C and C++ code should agree closely with the same discrete-time models executed within MATLAB. The accuracy of the fixed-point code will be limited by the quantization of the integer data formats used, which is dependent on the scaling vectors you select.

8.8 Summary

In this chapter, I began by showing how to convert a continuous-time state-space model of a controller (or observer-controller) in MATLAB to a discrete-time system. A number of different discretization methods are available and some of the benefits and drawbacks of each were discussed. If you do not have a particular reason to favor one of the discretization methods over the others, the first-order hold is a good general-purpose choice. This method provides a good match between the phase and magnitude responses of the continuous-time and discrete-time models over a wide range of frequencies.

When choosing a sampling period for the discrete-time model, a number of factors must be considered. A too-short sampling period requires excessive computation time and I/O activity. An excessively long sampling period can result in poor controller accuracy or even system instability. Selecting a suitable sampling period is a critical element of the control system design process.

A discrete-time controller model can be implemented with floating-point mathematics in C or C++ with the assistance of the `write_c_model.m` and `write_cpp_model.m` MATLAB M-files provided on the enclosed CD-ROM. These functions generate C and C++ source code to implement a discrete-time state-space model that uses floating-point math.

When the embedded processor used in the control system does not support floating-point mathematics or the resource requirements for floating-point math are excessive, fixed-point math can be used instead. In fixed-point mathematics, scaled integers represent continuous quantities. Although fixed-point math can be much more efficient than floating-point math, it has a couple of significant drawbacks: quantization and the potential for overflow.

Quantization occurs because the integer representation of the continuous values can only change in steps of the least significant bit. Overflow happens when a fixed-point value exceeds the maximum or minimum value the integer format can represent. Overflow is a very bad thing to happen in a controller, and you must take extreme care to ensure it does not occur.

Two M-files are provided to convert a discrete-time state-space MATLAB model to fixed-point C or C++ source code: `write_c_fixpt_model.m` and `write_cpp_fixpt_model.m`. The designer must provide maximum scale values for the input, output, and state vector elements to these functions. The scale factors must be selected carefully to ensure that the possibility of overflow is minimized under normal and extreme operating conditions. The resulting source code contains only integer operations and is suitable for deployment in embedded controllers that have stringent limits on resources such as memory usage and execution time.

8.9 Self-Test

1. The observer-controller developed in the Chapter 7 self-test is shown below. The states are $\mathbf{x} = [\theta \ \ x \ \ \dot{\theta} \ \ \dot{x}]^T$, the output is $\mathbf{y} = F$, and the inputs are $\mathbf{u} = [\theta \ \ x \ \ F]^T$. Create a continuous-time state-space MATLAB model of this system.

$$\dot{\mathbf{x}} = \begin{bmatrix} -126.8 & 0 & 1 & 0 \\ 0 & -55.07 & 0 & 1 \\ -5566 & 0 & 0 & 0 \\ 0 & -737.8 & 0 & 0 \end{bmatrix} \mathbf{x} + \begin{bmatrix} 126.8 & 0 & 0 \\ 0 & 55.07 & 0 \\ 5657 & 0 & -23.08 \\ -2.26 & 737.8 & 3.08 \end{bmatrix} \mathbf{u}, \qquad \mathbf{y} = \begin{bmatrix} 97.74 & 223.6 & 11.35 & 65.36 \end{bmatrix} \mathbf{x}$$

2. Discretize the continuous-time model of problem 1 with a step time of 10 milliseconds and a first-order hold approximation.
3. Plot the unit step response and frequency response from input 1 (θ) to the output (F) of the discrete-time observer-controller and compare them to the responses of the continuous-time observer-controller.
4. Implement the observer-controller in C++ with floating-point mathematics. Use `write_cpp_model()` for this.
5. Use the scaling vectors $\mathbf{u}_S = [4 \ \ 2 \ \ 1000]$, $\mathbf{x}_S = [2 \ \ 1 \ \ 100 \ \ 20]$, and $\mathbf{y}_S = [1000]$, to implement the observer-controller in C++ with fixed-point mathematics. Use `write_cpp_fixpt_model()` for this.
6. Write a C++ program that iterates the floating-point and fixed-point models created in the previous two problems for 10 time steps (0.1 seconds) and stores the results in a text file that can be read by MATLAB. Use $[1 \ \ 0 \ \ 0]^T$ as the system input vector and set the initial states to zero.
7. Plot the outputs of the fixed-point and floating-point models from the previous exercise along with the response of the continuous-time model in MATLAB.
8. In some situations, it is preferable to limit the results of integer additions rather than accept the possibility of overflow. This results in a more graceful degradation of controller behavior than when overflow is allowed to occur. Develop an algorithm that accepts two 32-bit two's complement integers (p and q) and determines whether their sum would cause an overflow. This procedure must use only integer operations on words no larger than 32 bits.
9. How would you modify the code of Listings 8.3 and 8.4 to perform limiting in the accumulation operations?
10. What are some drawbacks of performing limiting in the accumulation operations?

8.10 Answers

The answers to the Self-Test questions for this chapter can be found in the file `questions.m` in the `Self-Test\Ch08` directory of the accompanying CD-ROM.

1.

```
a = [  -126.8       0       1       0; ...
            0  -55.07       0       1; ...
        -5566       0       0       0; ...
            0  -737.8       0       0];

b = [   126.8       0       0; ...
            0   55.07       0; ...
         5657       0  -23.08; ...
        -2.26   737.8    3.08];

c = [   97.74  223.6  11.35  65.36];

d = 0;

sys = ss(a, b, c, d);
```

2.

```
Ts = 0.01;
method = 'foh';
dsys = c2d(sys, Ts, method);
```

3. The resulting plot appears in Figure 8.7.

Figure 8.7 Continuous- and discrete-time system comparison.

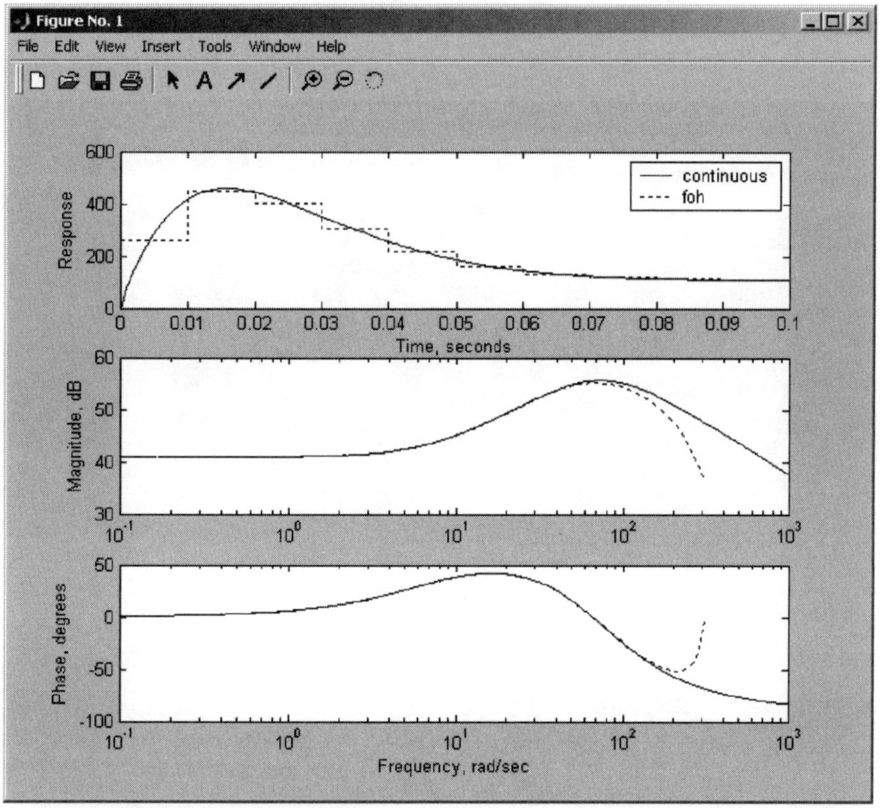


```
% Continuous system frequency response
w = logspace(-1, 3, 1000);
[mag_cont, phase_cont, w_cont] = bode(sys, w);
mag_cont = squeeze(mag_cont(:, 1, :));
mag_cont_db = 20*log10(mag_cont);
phase_cont = squeeze(phase_cont(:, 1, :));

% Continuous system step response
t = [0:0.001:0.1];
[y_cont, t_cont] = step(sys, t);
y_cont = y_cont(:, 1);

% Discrete-time system frequency response
```

```
[mag_foh, phase_foh, w_foh] = bode(dsys);
mag_foh = squeeze(mag_foh(:, 1, :));
mag_foh_db = 20*log10(mag_foh);
t = [0:Ts:0.1];
phase_foh = squeeze(phase_foh(:, 1, :));

% Discrete-time system step response
[y_foh, t_foh] = step(dsys, t);
y_foh = y_foh(:, 1);

% Plot the results
subplot(311)
plot(t_cont, y_cont, 'k-');
hold on
stairs(t_foh, y_foh, 'k:');
hold off
xlabel('Time, seconds')
ylabel('Response')
legend('continuous', method)

subplot(312)
semilogx(w_cont, mag_cont_db, 'k-', w_foh, mag_foh_db, 'k:');
ylabel('Magnitude, dB')

subplot(313)
semilogx(w_cont, phase_cont, 'k-', w_foh, phase_foh, 'k:');
xlabel('Frequency, rad/sec')
ylabel('Phase, degrees')
```

4.

```
write_cpp_model(dsys, 'pend_dsys.cpp')
```

5.

```
us = [4 2 1000];
xs = [2 1 100 20];
```

```
ys = [1000];

dsys_fixpt = dsys;
write_cpp_fixpt_model(dsys_fixpt, us, xs, ys, 'pend_dsys_fixpt.cpp');
```

6.

```
#include <cstdio>
#include <cassert>

#include "..\pend_dsys.cpp"
#include "..\pend_dsys_fixpt.cpp"

int main()
{
    dsys pend_dsys;
    dsys_fixpt pend_dsys_fixpt;

    // Initialize the floating-point model
    const double x0[dsys::n] = {0, 0, 0, 0};
    const double u0[dsys::r] = {1, 0, 0};

    pend_dsys.Initialize(x0);

    // Scale the inputs & states and initialize the fixed-point model
    const double us[dsys::r] = {4, 2, 1000};
    const double xs[dsys::n] = {2, 1, 100, 20};
    const double ys[dsys::m] = {1000};
    const double short_max = 32768;

    short u0_fixpt[dsys::r], x0_fixpt[dsys::n];

    for (int i=0; i<dsys::r; i++)
    {
        long l_val = long(u0[i] * short_max / us[i]);
        if (l_val > 32767) l_val = 32767;
        u0_fixpt[i] = short(l_val);
    }
```

```
    for (i=0; i<dsys::n; i++)
    {
        long l_val = long(x0[i] * short_max / xs[i]);
        if (l_val > 32767) l_val = 32767;
        x0_fixpt[i] = short(l_val);
    }

    pend_dsys_fixpt.Initialize(x0_fixpt);

    // Iterate the model for 11 steps & save the outputs
    FILE *iov = fopen("dsys_output.txt", "w");
    assert(iov);

    const double *y = pend_dsys.Output();
    const short *y_fixpt = pend_dsys_fixpt.Output();

    for (int n=0; n<=10; n++)
    {
        pend_dsys.Update(u0);
        pend_dsys_fixpt.Update(u0_fixpt);

        fprintf(iov, "%.16lf %.16lf\n",
            y[0], y_fixpt[0]*ys[0]/short_max);
    }

    fclose(iov);
    return 0;
}
```

7. The resulting plot appears in Figure 8.8.

```
load dsys_output.txt

pend_dsys_output = dsys_output(:, 1);
pend_dsys_fixpt_output = dsys_output(:, 2);

plot(t_cont, y_cont, 'k-');
```

```
hold on
stairs(t_foh, pend_dsys_output, 'k--');
stairs(t_foh, pend_dsys_fixpt_output, 'k:');
hold off
xlabel('Time, seconds')
ylabel('Response')
legend('continuous', 'floating-point', 'fixed-point')
```

Figure 8.8 Continuous-time, floating-point, and fixed-point discrete-time system responses.

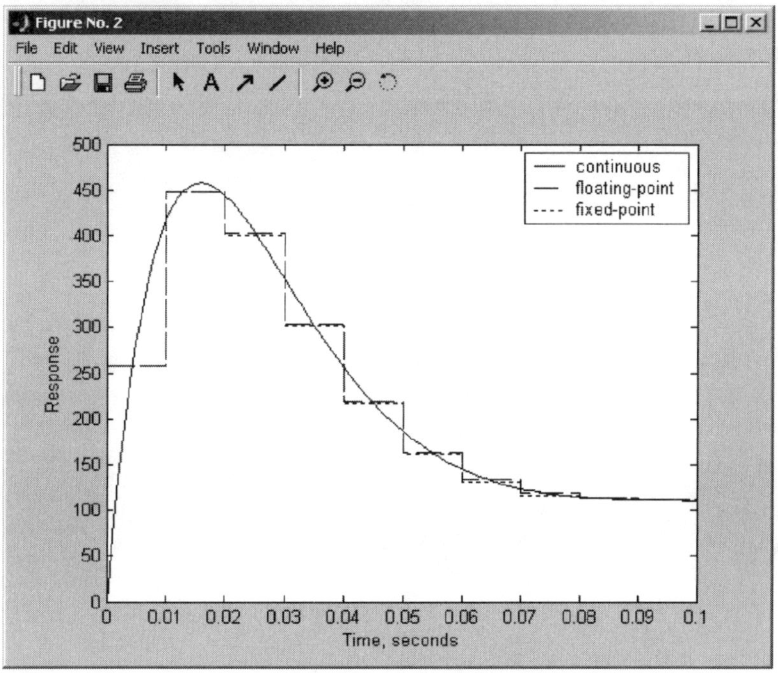

Note the slight differences between the results of the floating-point and fixed-point implementations as a result of quantization in the fixed-point implementation.

8. One approach is to divide both numbers by 2 (which can be done efficiently with a shift operation, assuming arithmetic shifting is performed) and add the results. If the sum is greater than $2^{30} - 1$ or less than -2^{30}, the addition of p and q would cause an overflow.
9. Replace each inner loop statement of the form `accum += a[n_offset+j]*x[j];` with the following steps.

- Assign `q = a[n_offset+j]*x[j];`
- Test whether the sum of `accum` and `q` would overflow using the algorithm developed in the previous problem.
- If the sum would overflow, set `accum` to the positive or negative full-scale value as appropriate.
- If the sum would not overflow, perform the addition and store the result in `accum`.

10. The testing required for limiting significantly increases the amount of computation required in the innermost loops of the `Update()` routine. The resulting code is also larger and more complex and requires additional effort to verify its correct operation.

8.11 References

1. Oppenheim, Alan V., and Ronald W. Schafer, *Discrete-Time Signal Processing* (Englewood Cliffs, NJ: Prentice Hall, 1989), §3.2.

CHAPTER 9

CONTROL SYSTEM INTEGRATION AND TESTING

9.1 Introduction

In this chapter, I cover the final steps in the development and test processes for embedded control systems. These topics include the addition of nonlinear features to the controller, the integration of the controller into the larger embedded system, and thorough testing of the complete system.

After completing a linear controller design with the techniques discussed in previous chapters, it is often necessary to include nonlinear elements such as limiting and gain scheduling to achieve satisfactory performance in all situations. These design components compensate for nonlinearities within the plant and for variations in a system's operational environment.

The control system must be integrated into the larger structure of the embedded system's software. The techniques for doing this vary depending on the operating system in use, or the lack thereof. Whether the embedded system's software environment supports real-time multitasking or uses a single thread of execution that polls a real-time clock, the controller algorithm must be carefully integrated with the other elements of the system software.

Following the integration of the controller into the embedded software environment, it is important to perform thorough testing of the complete system. System-level testing must ensure correct control system operation in normal situations, as well as under extreme conditions. I discuss two approaches for performing complete system-level tests in this chapter: simulation and operational testing.

System-level simulation is a valuable tool for performing many types of tests in a comparatively quick and low-cost manner. With simulation, it is possible to rapidly and thoroughly test the embedded system under a wide variety of conditions. These tests can exercise the simulated system in situations in which you would never willingly place the actual system, such as in dangerous emergency conditions. Simulation is also an excellent approach for performing regression testing following changes to a system design.

However, simulations can produce misleading results if the simulated system does not accurately represent the real-world system. Simulation verification and validation processes must be carried out to ensure the accuracy of simulation models and to provide confidence in the quality of the results produced by the simulation.

Operational testing involves tests of the actual system in its intended operational environment. One example is the flight testing of an aircraft. Operational testing provides the highest quality test data, but the results can be extremely expensive and time consuming to obtain. There might also be difficulties with the repeatability of results because of uncontrolled variations in the test environment.

A thorough system test plan employs a variety of test techniques to ensure that each system element performs as required under all operating conditions. By effectively combining simulation with operational testing, the cost and time required for test execution can be minimized while assuring complete test coverage. Thorough system testing leads to a high degree of confidence that the system will perform as required when placed into operation.

9.2 Chapter Objectives

After reading this chapter, you should be able to

- include nonlinear elements in appropriate locations in a controller design to accommodate plant or actuator nonlinearities such as saturation;
- understand the application of gain scheduling in controllers that must operate over widely varying plant and environmental conditions;
- use the Padé approximation to model a time delay;
- integrate a controller, developed with the methods described in earlier chapters, into an embedded system design;
- support any necessary controller mode switching required by the application;
- develop a set of tests to thoroughly exercise a controller design in its intended operating environment using simulation and operational testing; and
- evaluate the results of tests to determine whether the controller design is acceptable for the embedded system's intended uses.

9.3 Nonlinear Controller Elements

The controller design procedures I described in Chapters 2 and 4 through 7 focused primarily on the development of linear control systems. In Chapter 2, I also addressed the benefits of providing a nonlinear element in a system subject to actuator saturation. The nonlinear element in that case was a switch that reduced the integrator windup in a PID controller during periods of large error in the response. Another type of nonlinearity is the limiting of variable magnitudes to prevent overflow in fixed-point computations, as I discussed in Chapter 8 self-test questions 8 through 10.

A *limiter* is a common element in control system designs that simply limits its output to specified minimum and maximum values. When the limiter's input signal is between the minimum and maximum values, it is passed unchanged. A limiter is useful in situations in which the magnitude of a signal must be maintained within boundaries for smooth system operation. For example, in a design in which the error signal driving the controller can reach very large values, it might be best to limit the error magnitude at the controller input to prevent excessive controller output magnitude.

Important Point

Be careful when placing a limiter on a signal that is an output (even indirectly) from an integrator. Integration takes place in proportional plus integral (PI) and proportional plus integral plus derivative (PID) controllers and could occur in a transfer function or state-space linear system. A linear system performs integration if it has one or more poles located at the origin of the complex plane.

Placing a limiter on an integrator output leads to exactly the same problem discussed in Chapter 2: integrator windup. The actuator saturation described in that chapter has the same effect as placing a limiter on the controller output, which results in excessive overshoot, slow convergence to the commanded value, and potential oscillation and instability.

If a limiter must be placed on a signal that has been integrated, try using the approach described in Chapter 2 for turning off the integration action when limiting is occurring. This reduces integrator windup while allowing the benefits of limiting controller signal magnitudes.

9.4 Gain Scheduling

Control systems often operate under varying conditions that require changes to controller parameters for good performance. For example, an aircraft flight controller is expected to perform well under low-altitude, low-speed conditions near takeoff and landing, as well as at high-speed, high-altitude cruise conditions. The effectiveness of the control actuators (the moveable surfaces on the aircraft wings and tail) changes significantly between these flight regimes. It is not reasonable to expect to develop a controller with fixed parameters suitable for all of an aircraft's flight conditions. Instead, the control system must adapt as the flight conditions change in order to provide good control system performance at all times.

One way to implement these variations in control system parameters is to use the technique of *gain scheduling*. To use gain scheduling, you must develop a collection of controller designs in which each design is optimized for use under different system operating conditions. For example, in the aircraft controller case, you might create a two-dimensional grid of aircraft altitude versus airspeed covering the entire flight envelope and design a different controller for each point where the grid lines cross. The spacing between the grid lines must be chosen carefully so that the change in controller parameters between adjacent designs is not drastic. On the other hand, the grid spacing must not be so fine as to create excessive work in designing the different controllers or to consume excessive storage space in the embedded controller's memory.

In a gain-scheduled controller, the controller inputs must provide sufficient information for the control system to determine where the system is currently operating within its envelope. In the aircraft controller example (Example 7.2), these inputs would be the current measurements of altitude and airspeed. On each iteration of the controller algorithm, the appropriate set of controller parameters is selected from the grid on the basis of the current conditions.

To avoid abrupt transitions in moving from one grid point to the next, the technique of table interpolation is often used to smoothly adjust the values of controller gains as the operating conditions change. Table interpolation uses a mathematical algorithm to estimate the value of a function at points lying between a set of points where the function is known, called the breakpoints.

An interpolation function can have one or more inputs. The aircraft controller example has two inputs: the measured altitude and airspeed. However, as the number of inputs grows, the memory requirements and execution time for table interpolation will increase. In most cases, it is best to keep the number of inputs to a table interpolation as small as possible.

An example of a single-input interpolation table with eight equally spaced breakpoints appears in Figure 9.1. The span of the input variable x is [0, 0.7]. If the input variable precisely matches the x location of one of the breakpoints, it is a simple matter to return the corresponding y value as the result of the function evaluation. If the input value falls between the breakpoints, an interpolation must be performed.

One-dimensional linear interpolation can be performed graphically by drawing straight lines between adjacent breakpoints, as shown in Figure 9.2. The interpolated function is continuous and its derivative is discontinuous at the breakpoints.

You can implement one-dimensional linear interpolation with equally spaced breakpoints as follows. Assume there are N breakpoints with y-coordinates stored in a C/C++ language array. The values of $x(0)$ (the leftmost x-coordinate) and Δx (the interval between x coordinates) must also be provided.

1. Ensure that the input variable x_{in} has a value greater than or equal to $x(0)$ and less than or equal to $x(0) + (N - 1)\Delta x$. A limit function can be applied if appropriate. It is also possible to linearly extrapolate outside the table using the first (or last) two data points in the table to define a straight line. However, this approach could introduce significant errors if the extrapolation does not accurately model the desired behavior outside the range of the table and will not be considered here.

Figure 9.1 Example of a one-dimensional lookup table.

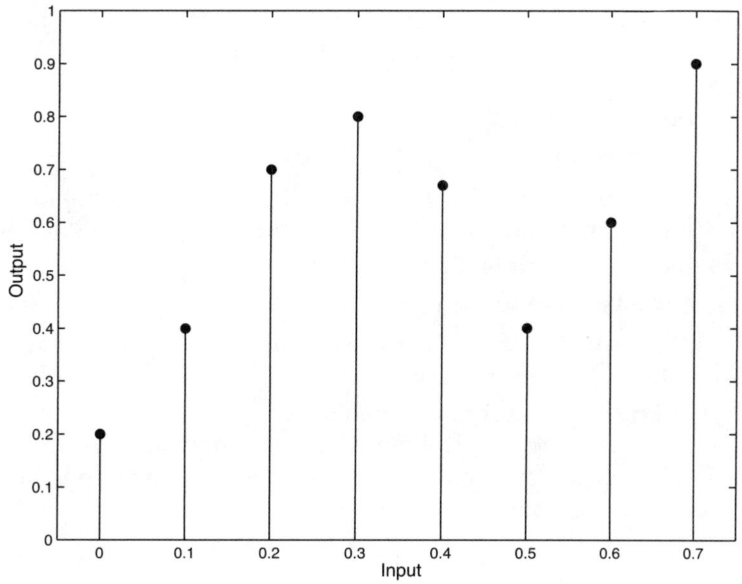

Figure 9.2 Linear breakpoint interpolation.

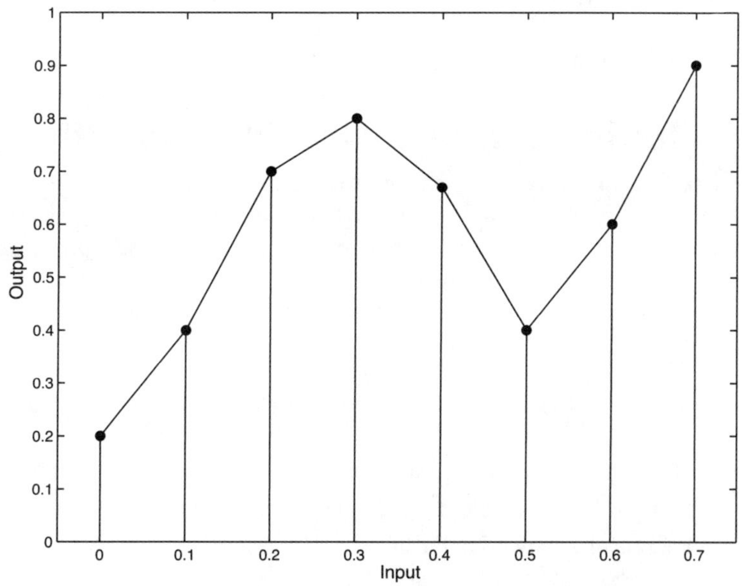

2. Determine the array index of the closest breakpoint with an x-coordinate that is less than or equal to the function input value. For equally spaced breakpoints, the lower breakpoint index is computed as shown in Eq. 9.1. Here, the *floor* operator returns the largest integer less than or equal to its argument.

$$L = \text{floor}\left(\frac{x_{\text{in}} - x(0)}{\Delta x}\right) \qquad \text{Eq. 9.1}$$

In Eq. 9.1, L is the index of the lower of the two breakpoints that surround the input value x_{in}, $x(0)$ is the x-coordinate of the first breakpoint in the array, and Δx is the x-interval between breakpoints. On the basis of the range limits placed on x_{in} in step 1, L will be in the range $0 \le L \le N - 1$.

3. Perform linear interpolation between the breakpoints with indices L and $L + 1$ as shown in Eq. 9.2. A special case occurs when $L = N - 1$, which is when x_{in} is located at the last breakpoint in the array and the correct interpolation result is $y = y(N - 1)$. When this happens, $y(L + 1)$ is undefined, although it ends up being multiplied by zero. It is important to handle this case properly to avoid potential memory access faults and floating-point exceptions.

$$y = y(L) + [y(L+1) - y(L)]\frac{x_{\text{in}} - x(L)}{\Delta x} \qquad \text{Eq. 9.2}$$

One-dimensional linear interpolation with equally spaced breakpoints is the simplest form of interpolation to implement. More complex variations involving smoother interpolating functions, unequally spaced breakpoints, and additional table dimensions are discussed in Ledin (2001) [1].

9.5 Controller Implementation in Embedded Systems

Figure 9.3 shows an approach for implementing a C or C++ discrete-time linear system developed with the techniques of Chapter 8 as a real-time controller. In this figure, n represents the time step number starting from 0, and h is the sampling interval of the discrete-time system, usually given in seconds.

The flow diagram in Figure 9.3 assumes that the real-time processor provides the following capabilities.

- A real-time clock enabling execution of the update loop at integer multiples of the sampling interval h.
- Input devices for reading the plant sensors.
- Output devices that enable the controller to drive the plant actuators.
- Sufficient execution speed so that the processing for each pass through the loop always takes less time than the step time h.

Figure 9.3 Embedded control system execution flow.

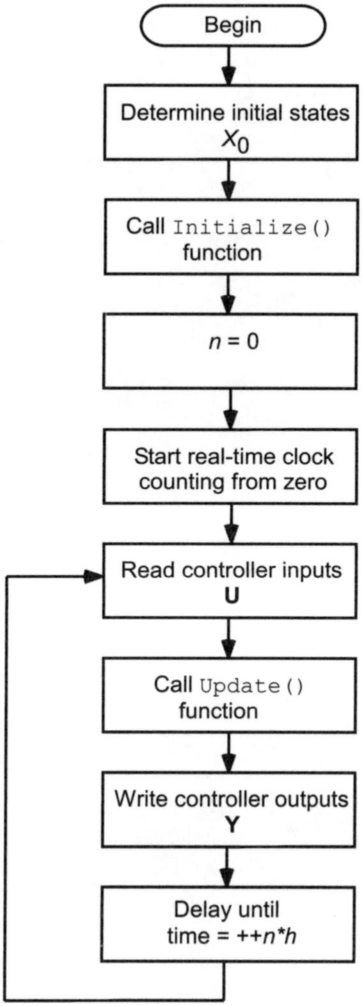

For best performance, the time between reading the controller inputs and writing the outputs should be small relative to *h*. In the mathematical analysis of discrete-time systems, the time between the input and output steps is often assumed to be zero. For example, when displaying the frequency response of a discrete-time system in MATLAB, zero processing time is assumed. The frequency response of the implemented system will deviate from the ideal response when the execution time is nonzero. This deviation is usually small if the execution time is small relative to *h*.

Even if the execution time consumes a large fraction of *h*, the difference in the frequency response will still be small if the sampling rate is sufficiently high compared to the bandwidth of the system. The only situation in which the execution delay might cause a problem is when the sampling rate is low relative to the system bandwidth and the processing time between input and output consumes a significant portion of the sampling interval. In this situation, it might be necessary to make another controller design iteration that accounts for the processing delay with the technique described in the following section.

9.5.1 The Padé Approximation

You can add a time delay to your linear plant model that represents the expected processing time with a Padé approximation. A Padé approximation is a continuous-time linear system with a response approximating that of a pure time delay. The MATLAB Control System Toolbox provides the command `pade()`, which requires two input parameters: the time delay (normally in units of seconds) and the desired model order. The `pade()` command returns continuous-time transfer function numerator and denominator polynomial coefficients implementing the time delay approximation.

When using the Padé approximation, you must select an appropriate order for the time delay transfer function. Larger orders produce more accurate representations of the time delay. However, a larger order for the time delay approximation also results in a higher order controller. To keep the controller order to a minimum, the order of the Padé approximation should usually be kept to a small value such as 2. This reduces the accuracy of the approximation, but avoids significant increases in the controller complexity that would lead to greater controller memory usage and execution time.

Appending the Padé approximation to the linear plant model takes the controller processing time into account when applying control system design methods such as pole placement and LQR design. The following steps demonstrate the addition of a 5-millisecond processing delay to a linear plant model named sys.

```
>> sys = ss(tf(1, [1 2 1]));
>> delay = 0.005;
>> order = 2;
>> [num, den] = pade(delay, order);
>> sys_delayed = sys * ss(tf(num, den));
>> bode(sys, sys_delayed, logspace(-2,2));
>> legend('Original', 'Delayed')
```

Figure 9.4 Effects of a 5-millisecond Padé delay approximation.

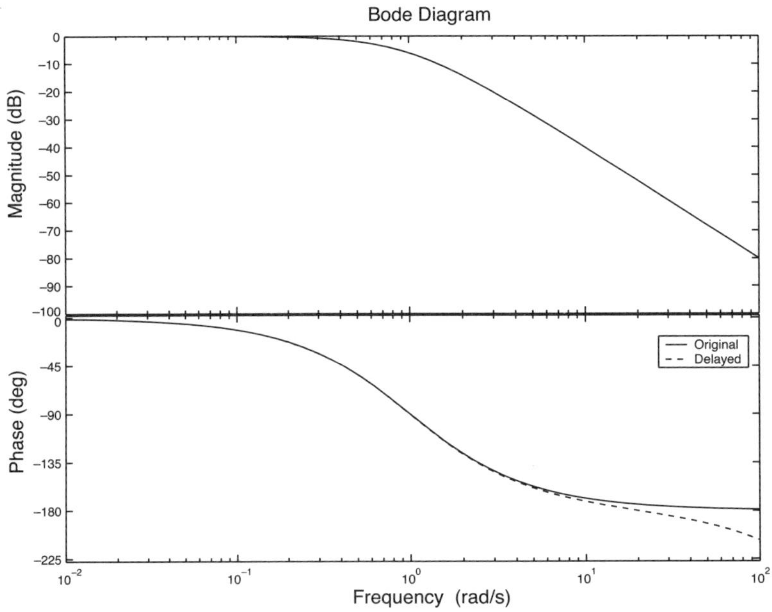

Figure 9.4 shows Bode plots of the original and delayed systems, which indicate that the magnitude response is essentially unchanged by the inclusion of the Padé approximation. However, the phase of the delayed system lags that of the original system by greater amounts at higher frequencies. This is indicative of a time delay, which is the effect you are trying to achieve. In this example, appending the second-order Padé approximation

to the original second-order system results in a fourth-order system. In general, the order of the plant model will increase by the order you choose for the Padé approximation.

If you add a time delay to your plant model, you must repeat the steps of designing the controller and observer for the modified plant model. Because the resulting controller will be a higher order system, its execution time might increase to the point that you need to adjust the time delay and perform a further design iteration.

9.5.2 Controller Initial Conditions

The first block at the top of Figure 9.3 might require some effort to implement. The initial states provided to the controller should be as accurate as possible to minimize startup transients. If measurements of the states are available, the problem is trivial. However, for states that are not measured, it is necessary to develop an initial estimate. If there is no information available to estimate a state's value, a reasonable default (say, zero) can be used. Errors in the initial estimates will lead to transients in the controller response as the observer converges to a more accurate state estimate.

9.5.3 Multitasking Operating Systems

Figure 9.3 represents a simplified control system that does not include other aspects of typical embedded systems such as an operator interface. Figure 9.3 also assumes controller operation takes place inside a loop that never exits. This is not a good design for all operating environments. For example, with a multitasking operating system that must perform other functions, such as providing an operator interface, the operations contained in the loop of Figure 9.3 should instead be placed inside a task that executes at the sampling interval h.

In a multitasking environment, many threads of execution can share processor time. In this situation, the processing should be separated into initialization and `Update()` functions, as shown in Figures 9.5 and 9.6.

The initialization function of Figure 9.5 sets up the initial controller states and schedules the update task for execution at regular intervals equal to the discrete-time system sampling interval h. Each time the update function of Figure 9.6 executes, it reads the inputs from the sensors, updates the discrete-time model, and writes the outputs to the actuators. The update function then returns, which stops its execution until the next time its task is scheduled.

This approach makes very efficient use of processing resources. Because the controller only consumes processing cycles when work needs to be done, enough free processor time could be available to perform a substantial amount of processing in addition to controlling the plant. Alternatively, in a situation where processor power usage must be minimized, the processor could go into a sleep mode following each execution of the `Update()` function and wait for the scheduling of the next update.

Figure 9.5 Initialization function for a controller in a multitasking environment.

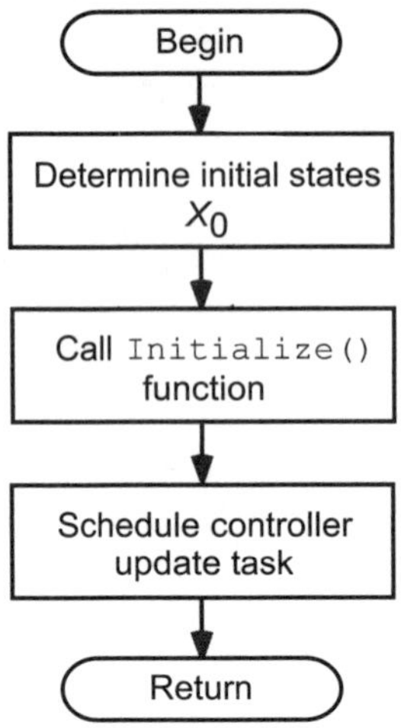

Figure 9.6 Update function for a controller in a multitasking environment.

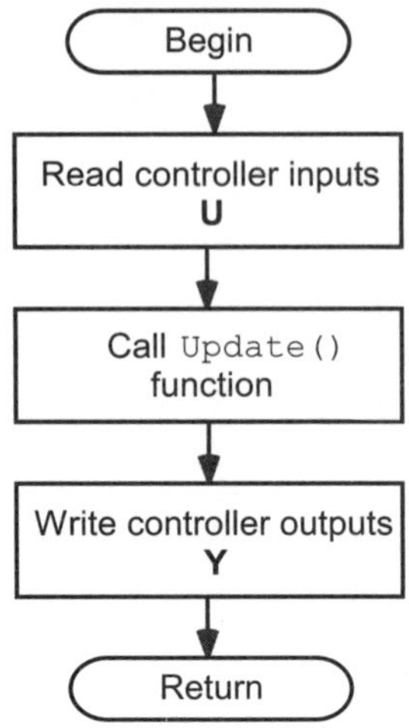

9.6 Control System Test Techniques

After the control system implementation has been completed and initial checkout of the system indicates correct operation, it is time to perform thorough system testing. This testing phase must exercise all controller modes throughout the system's entire operating envelope. The test process must ensure that the system and its embedded controller operate properly under nominal conditions, as well as in extreme situations.

I discuss two basic approaches for performing system testing in this section: system simulation and operational tests of the actual system. These are complementary techniques that enable different types of testing to be performed. By effectively combining simulation and system testing, it is possible to thoroughly test a complex embedded control system under a complete range of operating conditions while keeping testing costs to a minimum.

9.6.1 System Simulation

System simulation [1] is focused at the level of the entire system as it operates in its intended environment. This type of simulation permits testing of the system in its intended operational modes as well as under dangerous emergency conditions without risking loss of life or valuable assets. Environmental conditions that could be difficult or impossible to access for system tests (such as icy roads in the middle of summer or the conditions of outer space) can be simulated by computers running appropriate software algorithms. With simulation, intricate test sequences can be executed quickly and repeatably at comparatively low cost.

A system simulation is a software program developed with a simulation package like Simulink or in a programming language such as C++. The simulation contains mathematical models of the system components and their interactions with the environment. These models must possess sufficient fidelity to enable the execution of realistic tests.

Simulation development often starts early in the project life cycle with fairly simple models of the system components and the environment. As the project continues, the data from tests of hardware components and complete system prototypes enables the refinement of the simulation models to more accurately represent the real system.

The software-only simulation described above can form the basis for a hardware-in-the-loop (HIL) simulation. Prototype hardware and software can be tested in a HIL simulation long before a testable system prototype becomes available. HIL simulations run at real-time speeds and perform I/O operations with the system or subsystem under test so that the test item "thinks" it is operating as part of a real system in its operational environment. This enables the system or subsystem to be tested under simulated nominal conditions as well as at (and beyond) its intended operational boundaries.

HIL simulation provides the ability to thoroughly test subsystems early in the development process. This can greatly reduce the debugging time and project risk compared to the alternative approach of waiting until prototype hardware is available before performing system integration and testing.

Simulation verification and validation must be addressed carefully to gain the full range of potential benefits from a simulation effort. Verification is the process used to demonstrate that a simulation has been implemented according to its specifications. The validation process demonstrates that the simulation is a sufficiently good representation of the actual system it attempts to simulate. The primary goal of the verification and validation processes is to provide sufficient convincing evidence of the correctness of the simulation so that even skeptical observers will agree that it is credible and sufficiently accurate for its intended purposes.

Simulation will never completely replace tests of the actual system. However, in many cases, the thoughtful application of simulation techniques to an embedded control system development process can increase the overall test coverage while significantly reducing the test time required and the cost of the test program.

9.6.2 Operational Testing

Operational testing places the actual system into its intended operating environment for test execution. In this type of testing, you set up test scenarios that represent real-world situations the embedded system might encounter. You then observe the system's response to the situation, recording the data necessary to provide a complete picture of the system's behavior, as well as relevant attributes of the environment. Analysis of the test results leads to conclusions about whether the system performed properly and what type of performance improvements might be necessary.

Example 9.1 Testing an autonomous ground vehicle.

Suppose you are developing a small autonomous ground vehicle. This vehicle must be able to navigate over difficult terrain using a set of sensors to identify a path and with steering and drive systems to move along the chosen path. How would you go about setting up a set of operational tests for this vehicle?

First, you should identify the scope of the testing to be performed. In this case, the scope might be limited to having the vehicle travel between selected starting and ending points across various types of terrain. The types of terrain to be used for the testing must be identified carefully. External influences on the terrain, such as the presence of rain, must be understood and addressed.

A set of tests must be developed to exercise the system across its range of capability. Some of the dimensions explored in the testing might include

- terrain difficulty, from smooth and level to steep and rocky;
- time of day and corresponding light conditions;
- weather conditions: hot, cold, windy, rainy, foggy, etc.; and
- degraded modes of system operation (e.g., you might disable a sensor or actuator and observe how the system compensates).

As is clear from this short list, it is not a trivial job to set up and execute a comprehensive series of operational tests. Testing this system could involve long periods of waiting for the weather to cooperate. Alternatively, it might be necessary to use a water truck to provide a simulated rainstorm, for example.

Although operational testing is unquestionably a highly realistic way of testing the system, the method does present some problems. For one thing, operational testing can take a long time and cost a lot of money. Commercial airliners receive airworthiness certification after passing a rigorous series of flight tests. These tests often take over a year to complete. Great patience and deep pockets are required to conduct an operational test series of this magnitude. It makes sense to replace operational tests with quicker and lower cost forms of testing such as simulation whenever appropriate.

Another problem with operational testing is that it can be difficult to perform the tests repeatably. In a flight test, for example, the wind conditions and air temperature are factors that cannot be duplicated from one day to the next. When performing a regression test in an operational environment, it might be difficult to determine whether deviations from previously observed behavior are a result of system problems or differences in test conditions.

A combination of operational testing and simulation testing can help alleviate both of these problems. The operational tests should be designed to provide the maximum possible amount of data for use in validating the simulation under a variety of operating conditions. After the system simulation has been developed and validated, test runs can be performed with the simulation quickly and at low cost. This can eliminate the need for some operational tests, though not all of them. A number of real-world tests will always be required to validate the simulation.

9.7 Summary

In this chapter, I discussed the final steps in the embedded control system development process. Beginning with a linear controller design developed with the methods shown in previous chapters, it is often necessary to add nonlinear features such as limiting and gain scheduling. These elements compensate for nonlinearities within the plant and variations in the operational environment. It might also be necessary to modify the linear plant model by including a Padé time delay approximation if the control algorithm execution time is a significant portion of the sampling interval h.

Following the completion of the controller design, it is necessary to implement the design within the constraints of the embedded system software environment. The software environment can consist of anything from no operating system at all to a sophisticated multitasking real-time operating system.

With no operating system and no requirement to perform additional tasks other than the controller function, the simplest control system implementation is to initialize the controller and then execute a loop at timed intervals, as shown in Figure 9.3. On each pass through the loop, the processor reads the controller inputs from the sensors, executes the controller algorithm, and writes the outputs to the plant actuators.

When using a multitasking operating system, the controller software should be separated into an initialization function and an update function. The initialization function sets up the controller state and schedules the update function for execution at the sampling rate. On each execution, the update function reads the sensor inputs, computes the controller algorithm, and writes the actuator outputs.

When the implementation of the embedded controller has been completed, it is necessary to perform thorough testing to ensure correct operation of the system under all conditions. Two fundamental types of system testing were described in this chapter: system simulation and operational testing.

System simulation testing exercises a software model of the embedded system under simulated test conditions. To produce meaningful results, the simulation must have undergone a process of verification and validation. Verification demonstrates that a simulation has been implemented according to its specifications. Validation shows that the simulation is a sufficiently good representation of the real-world system it attempts to simulate. Given a valid simulation, thorough system testing can be performed quickly and inexpensively. Simulation also allows the testing of dangerous conditions in which the actual system would never intentionally be placed.

Operational testing exercises the actual system in its intended operating environment. This is the most realistic type of testing available. Sufficient data must be recorded during each test to understand the significant aspects of the system's behavior and its interaction with the surrounding environment. However, operational testing can be a slow and expensive way to collect test data. It can also be difficult to perform tests repeatably when operating in the uncontrolled environment of the real world.

For many development projects, the most cost-effective approach for system testing is to combine simulation testing with operational testing. One of the primary goals of the operational tests should be to provide data for simulation validation. With a validated simulation, additional testing can be performed much faster than equivalent operational tests and at comparatively low cost.

9.8 Self-Test

1. Develop a skeleton C++ program that implements the algorithm shown in the flowchart of Figure 9.3. In this initial version, just use comments to indicate where the Initialize, Update, I/O, and real-time clock–related operations would take place.
2. Integrate the C++ fixed-point controller code developed in Chapter 8 self-test problem 5 into the code from problem 1 above. This code provides the implementations of the Initialize and Update blocks in Figure 9.3. Note that the sampling interval for this system is 10 milliseconds.
3. Implement a MATLAB model of the inverted pendulum as shown in Chapter 7 self-test problem 1. Modify the model's **C** matrix so that its output is $\mathbf{y} = [\theta \; x]^T$, then augment the model to pass its input as an additional output at the end of the output vector. The resulting output vector should be $\mathbf{y} = [\theta \; x \; F]^T$. Execute `write_cpp_model()` to convert the model to C++ with a first-order hold and a 10-millisecond step time.
4. (a) Integrate the pendulum model with the results of problem 2 via the I/O blocks in the flow diagram of Figure 9.3. Use the system configuration shown in Figure 5.1. Set all controller and plant initial conditions to zero. Set up the program to run for 71 time steps (0.7 seconds).

   (b) Set up the commanded cart position x as the reference input. Include the feedforward gain value computed in Chapter 7 self-test problem 10. Use the constant value of 1 meter as the commanded cart position.

   (c) Add a data logging capability to the simulation. At each controller update, record the time, the cart position x, the pendulum angle θ, and the cart force F. Write this data to a text-format file with each update on one line and spaces separating the values. Don't write a header line or anything else to the file. This format can be read directly into MATLAB.
5. You now have a complete simulation of the plant and controller. Execute the simulation to produce the output file. Load the output file into MATLAB and plot each of the signals. Compare this plot to Figure 7.12. Explain any differences.
6. The simulation developed in the previous problems used a simplified linear model of the cart and the pendulum. Describe some limitations of this simulation and how you could make the simulation more realistic and useful for testing controller performance.

7. Assume you have a prototype cart and inverted pendulum system and a complete implementation of a control system for it. Describe a set of operational tests that will assess the performance of this system under a variety of operational conditions. Indicate how you could use the results of these tests for validating the simulation.

9.9 Answers

1. The following skeleton program implements the structure of Figure 9.1.

```
void main()
{
    // Determine initial states

    // Call the controller's Initialize function

    int n = 0; // Update counter

    // Start the real-time clock counting from zero

    for (;;)
    {
        // Read the controller inputs U

        // Call the controller's Update function

        // Write the controller outputs Y

        ++n;
        // Delay until time = n * h
    }
}
```

2. This program adds the inverted pendulum fixed-point controller class to the program and calls its `Initialize()` and `Update()` member functions.

```
#include "pend_dsys_fixpt.cpp"

void main()
{
    // Determine initial states
```

```
    short x0[4] = {0, 0, 0, 0};

    // Call the controller's Initialize function
    dsys_fixpt controller;
    controller.Initialize(x0);

    int n = 0; // Update counter
    double h = 0.01; // Sampling interval, seconds

    // Start the real-time clock counting from zero

    for (;;)
    {
        // Read the controller inputs U
        short u[3];

        // Call the controller's Update function
        controller.Update(u);

        // Write the controller outputs Y

        ++n;
        // Delay until time = n * h
    }
}
```

3. The following sequence of steps creates the inverted pendulum model and writes it to a C++ file named `pend_model.cpp`.

```
>> a = [0 0 1 0; 0 0 0 1; 90.55 0 0 0; -2.26 0 0 0];
>> b = [0; 0; -23.08; 3.08];
>> c = [1 0 0 0; 0 1 0 0];
>> d = 0;
>> ssplant_aug = ss(a, b, [c; zeros(1, 4)], [d; 1]);
>> h = 0.01;
>> pend_model = c2d(ssplant_aug, h, 'foh');
>> write_cpp_model(pend_model, 'pend_model.cpp');
```

4. The following C++ program combines the results of problem 4a through 4c.

```
#include "pend_dsys_fixpt.cpp"
#include "pend_model.cpp"

#include <cstdio>
#include <cassert>

void main()
{
    // Declare the plant and controller objects
    dsys_fixpt controller;
    pend_model plant;

    // Specify the initial states
    short controller_x0[4] = {0, 0, 0, 0};
    double plant_x0[4] = {0, 0, 0, 0};

    // Call the plant and controller intialization functions
    controller.Initialize(controller_x0);
    plant.Initialize(plant_x0);

    // Set up for the dynamic loop
    const short *controller_output = controller.Output();
    const double *plant_output = plant.Output();

    int n = 0;                // Loop counter
    double h = 0.01;          // Sampling interval, seconds
    const double r = 0.9;     // Reference input
    const double N = -223.6; // Feedforward gain
    const double short_max = 32768;

    const double us[dsys_fixpt::r] = {4, 2, 1000};
    const double ys[dsys_fixpt::m] = {1000};

    // Start the real-time clock counting from zero

    // Open the data logging output file
```

```
    FILE *iov = fopen("pend.txt", "w");
    assert(iov);

    while (n < 71)
    {
        // Set up the controller inputs U
        short controller_u[3];
        for (int i=0; i<dsys_fixpt::r; i++)
            controller_u[i] = short(short_max * plant_output[i] /
                                    us[i]);

        // Call the controller's Update function
        controller.Update(controller_u);

        // Combine the controller output and the reference input
        double pend_u = (ys[0]*controller_output[0])/
                                short_max + r*N;

        // Call the plant's Update function
        plant.Update(&pend_u);

        // Log the current plant and controller outputs
        fprintf(iov, "%lf %lf %lf %lf\n", n*h,
                plant_output[0], plant_output[1], plant_output[2]);

        ++n;
        // Delay until time = n * h
    }

    fclose(iov);
}
```

5. The following MATLAB script reads the file created by the C++ program shown above and plots the controller and plant outputs with the `plot()` command.

```
>> clear all
>> close all
>> load pend.txt
>> t     = pend(:, 1);
>> theta = pend(:, 2);
>> x     = pend(:, 3);
>> F     = pend(:, 4);
>> subplot(311), plot(t, theta), legend('theta')
>> subplot(312), plot(t, x), legend('x')
>> subplot(313), plot(t, F), legend('F')
```

The plot created by the above sequence of commands is shown in Figure 9.7. One difference from Figure 7.12 is that the x state does not converge to precisely 1 because of quantization.

Figure 9.7 Plot of controller and plant outputs.

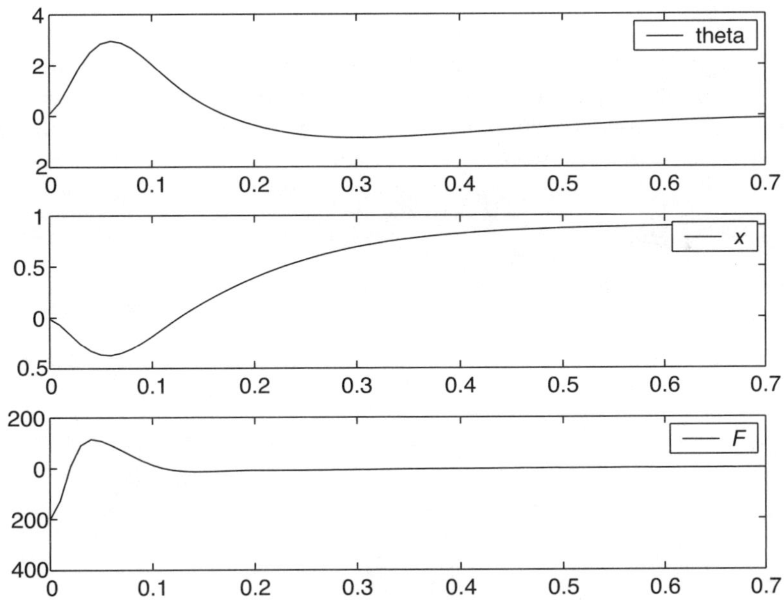

6. This plant model is a linear approximation of a nonlinear system. For pendulum angles more than about 5° from the vertical, this assumption becomes less and less reasonable. The angles reached in Figure 9.6 are far outside this limit. A better approach for testing this controller in a simulated environment would be to replace the linear plant model with a nonlinear model that accurately represents the dynamic behavior of the plant for both small and large pendulum angles. Other relevant aspects of the system also should be modeled in the simulation, such as sensor and actuator noise, drive motor dynamics, and friction in the drive system. System simulations commonly grow in complexity with the addition of more realistic models as the system design matures and validation test data becomes available.
7. The following list of tests might be appropriate for a system of this type.
   - Step commands into the reference input.
   - Sine wave commands at various frequencies into the reference input.
   - Pseudorandom noise passed through a lowpass filter with a suitable cutoff frequency into the reference input.
   - Parameter variations: increase and decrease the cart and pendulum masses, increase the drive system friction, and alter the motor power supply voltage to test controller performance in the presence of plant variations. These variations should be representative of the parameter ranges the actual system is expected to experience.

   To perform simulation validation, set up and execute simulation tests that duplicate the test scenarios described above. Compare the results of the simulation tests to the results of the operational tests. Identify cases where the differences between the results are caused by significant limitations of the simulation. Improve the simulation models to more accurately represent the behavior of the actual system.

9.10 References

1. Ledin, Jim, *Simulation Engineering* (Lawrence, KS: CMP Books, 2001).

CHAPTER 10

WRAP-UP AND DESIGN EXAMPLE

10.1 Introduction

In this chapter, I wrap up the discussion of control system design methods I covered in earlier chapters and provide a more comprehensive design example than the simpler examples given previously.

I will examine each of the control system design methods in terms of its benefits and its drawbacks. The objective here is to provide the designer with some insight as to how to select a suitable design approach for a given control system problem.

The design example I present in this chapter demonstrates how to break a complex control problem into a collection of simpler problems and then combine the resulting controllers into a complete control system. I develop a complete control system for a simplified helicopter that consists of a rigid body, a two-blade main rotor, and a two-blade tail rotor. The main rotor is the primary actuator for this system. By varying the blade's angle of attack as it rotates, it is possible to generate lifting force, a moment in the helicopter's front–back plane (pitching moment), and a moment in the side-to-side plane (rolling moment). The remaining actuator is the tail rotor, which generates a variable sideways force on the tail of the helicopter.

The helicopter control system must be able to control the roll, pitch, and yaw angular motion of the helicopter and must be able to fly the helicopter to a specified point in three-dimensional space. The helicopter moves forward or sideways by tilting the plane of the main rotor in the desired direction so that some of the rotor's lift force becomes a thrust in the horizontal direction. This results in a fairly complex control system design problem.

In this chapter, I develop a simulation of the helicopter's dynamic behavior and use that simulation as the basis for the control system design. I integrate the resulting controller with the helicopter simulation and examine the performance of the resulting system.

Emphasis is placed on the iterative nature of control system design. At the completion of this example, I examine some limitations of the resulting control system that might be addressed in a subsequent design iteration. In a real design project, the plant simulation would likely become more complex and realistic as new information becomes available about the behavior of the subsystems and their interactions with the external environment. As the simulation improves, problems with the existing control system design that require further design iterations could become apparent.

Operational testing of a system prototype is also likely to highlight areas in which the control system needs improvement. The first design iteration usually results in a controller that works to some degree but often has problems in some aspects of its performance. Tests of the resulting design are likely to point out areas in which controller improvement is needed, which leads to further design work and a new controller implementation. The cycle of design, implementation, and testing must be repeated until the controller's performance is judged to be satisfactory in all respects.

10.2 Chapter Objectives

After reading this chapter, you should be able to

- identify the strengths and weaknesses of the control system design techniques discussed in the earlier chapters of this book,
- break a complex control system design problem into a set of simpler subproblems,
- select and apply appropriate control system design techniques for each component of the controller design,
- combine the resulting control system components into a complete control system,
- test the resulting design to identify areas of inadequate performance, and
- perform additional design iterations to improve performance inadequacies while maintaining the satisfactory aspects of the existing design.

10.3 Control System Design Approaches

In this section, I list the control system design approaches covered in this book and identify the benefits and drawbacks of each. This list is intended to provide a summary to help you select an appropriate design method to use in a given situation.

10.3.1 PID Control (Chapter 2)

The actuator command developed by a PID controller is a weighted sum of the error signal and its integral and derivative. This type of controller is suitable for use with SISO plants.

Benefits This controller design is easy to get started with because it does not require a linear plant model. In cases where actuator saturation can occur, integrator windup reduction can be used to reduce overshoot and improve convergence to the reference command.

Disadvantages The PID gains must be selected through an iterative, experimental tuning procedure. Because this is a simple controller with only three adjustable parameters, it might not be possible to control complex plants in a satisfactory manner. This controller is not appropriate for MIMO plants.

10.3.2 Root Locus Design (Chapter 4)

In the root locus method, the designer creates a graph showing all possible values of the system transfer function poles as a design parameter (typically the controller gain) varies over a specified range. By selecting a gain value that places the poles within a particular region of the complex plane defined by damping ratio and settling time constraints, it is possible to determine the dynamic behavior of the controlled system. This design method is suitable for SISO plants.

Benefits When using the MATLAB Control System Toolbox (or similar control system design software), you can easily plot a root locus diagram and select an appropriate controller gain. When designing compensators, you can move the compensator poles and zeros and immediately observe the effects on the root locus. Pole cancellation can remove the effects of poles at undesirable locations and replace them with more suitably located poles.

Disadvantages A linear plant model is required. The resulting design is not likely to be optimal in any sense. If a simple gain variation does not result in a satisfactory controller design, some experimentation might be required with lead or lag compensators. This technique is not appropriate for MIMO plants.

10.3.3 Bode Design (Chapter 4)

Bode design is based on the use of open-loop frequency response plots of the plant plus controller. Gain margin and phase margin can be determined from these plots. Phase margin is approximately proportional to the damping ratio of the closed-loop system. Phase margin is most commonly used as a specification and performance metric for control system design. This design method is suitable for SISO systems.

Benefits A linear plant model is not necessary for this technique — the open-loop frequency response plots can be generated experimentally. Note, however, that this approach in MATLAB requires a linear model of the plant and controller. This technique can be applied to systems with complex and poorly understood dynamics, assuming experimentally determined open-loop frequency response plots are available.

Disadvantages The resulting design is not likely to be optimal in any sense. If a simple gain variation does not result in a satisfactory controller design, experimentation might be required with lead or lag compensators. This technique is not appropriate for MIMO systems.

10.3.4 Pole Placement (Chapter 5)

The pole placement design approach allows the closed-loop system poles to be located at arbitrarily selected points in the complex plane. Given an appropriate set of pole locations, the closed-loop system can exhibit any dynamic behavior desired, provided the plant and actuators are capable of producing an approximately linear response and the plant is observable and controllable. This technique is suitable for MIMO systems.

Benefits Any desired closed-loop response can be achieved, provided the plant and actuators are able to maintain approximately linear response. Given a linear model and the desired closed-loop pole locations, the controller design is developed without the need for iteration. The controller output is a simple linear combination of the state vector elements. This method supports MIMO systems.

Disadvantages This method does not take into account the control effort required to produce the desired response. If the system state is not completely measured, it is necessary to develop an observer to estimate the states for use with the control law. It is necessary to somehow select a set of closed-loop pole locations, which is unlikely to be an optimal set for the given application. Additional effort is required to implement integral control, if it is required.

10.3.5 Optimal Control (Chapter 6)

The optimal control design technique produces the best, or optimal, controller design for a given plant model and associated weighting criteria. In this approach, "best" is defined as a weighted trade-off between speed of system response and actuator effort. The optimal observer is the Kalman filter, which minimizes the mean-squared error in the state estimate. Optimal design techniques are widely used in applications where incremental improvements in control system performance can provide substantial benefits.

Benefits The resulting controller is optimal given the weighted trade-off between speed of response and actuator effort. Similarly, the Kalman filter observer is the optimal observer for estimating the state on the basis of noisy measurements. The control law and observer implementations are identical to those of pole placement, differing only in the method used to determine the gains. This method supports MIMO systems.

Disadvantages The optimality criteria for the controller and observer rely on the assumption of linearity, which might not be valid in the real-world plant. Iteration is usually necessary to develop appropriate controller design weighting matrices, the observer process noise model, and the process and measurement noise covariance matrices. Developing a suitable process noise model can be a difficult task.

10.4 Helicopter System

In earlier chapters, I discussed and demonstrated several different control system design methods with relatively simple example plants. The final example given below will be much more ambitious. In the remainder of this chapter, I develop a control system that stabilizes a helicopter and flies it from its starting position to a desired location in three-dimensional space.

The principal steps in this process will be to

- develop a nonlinear simulation of the helicopter,
- extract linear models of the relevant aspects of the helicopter's behavior from the simulation,
- design a control system that produces satisfactory system performance,
- implement the control system with the nonlinear helicopter simulation, and
- test the resulting control system in conjunction with the nonlinear plant model.

This basic approach is commonly used in real-world design applications for systems such as aircraft and spacecraft, in which control system design must proceed before a system prototype exists.

10.5 Helicopter Model

The helicopter model used in this example is highly simplified yet still contains enough realism to present a challenging design problem. Figure 10.1 is a diagram of the helicopter plant.

Figure 10.1 Helicopter configuration.

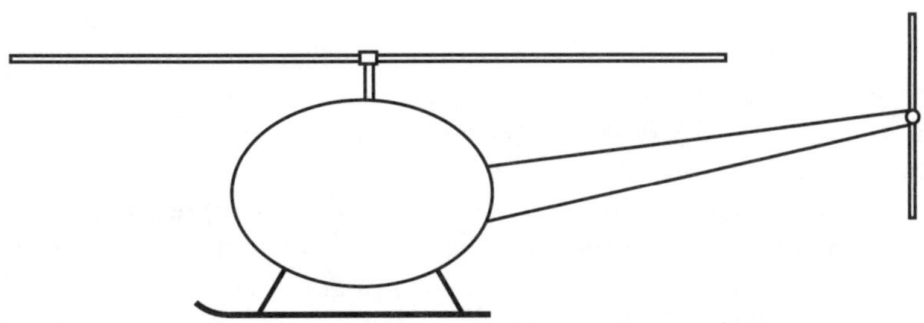

The helicopter configuration is typical of a small manned unit. The main rotor is located above the main cabin area and rotates in an approximately horizontal plane.

The tail rotor is mounted on a boom that extends to the rear and rotates in a vertical plane, with its axis of rotation aligned in the left–right direction.

I will model the helicopter as three rigid components: a two-blade main rotor, a tail rotor, and the helicopter body. The rotors are assumed to rotate at constant angular velocities. The standard helicopter control actuators will be used and are described in the "Helicopter Actuators" box.

Helicopter Actuators

Main rotor collective This actuator adjusts the angle of attack of both main rotor blades by the same amount. It controls the amount of lift generated by the main rotor.

Main rotor front–back cyclic This actuator adjusts the angle of attack of the blades in opposing directions but does so primarily during the portion of the blade rotation when it is in the front–back direction. This control has the effect of producing a moment that pitches the helicopter's nose up or down.

Main rotor left–right cyclic This actuator adjusts the angle of attack of the blades in opposing directions but does so primarily during the portion of the blade rotation when it is in the left–right direction. This control has the effect of producing a moment that rolls the helicopter to the left or to the right.

Tail rotor collective This actuator adjusts the angle of attack of the tail rotor blades by the same amount. It controls the side force generated by the tail rotor, which allows control of the yaw orientation of the helicopter.

I do not make any attempt to model the complexity and subtleties of the helicopter's aerodynamics. That's a topic that requires its own book. Instead, I assume that the forces and moments generated by each of the helicopter's control actuators is proportional to the control input. This first-order approximation is reasonably valid for control inputs that are not too aggressive. Aerodynamic modeling is limited to including the effects of drag, which limits the speed of the helicopter through the atmosphere.

I assume the helicopter possesses a navigation system that keeps track of the vehicle's position, velocity, body rotation rates, and angular orientation without error. In reality, such error-free navigation systems do not exist. However, the availability of small Global Positioning System (GPS) receivers and inertial sensors (gyros and accelerometers) means that the assumption of negligible navigation errors is not as unrealistic as it would have been a few years ago. I will not model the navigation system's behavior; instead, I will directly use the helicopter's position, velocity, and angular orientation from the simulation as inputs to the control system.

Figure 10.2 shows the top-level Simulink diagram representing the helicopter plant model. The plant inputs are the forces and torques generated by the four control actuators, all of which are scalar values. The outputs are the helicopter's position, velocity, angular rotation rate, and Euler angles (roll, pitch, yaw). All of the outputs are in the form of three-element vectors.

Figure 10.2 Top-level helicopter plant model.

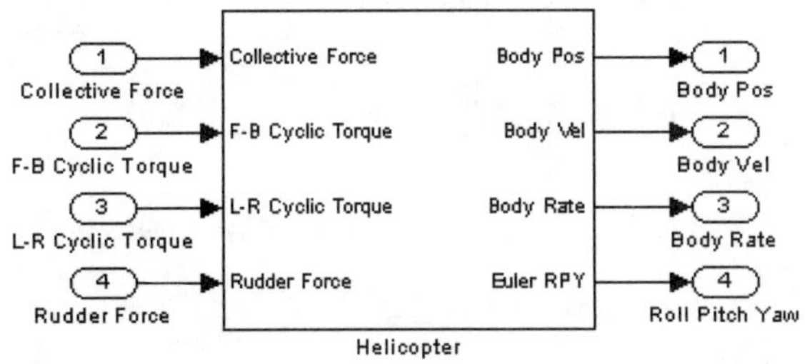

Figure 10.3 shows the contents of the `Helicopter` block of Figure 10.2. In this figure, the blocks with small squares or circles at the points where lines connect to them model the physical components of the helicopter and the mechanical joints between them. These blocks are from the SimMechanics library. SimMechanics is an add-on to Simulink that provides a capability for modeling systems composed of collections of moving rigid bodies interconnected with various types of mechanical joints. In this example, SimMechanics takes care of modeling the helicopter's equations of motion, including the effects of rotor dynamics.

The primary blocks in Figure 10.3 are described below.

- The `Ground` and `Six-DoF` blocks represent the fixed Earth coordinate system and its relation to the freely moving helicopter body. To keep things simple, the Earth is assumed to be flat and nonrotating.
- The `Helicopter Body`, `Main Rotor`, and `Tail Rotor` blocks represent the three rigid bodies that constitute the helicopter physical model.
- The `Main Hub` and `Tail Hub` blocks model the joints connecting the two rotors to the helicopter body. Each joint has one axis of rotational freedom aligned in the appropriate direction.
- The `Main Rotor Drive` and `Tail Rotor Drive` blocks contain subsystems (lower level Simulink diagrams) that drive both rotors at constant angular rates.
- The `Trim`, `Main Rotor Actuator`, and `Tail Rotor Actuator` blocks allow forces and moments to be applied to the helicopter body, main rotor, and tail rotor, respectively.
- The `Aero Drag` subsystem applies a force proportional to the square of the helicopter's speed in the negative velocity direction that simulates aerodynamic drag.
- The `Joint Sensor` and `Body Sensor` blocks enable measurement of the main rotor's angular orientation about its rotational axis and the body's position, velocity, angular rotation rate, and Euler angles.
- The `Collective Force` and `Rudder Force` inputs represent the lift force generated by the main rotor and the side force produced by the tail rotor, respectively.

Figure 10.3 Detailed helicopter plant model.

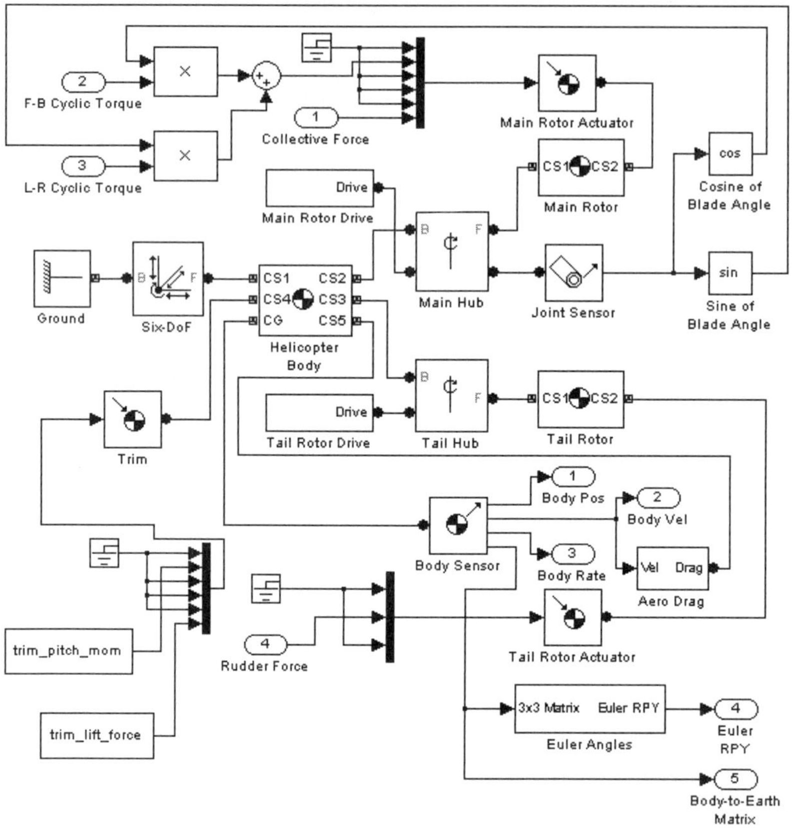

- The Sine of Blade Angle and Cosine of Blade Angle blocks compute the sine and cosine of the main rotor's angular position about its rotational axis. The resulting values multiply the L-R Cyclic Torque and F-B Cyclic Torque inputs, respectively. These computations model the moment produced by the variation of the blade's angle of attack resulting from cyclic control inputs.
- The trim_pitch_mom and trim_lift_force blocks represent constant values of pitching moment and lift force applied to the body to attain a trimmed configuration for the hovering helicopter. When trimmed, the main rotor axis is oriented vertically and there is no net translational or angular acceleration on the helicopter.

The mass properties selected for the helicopter body, main rotor, and tail rotor are representative of a model helicopter. To simplify the determination of the mass properties of the three components, each is approximated as a cylinder in terms of mass, length, and radius. A shorter, thick cylinder represents the helicopter body/tail boom assembly, and the blades are modeled as relatively long, thin cylinders.

The rotational velocities of the main and tail rotors are representative of the rotor speeds of a model helicopter. The simulated drive mechanism forces the blades to rotate at a constant angular velocity. This is a simplification; a more realistic blade speed model would account for the torques produced by blade aerodynamic loads and model the response of the engine and drive train to those loads and to variations in the throttle setting.

In operation, this plant model must execute with a step time short enough that several samples are taken for each rotation of the main rotor blade. This is because (assuming a fixed, nonzero cyclic control input) the moment produced by the main rotor varies sinusoidally during each rotation of the main rotor. A step time of 1.0 millisecond is sufficient for modeling the moment variations resulting from the collective control.

This description only covers the highlights of the helicopter model. To gain additional insight, examine the model contained in `Helicopter.mdl` in the `Examples\Ch10` directory of the accompanying CD-ROM. You will need MATLAB, Simulink, and SimMechanics to examine and execute this model. Remember, you can get a free 30-day trial license for these products from The MathWorks (`http://www.mathworks.com`) if you don't already own them.

10.6 Helicopter Controller Design

Once the helicopter model described in the previous section has been developed, the design of the control system can begin. This is a complex system, so I will develop the controller in steps. One of the most important points of this example is that when designing controllers for complex systems such as this, it is often necessary to do so incrementally.

Although it would be straightforward to develop a high-order linear model of this plant with the tools provided by MATLAB and Simulink, it often is not feasible to use such a model directly in designing a controller. The resulting controller would be a complex linear system that is likely to be subject to numerical instability and sudden failure in situations in which the actual system's behavior deviates from that of the linear model.

Instead, as a first step, I assume this MIMO system can be modeled as a collection of SISO systems. Although some degree of cross-coupling is likely, the assumption of SISO systems enables straightforward application of any of the design procedures covered in the earlier chapters. Assuming the control system design resulting from this approach is at least somewhat stable and controllable, it will then be possible to experiment with it to determine which controller elements would most benefit from the application of MIMO design techniques.

Although the ultimate goal for this control system is to control the motion of the helicopter in three-dimensional space, it is first necessary to control its angular orientation. In fact, if I have good control of the helicopter's Euler angles, I can use that capability to control the helicopter's horizontal motion by altering the pitch and roll Euler angles. Pitch and roll motions tilt the main rotor disk relative to the vertical, which results in a net force from the main rotor in the horizontal plane. This force moves the helicopter in the desired horizontal direction.

In summary, the design approach for this system will consist of the following steps. Starting with the nonlinear helicopter simulation,

- develop linear models for Euler angle controller design assuming each angle is primarily controlled by one associated actuator,
- design SISO Euler angle controllers for each of the three rotational axes,
- implement and test the Euler angle controllers,
- design a SISO altitude controller,
- design two SISO controllers for moving the helicopter in the horizontal plane: one for the front–back motion and the other for left–right motion, and
- implement and test the position controllers.

10.6.1 Euler Angle Control

To begin the development of the Euler angle controllers, it is first necessary to select an equilibrium operating condition about which to linearize the nonlinear model of Figure 10.3. I will use a hovering condition for this purpose. In hover, the net lift from the main rotor equals the sum of the weights of the helicopter components. The net moment produced by the main rotor must be equal and opposite to the moment produced by the weights and moment arms of the helicopter components.

Because this model assumes the helicopter body and rotors are rigid bodies at fixed relative locations, it is a straightforward matter to compute the net lift force and pitching moment the main rotor must produce to maintain equilibrium. These constants must be placed in the `trim_pitch_mom` and `trim_lift_force` blocks in preparation for the linearization procedure. The helicopter must also be initialized with zero translational and angular velocity and with the main rotor axis aligned with the vertical.

Advanced Concept

In addition to the steps given above, I will take the additional step of stopping the rotor motion during linearization. Although not realistic for modeling purposes, this method avoids introducing the dynamics of the rotor motion into the linear system model, which simplifies the process of generating the linear model and reduces the order of the resulting model. It also allows fixing the main rotor blade's rotation angle to enable control about the desired axis. Placing the blade at 0° (aligned front–back) allows a moment produced by the front–back cyclic control actuator to control the helicopter's pitch motion. Placing the blade at 90° (aligned sideways) allows a moment produced by the left–right cyclic to control the helicopter's roll motion.

As the blade rotates, the angle of attack due to a constant cyclic control input varies sinusoidally. The length of the blade's moment arm in the controlled direction also varies sinusoidally. For example, with a pure roll command applied to the left–right cyclic, the main rotor will exert a maximum moment when it is aligned in the sideways direction. When it is in the front–back orientation, it generates no moment because at that point, there is no angle of attack due to the cyclic input and there is no moment arm allowing the blade to produce a rolling torque.

The result of these effects is that the roll moment produced by the blade in response to a fixed left–right cyclic control input varies in proportion to $\sin^2 \psi$, where ψ is the main rotor rotation angle about the vertical axis. The angle $\psi = 0$ when the rotor is aligned in the front–back direction.

The linear model derived with the use of a stationary main rotor blade assumes the blade remains stationary. Because the moment resulting from a control input varies with $\sin^2 \psi$, it is necessary to account for this effect. The moment produced over each half cycle is identical, so I can limit the analysis to a half cycle. Integrating $\sin^2 \psi$ over a half cycle (from 0 to π) produces the result $\pi/2$. A fixed blade orientation would have a multiplier of 1 instead of the $\sin^2 \psi$ variation. Integrating 1 from 0 to π gives the result π. Because $\pi/2$ is half of π, the control effectiveness of the rotating blade is exactly half that of the stationary blade used in the linearization.

To compensate for this effect in the resulting linear models, I simply multiply the linear model by 0.5. This accounts for the diminished effectiveness of the cyclic control inputs relative to the fixed blade positions used in the linearization.

[redacted]

With the trim values and initial state (including main rotor orientation) specified, the following commands produce a linear state-space model of the helicopter.

```
>> [a,b,c,d] = linmod2('Helicopter');
>> sys = ss(a,b,c,d);
```

The `linmod2()` command creates a set of state-space matrices with the inputs and outputs shown in Figure 10.2. The resulting linear model has 4 inputs, 12 outputs (four three-element vectors), and 16 states.

The next step is to extract SISO models from the 16-state system model that represent the transfer function from each of the angular control inputs (the two cyclic controls and the tail rotor collective) to its respective Euler angle. For example, pitch motion is controlled by the front–back cyclic. The command to extract the linear model from pitch cyclic input (input 2; see Figure 10.2) to pitch Euler angle (output 11) is as follows.

```
>> pitch_sys = minreal(sys(11, 2));
```

In the previous statement, `minreal()` eliminates states from the model that do not affect the dynamics between the SISO system's input and output. The result is the second-order system $\theta/M_{FB} = 11.3746/s^2$, where θ is the pitch Euler angle and M_{FB} is the moment applied to the main rotor blade in the front–back plane. It is not surprising that the 16-state full system model reduces to such a simple form when considered as a SISO system: This is just a moment applied to a collection of rigid bodies at fixed positions relative to each other. Although this is not a precise description of the helicopter in operation, it captures the relevant plant aspects necessary for use in controller design.

I will apply the pole placement design method here because of its directness and simplicity. To produce a system with satisfactory response, I select the specifications of a 1.0-second settling time and a damping ratio of 0.8. Although the pole placement method does not take into account the actuator effort, I can examine the performance of the resulting controller and adjust the settling time to a different value in subsequent design iterations if I find the actuator effort to be excessive.

The observer pole locations are selected to be the closed-loop poles multiplied by 3. This results in observer poles that converge rapidly in comparison to the closed-loop response while minimizing the sampling rate required for a discrete controller implementation.

The following commands design the observer-controller for the pitch motion. Note that I have included a factor of 0.5 to account for the diminished effectiveness of the cyclic control as a result of the rotation of the main rotor.

```
>> t_settle = 1;
>> damp_ratio = 0.8;
>> obs_pole_mult = 3;
>> [N_p, ssobsctrl_p, sscl_p] = ss_design(0.5*pitch_sys, ...
                                   t_settle, damp_ratio, ...
                                   obs_pole_mult);
```

The feedforward gain (`N_p`) and the state-space observer controller (`ssobsctrl_p`) are integrated into the Simulink diagram as shown in Figure 10.4. The controller's *r* input receives the commanded pitch angle, and the *y* input is the measured pitch angle. The output *u* is the moment applied to the main rotor by the front–back cyclic.

Figure 10.4 Pitch observer-controller in Simulink.

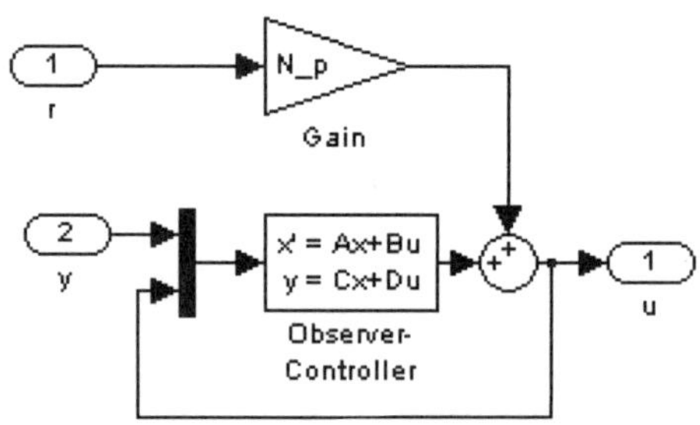

Controllers for the roll Euler angle and the yaw Euler angle are designed with similar procedures, except that the yaw controller has a settling time specification of 4 seconds to limit the magnitude of the yaw rate. After integrating the controllers with the helicopter plant model, the resulting system is shown in Figure 10.5. The inputs are now the main rotor collective force and the three commanded angular orientations for the helicopter.

It is now possible to test the Euler angle control system. Remember, the model has been set up at a trim condition for hovering. The four inputs in Figure 10.5 represent variations from the hovering condition. With all four inputs set to zero, the system should hover in place. Because the position of the helicopter is not yet being controlled, I can expect it to drift away from its initial position over time.

The stability and responsiveness of the angular orientation controllers and the cross-coupling between them can be tested by putting a small step command (say, 1°) into each of the pitch, yaw, and roll angle commands and observing the response. Note that changes to the pitch and roll of the rotor disk will introduce a force in the horizontal direction, which will cause the helicopter to begin moving. However, for the small step angle I am using, the horizontal force will be quite small.

Figure 10.5 Helicopter with angular orientation controllers.

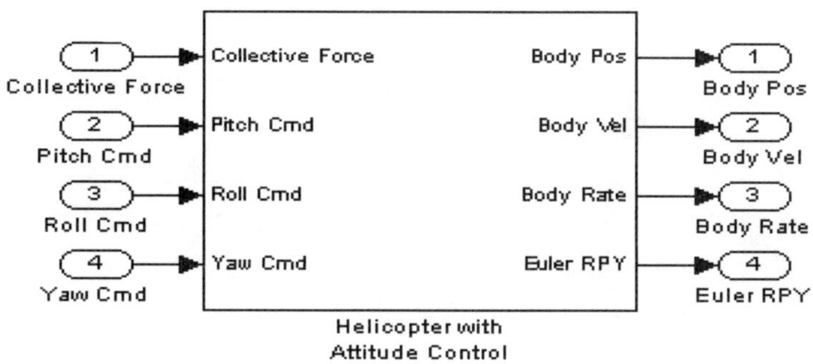

Figure 10.6 displays the responses to 1° step commands applied separately to each of the pitch, yaw, and roll axes. This figure shows that the angular orientation control is stable in response to each of these inputs, and the responses converge to the commanded values.

However, note that in the top plot of Figure 10.6, there is significant cross-coupling from the pitch angle command into the helicopter's roll angle. This degree of cross-coupling might be unacceptable for a final design, but for now, I will simply note its presence and continue with the design. The cross-coupling resulting from the yaw and roll step inputs is at a much lower level compared with the pitch response.

The next step in the design is to develop a vertical position (altitude) controller. I will again assume a SISO controller is appropriate. The input to the controller is the desired altitude, and the plant output is the true helicopter altitude. The actuator is the main rotor collective force. The following commands design the altitude controller.

```
>> t_settle = 4;
>> damp_ratio = 0.8;
>> obs_pole_mult = 3;
>> [N_v, ssobsctrl_v, sscl_v] = ss_design(vert_sys, t_settle, ...
                                        damp_ratio, ...
                                        obs_pole_mult);
>> N_v = -N_v; % Sign change
```

Figure 10.6 Step responses of angular orientation controllers.

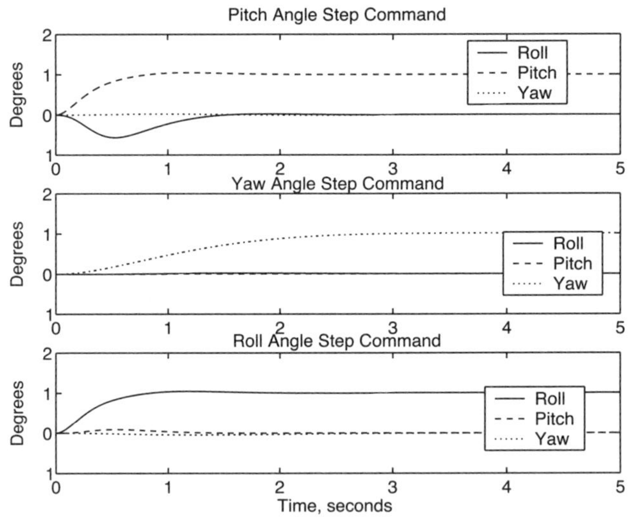

The sign change for the feedforward gain (N_v) is necessary because the vertical dimension of the position vector is positive downward, but altitude commands are positive in the upward direction. The resulting observer-controller has the same form as the pitch observer-controller shown in Figure 10.4.

A plot of the step response of a 1-meter change in altitude, along with the responses of the three Euler angle controllers, appears in Figure 10.7. Note that cross-coupling into the Euler angles is present, but the magnitudes of the responses are a fraction of a degree about each axis.

Figure 10.7 Step response of altitude controller.

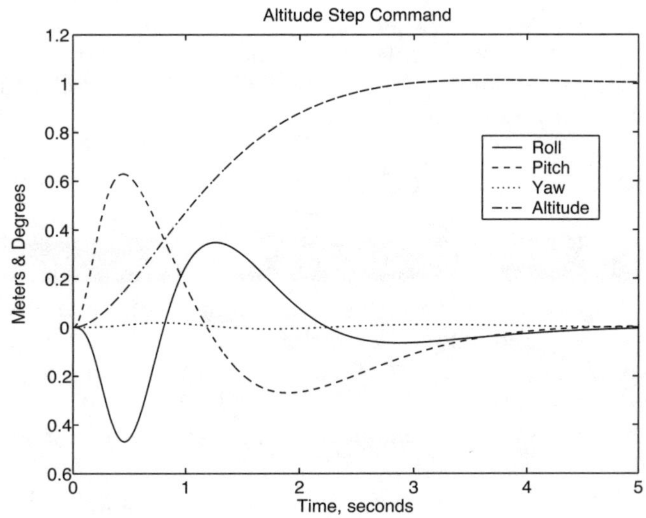

It is necessary to use limiting in the altitude control loop because the altitude command could become quite large. For instance, suppose the helicopter is commanded to an altitude of 1,000 meters instead of 1 meter. A truly linear response would amplify each of the traces in Figure 10.7 by a factor of 1,000, which is clearly unacceptable. A limiter applied to the output of the altitude controller restricts the amount of force applied by the main rotor collective and restricts the magnitude of the cross-coupling into the Euler angles from the altitude control system.

The remaining dimensions of control relate to the helicopter's motion in the horizontal plane. I can break this motion into two components relative to the helicopter body: motion in the forward–backward directions and side-to-side motion. The forward–backward motion is affected primarily by the tilt of the main rotor about the helicopter pitch axis. For example, pitching the helicopter nose downward results in a horizontal force from the main rotor in the forward direction. Similarly, side-to-side motion is affected by the tilt of the main rotor about the helicopter roll axis.

Looked at in this way, the actuator input for horizontal motion is the commanded main rotor tilt in the desired direction, and the output is the helicopter horizontal position in that direction. In principle, I can use any of the SISO design methods discussed in this book to develop controllers for motion in the forward–backward and side-to-side directions.

However, a linear model of the dynamic behavior from the commanded main rotor tilt angle to horizontal motion would be quite complex. This model would contain not only the dynamics of the helicopter system, it would also include the observer-controllers that control the rotor tilt angle. The observer-controller resulting from such a model would be of high order and could be susceptible to numerical difficulties. To bypass (at least temporarily) the complexity and difficulty of this approach, I can attempt to use PID control for the horizontal motion instead.

PID control is often used in applications where the plant is of high order and its dynamic behavior is not well understood. For this helicopter model, although I have a complete model of the plant dynamics, the high-order controller that would result from its use is likely to be unacceptable.

10.6.2 Model Order Reduction

Advanced Concept

An alternative approach for working with a high plant model order is to use the technique of model order reduction. This technique requires that the plant model is controllable, observable, and stable. Starting with a linear plant model, the first step is to use `balreal()` to convert the plant model to a "balanced" realization. A balanced realization of a linear system is in a format in which the states are ordered from the most to the least controllable and observable.

The `balreal()` function also returns a vector containing the Hankel singular values of the balanced realization. A small Hankel singular value indicates that the corresponding state is weakly coupled and is suitable for removal from the model. You must examine the elements of this vector and determine the number of states you would like to remove.

After you determine how many states to remove from the model, `modred()` performs this task, eliminating the specified states from the model. For example, given the linear model `sys`, create a balanced realization as follows.

```
>> [sys, G] = balreal(sys); % Convert to a balanced realization
```

After executing `balreal()`, you must examine the contents of `G` to determine which of the last states to delete. For example, suppose the model has 16 states and you want to delete the last five because the corresponding values in the G vector are small relative to the others. Eliminate these states with `modred()`.

```
>> sys = modred(sys,12:16); % Delete the last 5 states
```

The resulting model has 11 states. After performing these steps, you should examine the reduced-order model's step response and frequency response to ensure that it is a satisfactory approximation of the original plant model before using it in the design process.

I will use PID controllers to drive the helicopter to a specified point in space, which is called a waypoint. A higher level guidance function can select and sequence through waypoints, allowing the helicopter to be flown along an arbitrary trajectory. For design purposes, however, I will assume only one waypoint is given.

The horizontal position controller error is the vector (in helicopter body coordinates) from the helicopter's current position to the position commanded by the waypoint. Because the position error might have an arbitrarily large magnitude, it is necessary to place limiters on the output of the PID controller, which limits the commanded main rotor tilt angle to a maximum magnitude (selected to be 10°) in the forward–backward and side-to-side directions.

Because the plant model does not include any effects (such as wind) that would lead to a steady-state horizontal position error, it is not necessary to use an integral term in the position controller implementation. This simplifies the PID controller to a PD controller. After implementing the two PD controllers in the simulation, it is a straightforward matter to follow the procedures of Chapter 2 to iteratively determine proportional and derivative gains that result in satisfactory system performance.

Figure 10.8 shows the resulting system's response to a step command to move forward 400 meters at constant altitude. Starting from a trim hovering condition at the Earth coordinate system origin, the main rotor tilts –10° in pitch to produce a force moving the helicopter forward while maintaining constant altitude. The model includes the effect of aerodynamic drag, so the helicopter soon reaches an equilibrium cruising speed. After about 40 seconds, the PD controller commands the rotor to pitch in the positive direction, slowing the helicopter as it approaches the waypoint. The helicopter stops at the waypoint and hovers there. Some cross-coupling is noticeable from the pitch motion into the roll, but at least the current design is stable.

Figure 10.8 Step response of position controller.

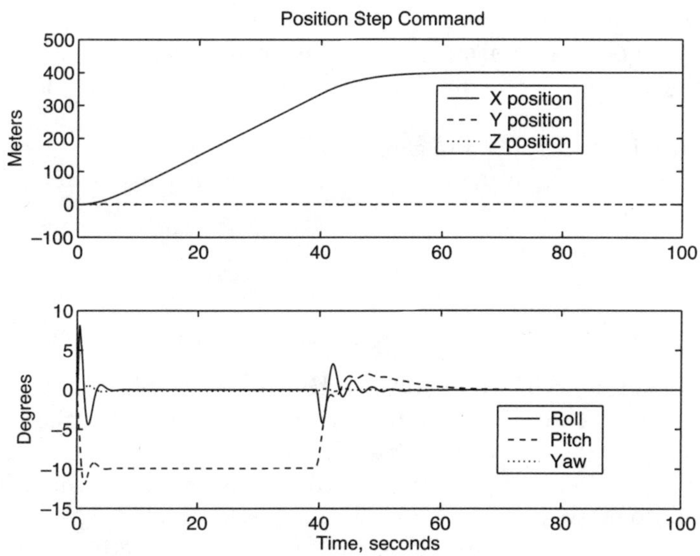

This completes the initial iteration of the helicopter control system design. I have observed some areas of the existing design in which improvement is possible. In particular, the cross-coupling of the pitch angle control into roll has a noticeable effect on performance. A second design iteration could address this issue by using a MIMO design approach to develop a coupled pitch/roll controller that minimizes the cross-coupling effects.

Another way to improve the controller design would be to work with a more realistic helicopter model. For example, instead of assuming a perfect inertial measurement system, realistic errors could be added to the simulated position and angular orientation measurements. A further design iteration could optimize controller performance in the presence of these errors with LQR controllers and Kalman filter observers.

10.7 Controller Implementation in C++

Assume that the implementation language for the control system software is C++ with floating-point mathematics. If desired, implementation in fixed-point math would be straightforward using the techniques described in Chapter 8.

The design developed in the previous section consists of four state-space observer-controllers and two PD controllers. The observer-controllers can be implemented in C++ with the techniques described in Chapter 8. Before I can complete the implementation, it is necessary to make two decisions: I must choose a sampling interval and select a discretization method.

The fastest closed-loop responses of the system are in the pitch and roll controllers, which both have a 1-second settling time requirement. A rule of thumb is to take the settling time divided by 20 to get an approximate value for the largest acceptable sampling interval. This results in a sampling interval of 50 milliseconds. Lacking any reason to select one of the more specialized discretization methods, I will use the first-order hold technique.

I discretize the controller and generate C++ code for the pitch axis controller with the following steps. Note that the name of the state-space observer controller created in the previous section is `ssobsctrl_p`.

```
>> Ts = 0.05; % Sampling interval
>> dssobsctrl_p = c2d(ssobsctrl_p, Ts, 'foh');
>> write_cpp_model(dssobsctrl_p, 'dssobsctrl_p.c')
```

Similar procedures produce C++ code implementing the roll, yaw, and altitude controllers.

The remaining controllers are the two PD controllers for the horizontal helicopter motion. Consider the forward–backward horizontal position controller. The error term at the input to this controller is the horizontal distance from the helicopter to the waypoint in the forward–backward axis in body coordinates. The derivative of the error term is the helicopter velocity along the forward–backward axis in body coordinates. Both the position error and the velocity in body coordinates can be computed directly from information that is available in the system, so the PD controller can be implemented as shown in Eq. 10.1.

$$u_p = K_p(\mathrm{WP}_x - P_x) + K_d V_x \qquad \text{Eq. 10.1}$$

In Eq. 10.1, u_p is the commanded pitch angle, K_p is the proportional gain, WP_x is the waypoint position in the body x direction, P_x is the helicopter's current position in the body x direction, K_d is the derivative gain, and V_x is the helicopter velocity in the body x direction. A similar equation describes the PD controller for the side-to-side axis. u_p must then be limited to the range [–10°, +10°].

The remaining code for the controller consists of limit functions, a translation of the vector from the helicopter to the waypoint from earth coordinates to body coordinates, I/O operations to read sensors and write to actuators, and a scheduling structure that executes it at 50-millisecond intervals.

10.8 System Testing

I'll step back for a moment and take a look at what has been accomplished in this example. A helicopter is a difficult aircraft for a human pilot to control. Starting with a simulation of a helicopter and with the help of some fairly straightforward MATLAB commands, I've developed a complete control system for this helicopter that rivals the performance of a skilled human pilot, at least in the simple test scenario of Figure 10.8. This should give you a feeling of the power and accessibility of the design methods discussed in the chapters of this book.

The controller design I've developed should not be considered complete yet. In a real-world design project for a system like this, the helicopter model would undergo many iterative revisions to make it a more realistic representation of the actual system [1]. Each improvement to the helicopter model requires testing with the control system to ensure that performance remains adequate. It is likely that enhancements to the control system will be required as the tests uncover problems.

Finally, after the simulation is deemed sufficiently realistic and controller performance with the simulation is satisfactory in all respects, the control system is ready to be used in flight tests with a prototype helicopter. If the helicopter simulation has been properly validated, there should be a high probability that initial flight tests with the control system will exhibit good controller performance.

Initial operational tests for this type of system should consist of simple checks of basic control system functionality. Safety is an overriding concern, so the emphasis must be on performing the tests and ensuring that the helicopter lands safely. Later, after a high level of confidence has been achieved in the control system's basic capabilities, more advanced testing is appropriate. The complete series of tests must ensure that the controller provides acceptable performance over the system's entire operating envelope. Performance under environmental variations (such as temperature, wind, rain, etc.) must also be tested sufficiently.

It is possible, and perhaps likely, that significant problems with the control system's performance will be uncovered during this testing. These issues are usually resolved by performing additional design iterations. If changes must be made to the helicopter or its control system, a sufficient amount of regression testing must be performed in both simulated and actual flights to ensure that the problem has been resolved and other aspects of performance have not been degraded by the changes.

10.9 Summary

In the first part of this chapter, I provided a summary of the control system design methods discussed in earlier chapters. I described each method and listed its benefits and disadvantages. This information enables the designer to select an appropriate approach to use in solving a given design problem.

The remainder of the chapter consists of a comprehensive control system design example for a helicopter. I developed a nonlinear helicopter model with Simulink and SimMechanics. The model was used as the basis for designing controllers for angular motion about the roll, pitch, and yaw axes. These controllers were integrated with the helicopter model, and I designed and integrated additional controllers for translational motion in the vertical and horizontal directions.

I ended the chapter with a discussion of the approach to be taken in refining this initial design with a more realistic helicopter model and the need for comprehensive operational testing.

10.10 Self-Test

1. Suppose you are designing an automotive cruise control system. The sensor is the measured vehicle speed and the actuator is the engine throttle setting. The reference input is the commanded speed, set by the operator. There is no mathematical model of the vehicle's dynamic behavior in response to throttle inputs. Identify an approach for developing a prototype control system quickly using no plant model. The controller must converge to the commanded speed on a level road and also when traveling up and down constant slopes.
2. What is a potential drawback of the design developed in the previous problem?
3. Suppose you have the ability to program a timed sequence of reference inputs into the cruise control developed in problem 1. How could you use this capability to develop a linear model of the vehicle's speed response to the throttle input, including the effects of road slope?
4. Now suppose a tilt sensor is included in the automobile to measure the instantaneous slope of the road. Integrating this sensor into the cruise control system will enable it to, for example, avoid the momentary slowdown that otherwise occurs when transitioning from a level road section to a section with an upward slope. Identify an approach that uses the linear plant model from problem 3 to develop a controller.

5. What type of nonlinear control system element is likely to be necessary for the controllers developed in the previous problems?
6. What potential benefits can you identify from the use of optimal control design techniques for this application?
7. Identify several conditions in which the automobile must be placed during system testing to assure correct operation of the cruise control over the vehicle's entire operating envelope.
8. What sort of dangerous emergency conditions should be tested for an automotive cruise control?
9. How can simulation minimize the difficulty and danger of performing the tests of problem 8?

10.11 Answers

1. Implement a PID controller with the techniques described in Chapter 2. The integral term in the controller will assure convergence to the commanded speed even on a sloped road.
2. The PID controller is not likely to be an optimum solution to the problem. In general, better performance results from a controller design that is matched to the dynamic behavior of the plant.
3. Perform a series of step changes of the reference input at varying frequencies and record the throttle setting and vehicle speed during the tests. Repeat the tests on road sections with differing known slopes. Use this data as input to a system identification procedure as discussed in Chapter 3. The result will be a linear model of the automobile's speed response to the throttle input under varying road slope conditions.
4. The plant is now a MIMO system with two sensors (speed and road slope) and one actuator (throttle setting). The pole placement technique described in Chapter 5 is suitable for this situation. The damping ratio should be selected to produce little or no overshoot. The settling time should be chosen fast enough to give reasonably quick response, but slow enough to avoid large throttle commands.
5. It might be necessary to limit the magnitude of the command the controller gives to the throttle. For example, if the reference input is set to a speed that is much higher than the current speed (perhaps with a "resume" function), the throttle command might be unacceptably large. A limiter can keep the commanded throttle magnitude within an acceptable range.
6. The use of LQR controller design can minimize the control effort used to reach a desired cruise speed. This results in "smoother" cruise control performance. A Kalman filter minimizes the mean-squared estimation error of the observer, again potentially resulting in smoother performance.
7. Several combinations of wind conditions, road slope, road surface (pavement, gravel, etc.), altitude (sea level, mountains), and road conditions (dry, wet, snow-covered, etc.) must be tested.

8. Some examples are a tire blowout, a loss of traction on ice, and an accident that leaves the wheels off the ground. With the wheels off the ground, an attempt by the cruise control to maintain cruising speed could be exceptionally hazardous to the occupants of the vehicle and their rescuers.
9. If a validated plant model with sufficient fidelity is available, dangerous tests involving component failures (tire blowouts), environmental extremes (loss of traction on ice), and unusual configurations (wheels off the ground) can be simulated. A simulated implementation of the cruise control system could be used, or the actual controller hardware and software can be employed in a HIL simulation environment.

10.12 References

1. Ledin, Jim, *Simulation Engineering* (Lawrence, KS: CMP Books, 2001).

Glossary

Actuator Saturation

Actuator saturation occurs when an actuator reaches a limit of its capabilities. These limits typically appear in the form of position or rate-of-change bounds. When actuator saturation occurs, the system's response to increasing controller gains becomes nonlinear and might be unacceptable.

Block Diagram

A block diagram of a plant and controller is a graphical means to represent the structure of a controller design and its interaction with the plant. Each block represents a system component. Solid lines with arrows indicate the flow of signals between the components. In block diagrams of SISO systems, a solid line represents a single scalar signal. In MIMO systems, a line can represent multiple signals. Circles represent summing junctions, which combine their inputs by addition or subtraction depending on the + or – signs displayed next to each input.

Bode Diagram

Bode diagrams display the magnitude and phase of the open-loop frequency response of the combined plant and controller. The horizontal axis of both diagrams is frequency, displayed on a logarithmic scale. The magnitude diagram is displayed in units of decibels, and the phase diagram is in units of degrees. Together, the Bode diagrams represent the steady-state amplitude and phase of an output sine wave relative to an input sine wave at each frequency shown on the horizontal axes of the diagrams.

Continuous-Time System

A continuous-time system has outputs with values defined at all points in time. Real-world plants are usually best represented as continuous-time systems. In other words, such systems have parameters such as speed, temperature, weight, and so on, available for measurement at all points in time.

Controllability

A plant is controllable if it contains sufficient actuators to drive all of its internal variables to commanded values. The controllability of a linear time-invariant state-space model is determined from an examination of the **A** and **B** matrices. The controllability matrix (computed by the MATLAB `ctrb()` command) must be of full rank for the system to be controllable.

Controller

The function of a controller is to manage a system's operation so that its response approximates commanded behavior. In modern system designs, embedded processors have taken over many control functions. A well-designed embedded controller can provide excellent system performance under widely varying operating conditions.

Decibel

The decibel measures the ratio of two signal power values. Given two power values, the formula for computing the decibel ratio is 10 log 10($power_1/power_2$). If the signal amplitude is used instead of the power, the expression for computing the decibel ratio is 10 log 10($amplitude_1/amplitude_2$). The reason for the difference in the multiplying factors is that power is proportional to the square of the signal amplitude.

Difference Equation

Difference equations model the behavior of discrete-time systems. A difference equation is a recursive algebraic equation that computes the next value of a discrete state variable as a function of current and previous values of the state variable and equation input variables. Difference equations are used in control system algorithms to approximate the solution of continuous-time differential equations on digital computers.

Differential Equation

A differential equation is an equation containing one or more derivatives of an unknown function. In control systems development, it is common to compute an estimate of the unknown function in a differential equation with difference equations.

Discrete-Time System

The outputs of a discrete-time system are only updated or used at discrete points in time. The discrete-time systems of interest in this book are embedded processors and their associated input/output (I/O) devices. An embedded computing system measures its inputs and produces its outputs at discrete points in time. The embedded software typically runs at a fixed sampling rate, resulting in I/O device updates at equally spaced points in time.

Eigenvalue

An eigenvalue is a characteristic root (pole) of a linear system model. In the state-space model representation, the eigenvalues can be determined from the **A** matrix using MATLAB's `eig()` command. An *n*th order system has *n* eigenvalues, which need not be distinct. The locations of a linear system's eigenvalues in the complex plane determine the system's stability, damping, and response speed characteristics.

Equilibrium Point

An equilibrium point is an operating point at which a continuous-time plant is in a steady state and all the derivatives in its equations are zero. For many systems of interest, the response of the plant to small perturbations about an equilibrium point is approximately linear.

Feedback Control

A feedback control system measures one or more attributes of the system being controlled (the plant) and uses that information to develop actuator commands that drive the system toward a commanded state as specified by the reference input. In comparison to open-loop control, which develops actuator commands without any information about the plant's state, feedback control provides generally superior performance.

Frequency Response Format

The frequency response representation of a linear or nonlinear system is described by a Bode diagram. A Bode diagram shows the ratio of the magnitude of the output signal to a sine wave input signal in decibels and the phase of the output signal relative to the input in degrees. The horizontal axis in both plots is the frequency of the input signal in radians per second displayed on a logarithmic scale.

Gain Margin

On Bode diagrams, the gain margin is defined as the negative of the open-loop gain at the frequency at which the phase is –180°. A stable system has a gain less than 0dB at that frequency, so the negative of that value results in a positive gain margin. The gain margin indicates the amount by which the compensator gain can be increased before the system becomes neutrally stable.

Gain Scheduling

Gain scheduling involves the development of a collection of controller designs in which each design is optimized for use under different operating conditions. As an example, in an aircraft flight controller design, you might create a two-dimensional grid of aircraft altitude versus airspeed covering the entire flight envelope and design a different controller for each point where the grid lines cross. Table interpolation can be used to smoothly adjust the controller gains as the plant operating point moves across its operating envelope.

Integrator Windup

Integrator windup is the result of integrating a large error signal during periods when the actuator is unable to respond fully to its commanded behavior. The integrated error term can reach a very large value during these periods, which results in significant overshoot in the system response. Oscillation is also a possibility, with the actuator banging from one end of its range of motion to the other. One way to reduce the effect of integrator windup is to turn integration off when the amplitude (absolute value) of the error signal is above a cutoff level. This result can be achieved by setting the integrator input to zero during periods of large error.

Kalman Filter

The Kalman filter forms an optimal state estimate for a given state-space plant model in the presence of process and measurement noise. The optimality criterion for the steady-state Kalman filter is the minimization of the steady-state error covariance matrix $\mathbf{P} = \lim_{t \to \infty} E(\{\hat{\mathbf{x}} - \mathbf{x}\}\{\hat{\mathbf{x}} - \mathbf{x}\}^T)$ where E represents the expectation, or mean, of the elements of $\mathbf{P}$; $\hat{\mathbf{x}}$ is the state estimate; and $\mathbf{x}$ is the true state vector. The term $\{\hat{\mathbf{x}} - \mathbf{x}\}$ is the state estimation error. The diagonal elements of **P** contain the variance (the square of the standard deviation) of the state estimation error. The off-diagonal terms represent the correlation between the errors of the state vector elements.

Limiter

A limiter restricts its output signal to a range between specified minimum and maximum values. When the limiter's input signal is between the minimum and maximum values, it is passed unchanged. A limiter is useful in situations in which the magnitude of a signal must be maintained within boundaries for smooth system operation.

Linear Quadratic Regulator

A linear quadratic regulator minimizes the cost function $J(\mathbf{u}) = \int_0^\infty \mathbf{x}^T\mathbf{Q}\mathbf{x} + \mathbf{u}^T\mathbf{R}\mathbf{u}\,dt$ in which the elements of **Q** and **R** have been chosen so the scalar terms $\mathbf{x}^T\mathbf{Q}\mathbf{x}$ and $\mathbf{u}^T\mathbf{R}\mathbf{u}$ are greater than or equal to zero for all possible values of **x** and **u**. This is the optimal controller for the given **Q** and **R** weighting matrices. The elements of **Q** and **R** must be selected by the designer so that the controller satisfies performance requirements.

Linearization

Linearization is the process of converting a nonlinear model of a dynamic system into a linear model that approximates the response of the nonlinear model in the vicinity of an equilibrium point.

Measurement Noise

Measurement noise is the result of errors in the measurement of plant outputs. The modeling of measurement noise typically relies on manufacturer's data describing the accuracy of sensor measurements. One example of measurement noise is the quantization of analog-to-digital converter (ADC) samples.

MIMO System

A control system with more than one input or output is called a MIMO system, which stands for a multiple-input–multiple-output system.

Neutral Stability

A system with neutral stability oscillates indefinitely in response to a change in its input. A neutrally stable system has one or more pairs of complex eigenvalues with a real part of zero. Although neutral stability is generally undesirable in control systems, this concept is useful in the design of electrical oscillator circuits.

Observability

A plant is observable if it is possible to form an accurate estimate of all of its internal states using only the plant inputs and measured plant outputs. The observability of a linear time-invariant state-space model is determined from an examination of the **A** and **C** matrices. The observability matrix (computed by the MATLAB `obsv()` command) must be of full rank for the system to be observable.

Open-Loop Control

An open-loop control system does not use feedback describing the current plant state in determining the actuator command. Feedback control systems provide generally superior system performance in comparison to open-loop controllers.

Phase Margin

On Bode diagrams, the phase margin is defined as the number of degrees the phase curve is above –180° at the frequency in which the gain plot passes through 0dB. For good transient response characteristics, the phase margin should normally be at least 60°. A value of less than 45° tends to produce unacceptable overshoot and ringing in the response.

PID Controller

The PID controller's output signal consists of a sum of terms proportional to the error signal, as well as to the integral and derivative of the error signal—hence, the name PID. This is the most commonly used controller structure.

Plant

A plant is a system to be controlled. From a feedback controller's point of view, the plant has one or more outputs and one or more inputs. Sensors measure the plant outputs and actuators drive the plant inputs. The behavior of the plant itself can range from trivially simple to extremely complex.

Pole Cancellation

Pole cancellation involves the placement of compensator zeros at the locations of undesired plant poles, thus canceling out the dynamic behavior due to those poles. This technique is used in the root locus design method. Pole cancellation generally fails to produce a stable design if any of the cancelled poles are unstable.

Process Noise

Process noise is a model of the deviation of the actual plant behavior from its linear model. These deviations could result from unmodeled disturbance inputs the plant receives or they could be caused by nonlinearities within the plant itself. It is possible to develop a process noise model analytically, or a simplified model can be used that assumes some noise is added to each plant input signal.

Regulator

A control system that attempts to maintain the output signal at a constant level for long periods of time is called a regulator. In a regulator, the desired output value is called the reference input or set point.

Sampling Frequency

The sampling frequency of a discrete-time system is the inverse of its sampling period. The sampling frequency is usually expressed in units of samples per second.

Sampling Period

The sampling period of a discrete-time system is the time interval between input samples. Output signals are updated at the same interval. The sampling period is usually expressed in units of seconds.

Servomechanism

A servomechanism is a control system that attempts to track a reference input signal that changes frequently (perhaps continuously.)

SISO System

The simplest form of feedback control system has one input and one output. This is called a single-input–single-output (SISO) system.

State-Space Representation

The state-space representation models a linear time-invariant SISO or MIMO system as a set of first-order linear differential equations using matrix methods. The behavior of the system is fully described by four matrices: **A**, **B**, **C**, and **D**. When using control system design software such as the MATLAB Control System Toolbox, state-space is the preferred linear model representation. The state-space representation exhibits superior numerical properties and provides more precise results compared with the transfer function representation.

System Identification

System identification is the development of dynamic system models from experimental input and output data. To perform system identification, one or more test input data sequences and the corresponding measured output data sequences are required for the system being modeled. Typically, tests of a real-world system are designed and executed to generate this data. By applying system identification algorithms, it is possible to derive an estimate of the system transfer function from input to output.

Transfer Function Representation

The transfer function representation is based on the Laplace transform of a linear differential equation with constant coefficients. A transfer function is a ratio of polynomials in the variable s that represents the ratio of a system's output to its input. Each transfer function corresponds directly to a linear differential equation. Transfer functions are widely applied in classical control system analysis and design, where they are used to represent linear models of SISO components such as controllers, plants, actuators, and sensors.

White Noise

White noise is composed of signals of all possible frequencies, with all frequencies represented equally. The adjective "white" is used because white light is similarly composed of light of all colors. White noise is a mathematical abstraction. True white noise would contain infinite energy, which is not possible. Nevertheless, the concept of white noise is an extremely useful approximation in applications such as Kalman filtering.

Index

Bold page numbers refer to term definitions.

I

K

L

M

N

O

P

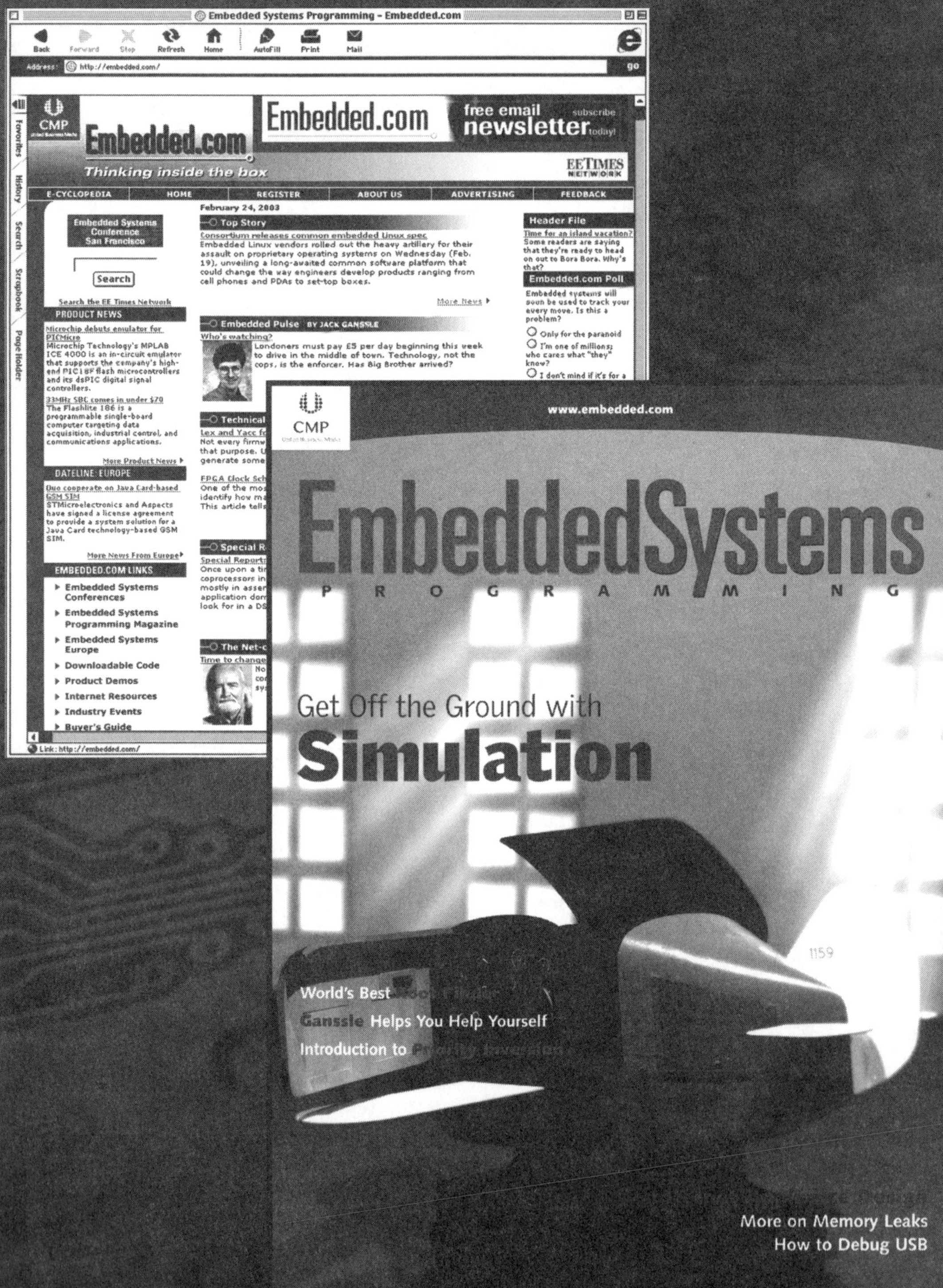
Embedded Systems Programming – Embedded.com
Back
Forward
Stop
Refresh
Home
AutoFill
Print
Mail
Address: http://embedded.com/
go
CMP
Embedded.com
Thinking inside the box
Embedded.com
free email newsletter
subscribe today!
EETIMES NETWORK
E-CYCLOPEDIA
HOME
REGISTER
ABOUT US
ADVERTISING
FEEDBACK
February 24, 2003
Embedded Systems Conference San Francisco
Search
Search the EE Times Network
Top Story
Consortium releases common embedded Linux spec
Embedded Linux vendors rolled out the heavy artillery for their assault on proprietary operating systems on Wednesday (Feb. 19), unveiling a long-awaited common software platform that could change the way engineers develop products ranging from cell phones and PDAs to set-top boxes.
More News
Header File
Time for an island vacation?
Some readers are saying that they're ready to head on out to Bora Bora. Why's that?
Embedded.com Poll
Embedded systems will soon be used to track your every move. Is this a problem?
Only for the paranoid
I'm one of millions; who cares what "they" know?
PRODUCT NEWS
Microchip debuts emulator for PICMicro
Microchip Technology's MPLAB ICE 4000 is an in-circuit emulator that supports the company's high-end PIC18F flash microcontrollers and its dsPIC digital signal controllers.
33MHz SBC comes in under $70
The Flashlite 186 is a programmable single-board computer targeting data acquisition, industrial control, and communications applications.
More Product News
DATELINE: EUROPE
Duo cooperate on Java Card-based GSM SIM
STMicroelectronics and Aspects have signed a license agreement to provide a system solution for a Java Card technology-based GSM SIM.
More News From Europe
EMBEDDED.COM LINKS
Embedded Systems Conferences
Embedded Systems Programming Magazine
Embedded Systems Europe
Downloadable Code
Product Demos
Internet Resources
Industry Events
Buyer's Guide
Embedded Pulse BY JACK GANSSLE
Who's watching?
Londoners must pay £5 per day beginning this week to drive in the middle of town. Technology, not the cops, is the enforcer. Has Big Brother arrived?
Link: http://embedded.com/
CMP
www.embedded.com
EmbeddedSystems
PROGRAMMING
Get Off the Ground with
Simulation
World's Best
Ganssle Helps You Help Yourself
Introduction to
More on Memory Leaks
How to Debug USB

CD-ROM accompanying Embedded Control Systems in C/C++

The CD-ROM accompanying this book contains MATLAB M-files (MATLAB language source code) and Simulink block diagram models for designing, implementing and testing control systems.

The top-level directories on the CD-ROM are organized as follows:

Design: The Design directory contains the main MATLAB M-files described in the book for performing control system design and implementation in the C/C++ languages. You may wish to copy these files to a directory on your MATLAB path for future use. The MATLAB Control System Toolbox is required for many of these functions.

ss_design.m Design a state space observer-controller and feedforward gain for a SISO plant using the pole placement method.

optimal_design.m Design a state space observer-controller and feedforward gain for a SISO plant using the linear quadratic regulator and steady-state Kalman filtering approaches.

select_poles.m Determine a set of pole locations for use in pole placement design.

plot_poles.m Plot system pole locations along with settling time and damping ratio constraints.

write_c_model.m Write a C language implementation of a discrete-time state-space controller using floating-point mathematics.

write_c_fixpt_model.m Write a C language implementation of a discrete-time state-space controller using fixed-point mathematics.

write_cpp_model.m Write a C++ language implementation of a discrete-time state-space controller using floating-point mathematics.

write_cpp_fixpt_model.m Write a C++ language implementation of a discrete-time state-space controller using fixed-point mathematics.

Examples: The Examples directory contains many of the MATLAB M-file and Simulink model examples presented in the book organized by chapter number.

Self-Test: The Self-Test directory contains partial and complete solutions for many of the Self-Test questions given at the end of each chapter.

Those of you who would like to sign up for email news updates can send a blank email to controlsystems@news.cmpbooks.com. If you have a suggestion or correction, please email your comments to: jim@ledin.com